Garfield rolls on

BY JIM DAVIS

Ballantine Books • **New York**

2005 Ballantine Books Trade Paperback Edition

Copyright © 1984, 1985, 2005 by PAWS, Inc. All Rights Reserved.

Published in the United States by Ballantine Books, an imprint of The Random House Publishing Group,
a division of Random House, Inc., New York.

Ballantine and colophon are registered trademarks of Random House, Inc.

"GARFIELD" and the GARFIELD characters are registered and unregistered trademarks of PAWS, Inc.

Originally published in slightly different form in the United States by Ballantine Books, an imprint of
The Random House Publishing Group, a division of Random House, Inc., in 1985.

Library of Congress Control Number: 2005903205

ISBN 0-345-47561-5

Printed in the United States of America

www.ballantinebooks.com

9 8 7 6 5 4 3 2 1

First Colorized Edition

TO THE PROSPECTIVE CARTOONIST

Al Capp once said, "You must have two qualities to be a successful cartoonist. First, it helps to have been dropped on your head as a small child. Second, you must have no desire, talent, or ability to do anything useful in life."

While his may seem a somewhat flippant observation, it nevertheless reflects how seriously cartoonists take themselves and their art. If I had only one piece of advice to give a prospective cartoonist, it would be: HAVE FUN WITH YOUR FEATURE!

If you have fun doing it, people have fun reading it. Your enthusiasm comes through.

Most hopeful cartoonists labor over their creations. An overworked, heavily laden cartoon strip or panel doesn't have the charm or witty appeal of a simply drawn, simply stated sentiment. All a cartoonist has to do is hold a mirror to life and show it back with a humorous twist. More often than not, when a reader laughs at a strip, it's not because it's funny but because it's true.

PREPARE YOURSELF . . .

HERE ARE SOME GENERAL RECOMMENDATIONS TO LAY THE GROUNDWORK FOR A CAREER IN CARTOONING . . .

1) GET A GOOD LIBERAL ARTS EDUCATION. Enroll in journalism courses, as well as art classes. DO A LOT OF READING. The better read you are, the more natural depth your writing will have. Learn to draw realistically. It helps any cartooning style.

2) SEEK AN ART OR JOURNALISM RELATED JOB. This affords you the luxury of having food to eat until you make a go of it in cartooning.

3) EXPERIMENT WITH ALL KINDS OF ART EQUIPMENT AND MATERIALS. I use India ink and a #2 Windsor-Newton sable brush. For lettering, I use a Speedball B-6 point. I work on Strathmore 3-ply bristol board, smooth surface.

4) STAY MOTIVATED. Try to get your work published in a school paper, local newspaper, or local publication. Many cartoonists give up the quest a year or two before they would have become marketable.

5) PREPARE NEAT, THOUGHTFUL SUBMISSIONS FOR THE SYNDICATE EDITORS. Send only your best work, and be prepared to submit it many times. I could wallpaper a bedroom with *my* rejection slips.

Again, don't forget to keep it simple and have fun. Oh, yes . . . a little luck along the way never hurts.

GOOD LUCK!

Jim Davis

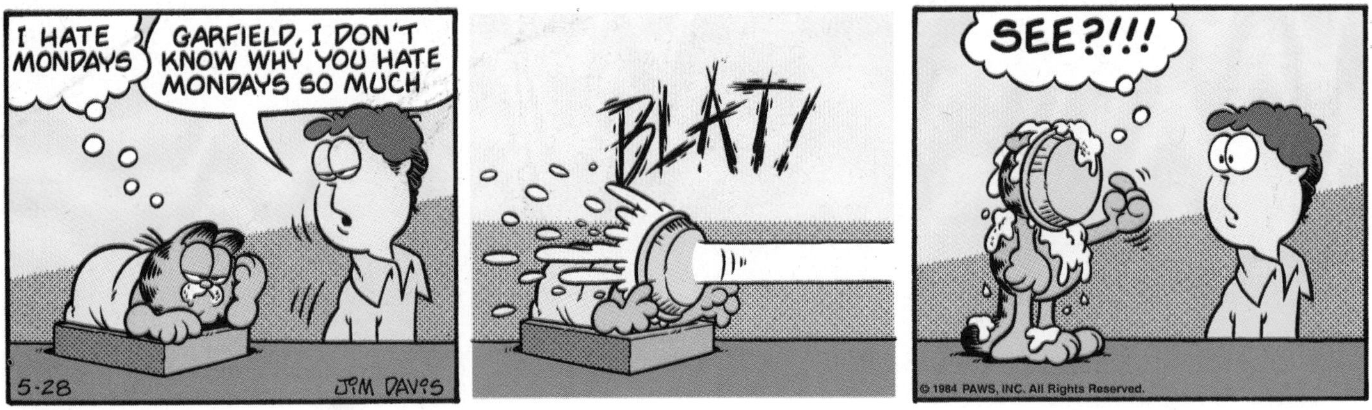
I HATE MONDAYS
GARFIELD, I DON'T KNOW WHY YOU HATE MONDAYS SO MUCH
5-28
JIM DAVIS
BLAT!
SEE?!!!
© 1984 PAWS, INC. All Rights Reserved.

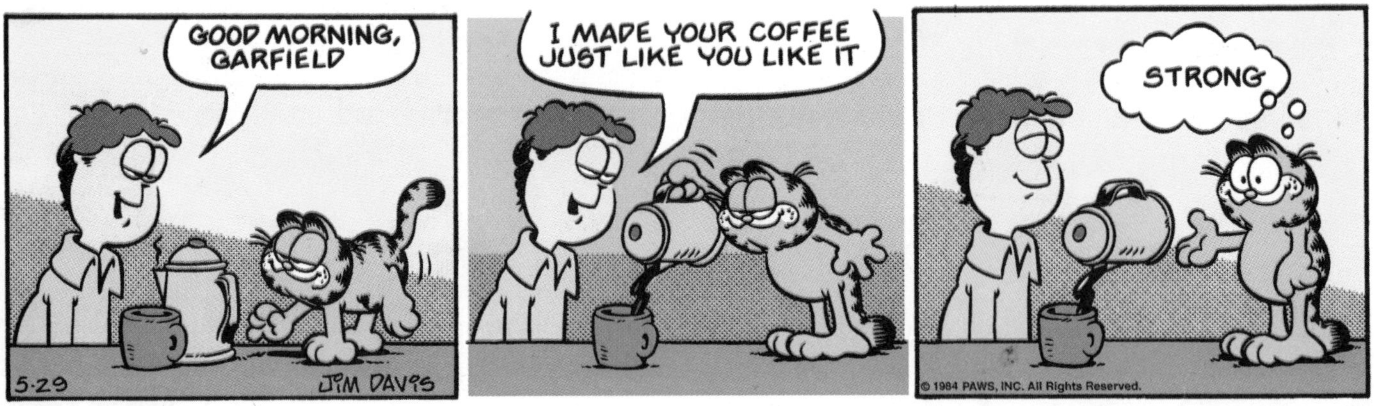
GOOD MORNING, GARFIELD
5-29
JIM DAVIS
I MADE YOUR COFFEE JUST LIKE YOU LIKE IT
STRONG
© 1984 PAWS, INC. All Rights Reserved.

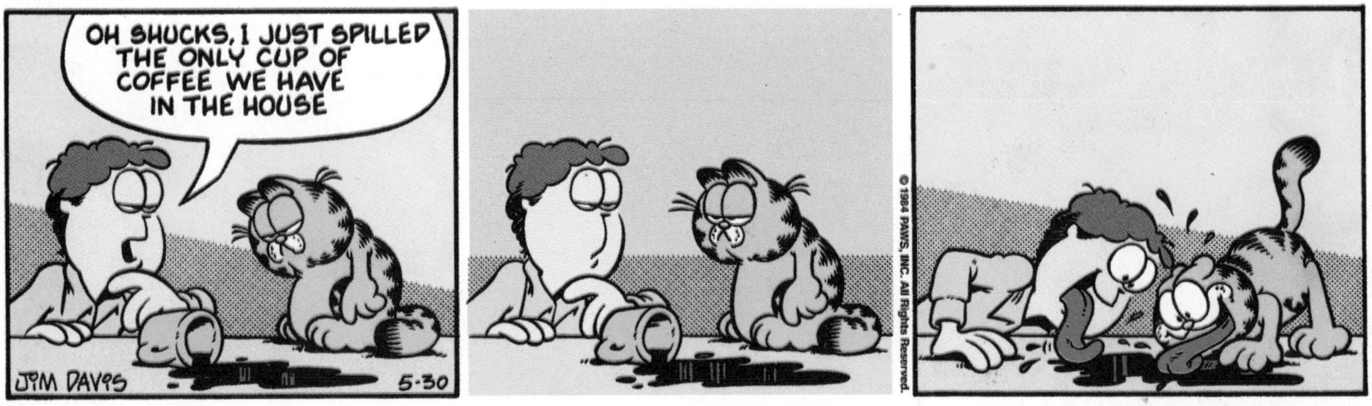
OH SHUCKS, I JUST SPILLED THE ONLY CUP OF COFFEE WE HAVE IN THE HOUSE
JIM DAVIS
5-30
© 1984 PAWS, INC. All Rights Reserved.

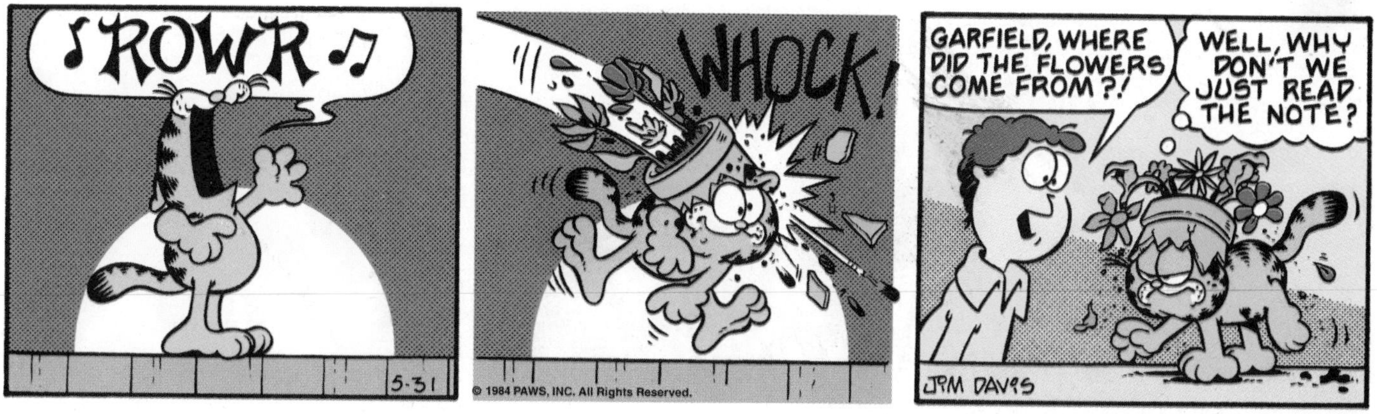
ROWR
5-31
WHOCK!
© 1984 PAWS, INC. All Rights Reserved.
GARFIELD, WHERE DID THE FLOWERS COME FROM ?!
WELL, WHY DON'T WE JUST READ THE NOTE?
JIM DAVIS

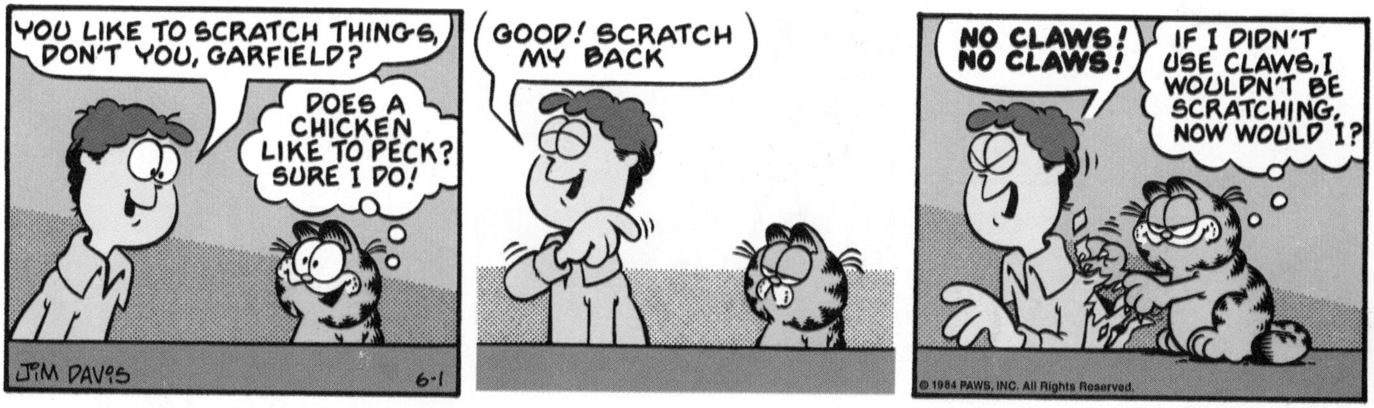
YOU LIKE TO SCRATCH THINGS, DON'T YOU, GARFIELD?
DOES A CHICKEN LIKE TO PECK? SURE I DO!
JIM DAVIS
6-1
GOOD! SCRATCH MY BACK
NO CLAWS! NO CLAWS!
IF I DIDN'T USE CLAWS, I WOULDN'T BE SCRATCHING, NOW WOULD I?
© 1984 PAWS, INC. All Rights Reserved.

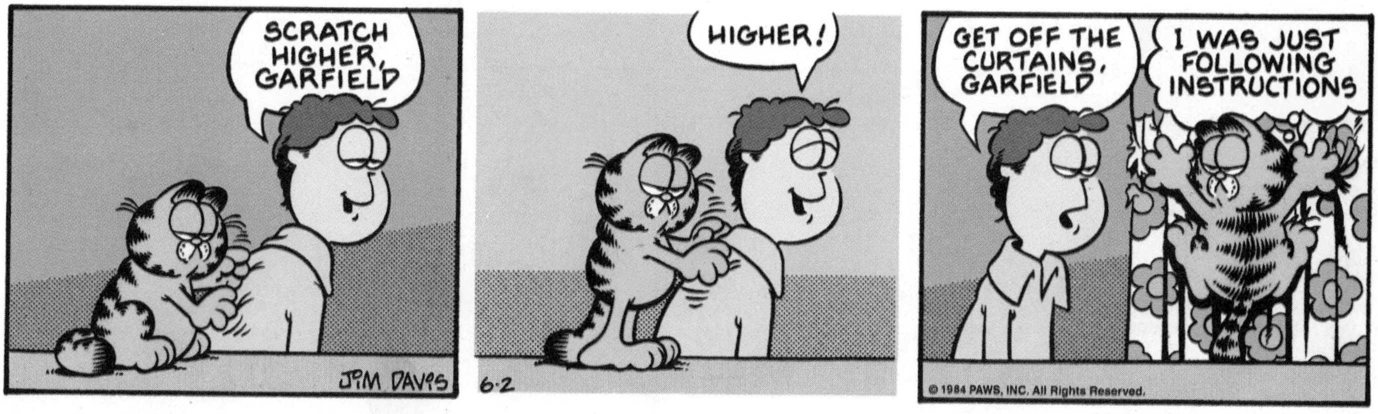
SCRATCH HIGHER, GARFIELD
JIM DAVIS
6-2
HIGHER!
GET OFF THE CURTAINS, GARFIELD
I WAS JUST FOLLOWING INSTRUCTIONS
© 1984 PAWS, INC. All Rights Reserved.

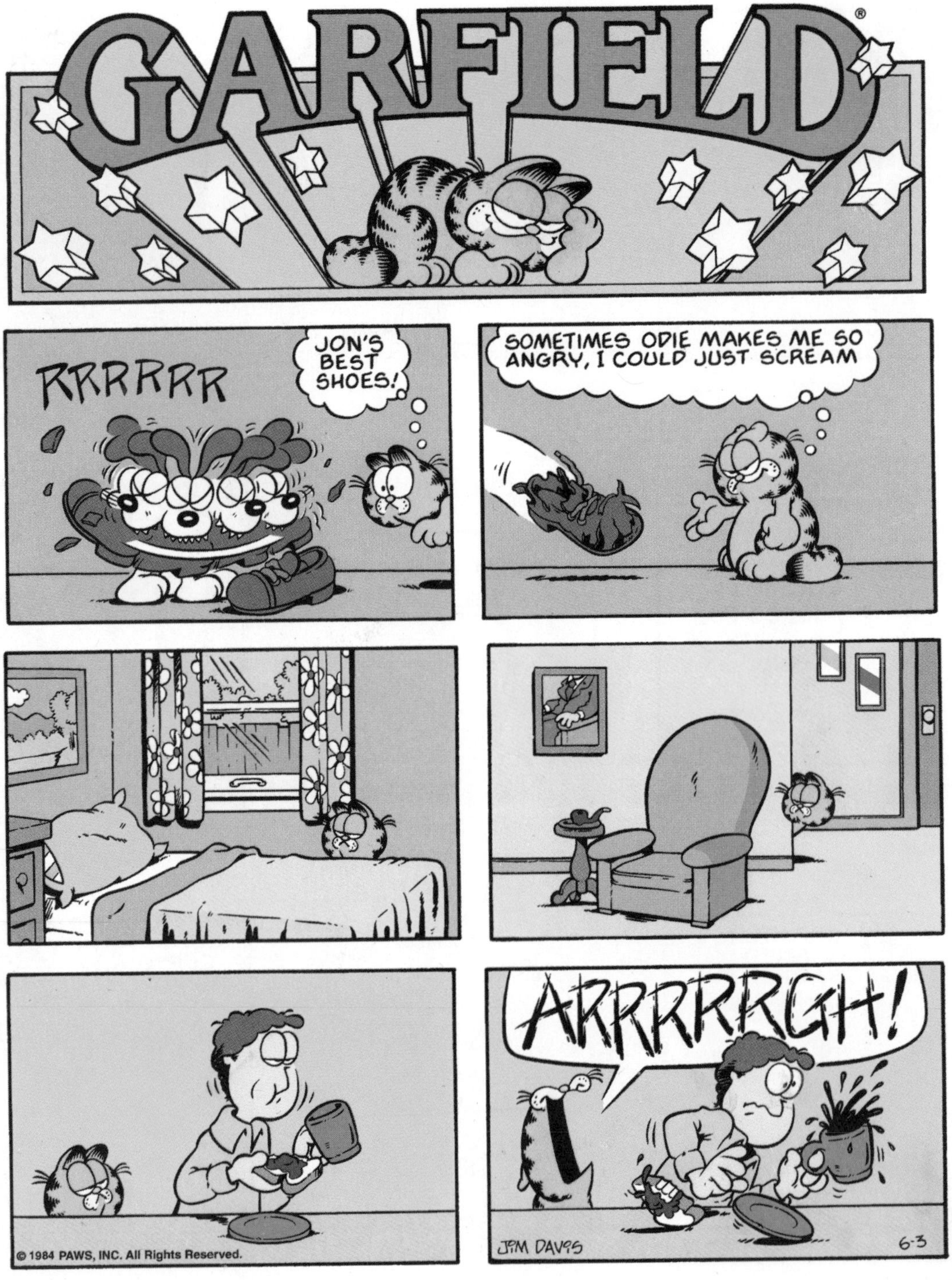
GARFIELD®
RRRRRR
JON'S BEST SHOES!
SOMETIMES ODIE MAKES ME SO ANGRY, I COULD JUST SCREAM
ARRRRRGH!
JIM DAVIS
6-3

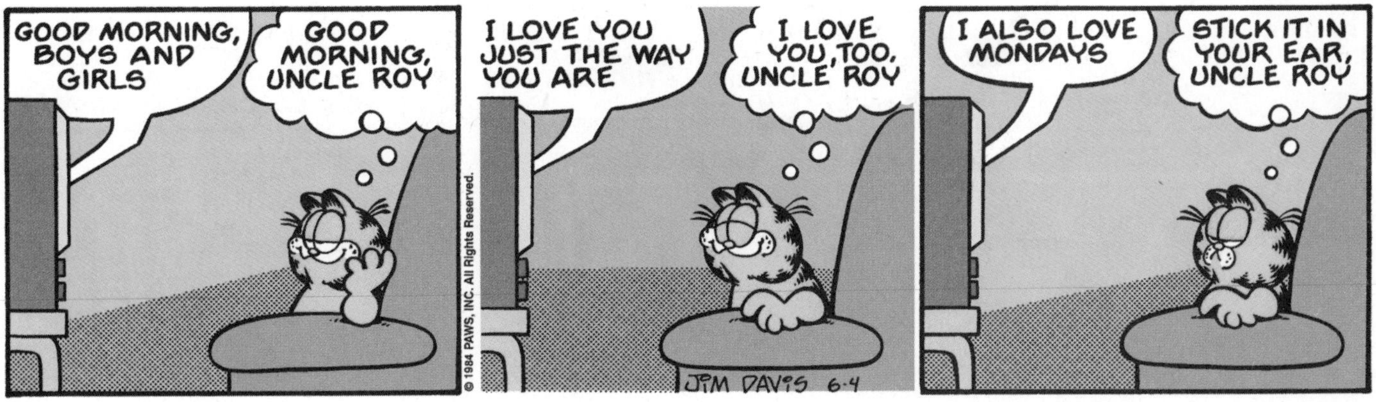
GOOD MORNING, BOYS AND GIRLS
GOOD MORNING, UNCLE ROY
I LOVE YOU JUST THE WAY YOU ARE
I LOVE YOU, TOO, UNCLE ROY
I ALSO LOVE MONDAYS
STICK IT IN YOUR EAR, UNCLE ROY
JIM DAVIS 6-4

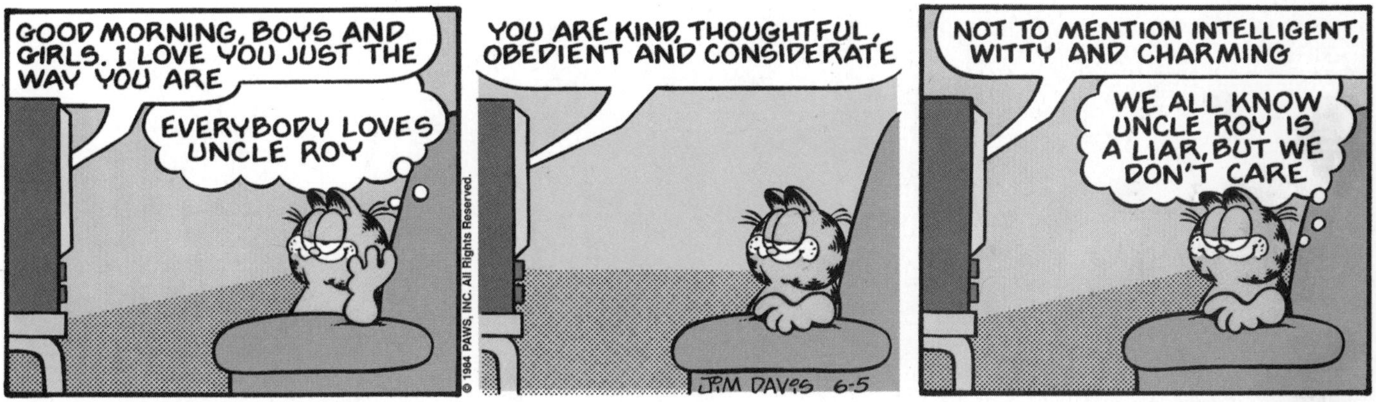
GOOD MORNING, BOYS AND GIRLS. I LOVE YOU JUST THE WAY YOU ARE
EVERYBODY LOVES UNCLE ROY
YOU ARE KIND, THOUGHTFUL, OBEDIENT AND CONSIDERATE
NOT TO MENTION INTELLIGENT, WITTY AND CHARMING
WE ALL KNOW UNCLE ROY IS A LIAR, BUT WE DON'T CARE
JIM DAVIS 6-5

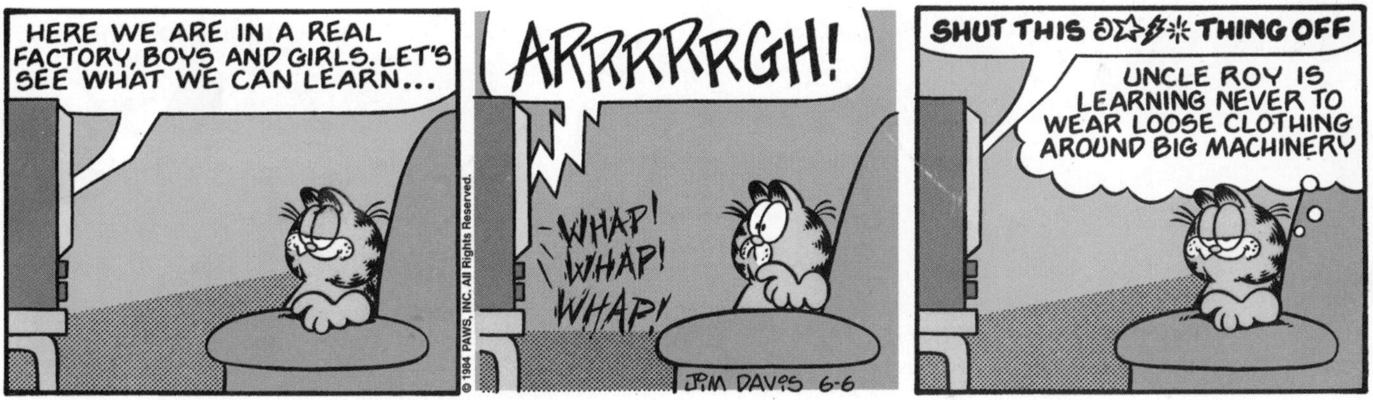
HERE WE ARE IN A REAL FACTORY, BOYS AND GIRLS. LET'S SEE WHAT WE CAN LEARN...
ARRRRRGH!
WHAP! WHAP! WHAP!
SHUT THIS ∂☆⚡✳ THING OFF
UNCLE ROY IS LEARNING NEVER TO WEAR LOOSE CLOTHING AROUND BIG MACHINERY
JIM DAVIS 6-6

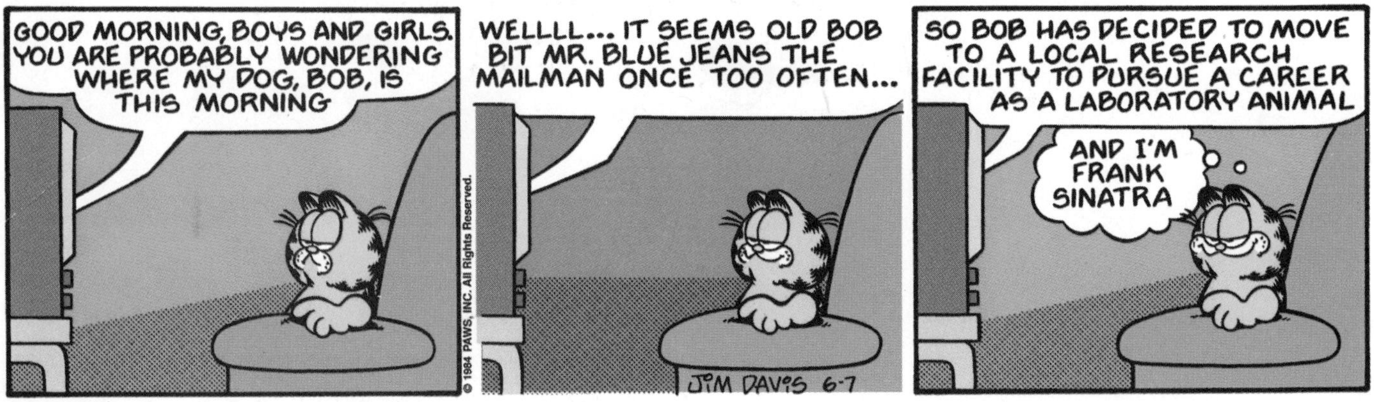
GOOD MORNING, BOYS AND GIRLS. YOU ARE PROBABLY WONDERING WHERE MY DOG, BOB, IS THIS MORNING
WELLLL... IT SEEMS OLD BOB BIT MR. BLUE JEANS THE MAILMAN ONCE TOO OFTEN...
© 1984 PAWS, INC. All Rights Reserved.
JIM DAVIS 6-7
SO BOB HAS DECIDED TO MOVE TO A LOCAL RESEARCH FACILITY TO PURSUE A CAREER AS A LABORATORY ANIMAL
AND I'M FRANK SINATRA

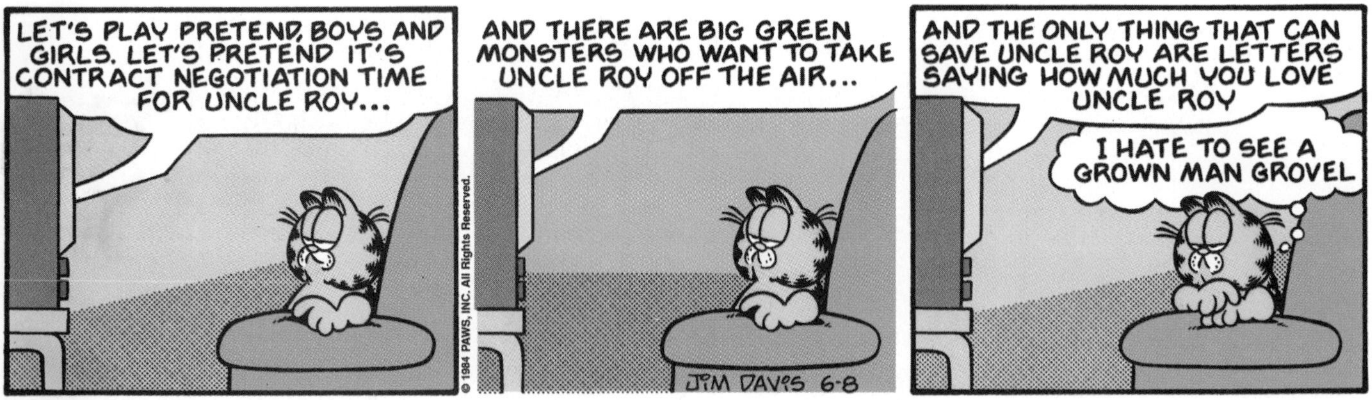
LET'S PLAY PRETEND, BOYS AND GIRLS. LET'S PRETEND IT'S CONTRACT NEGOTIATION TIME FOR UNCLE ROY...
AND THERE ARE BIG GREEN MONSTERS WHO WANT TO TAKE UNCLE ROY OFF THE AIR...
© 1984 PAWS, INC. All Rights Reserved.
JIM DAVIS 6-8
AND THE ONLY THING THAT CAN SAVE UNCLE ROY ARE LETTERS SAYING HOW MUCH YOU LOVE UNCLE ROY
I HATE TO SEE A GROWN MAN GROVEL

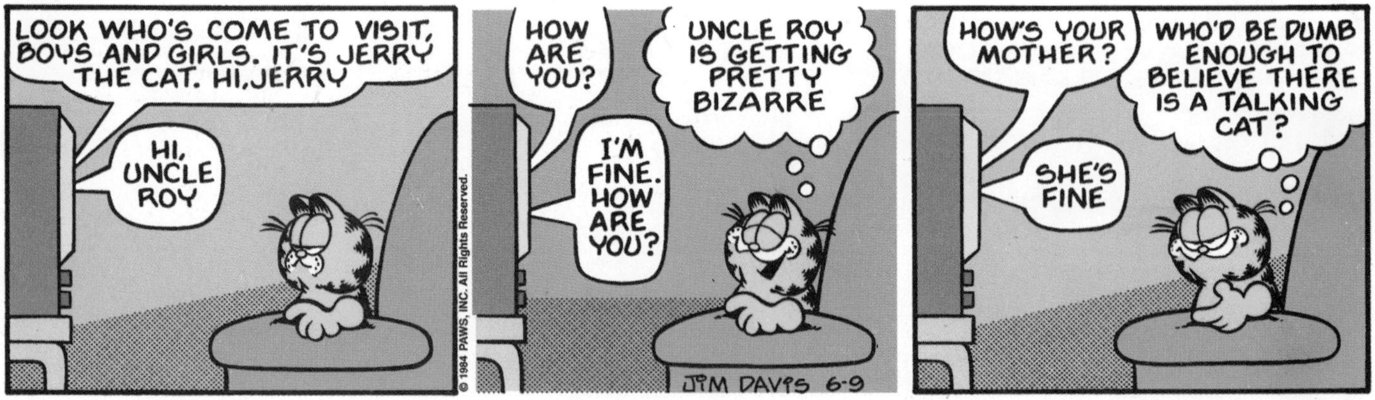
LOOK WHO'S COME TO VISIT, BOYS AND GIRLS. IT'S JERRY THE CAT. HI, JERRY
HI, UNCLE ROY
HOW ARE YOU?
I'M FINE. HOW ARE YOU?
UNCLE ROY IS GETTING PRETTY BIZARRE
© 1984 PAWS, INC. All Rights Reserved.
JIM DAVIS 6-9
HOW'S YOUR MOTHER?
SHE'S FINE
WHO'D BE DUMB ENOUGH TO BELIEVE THERE IS A TALKING CAT?

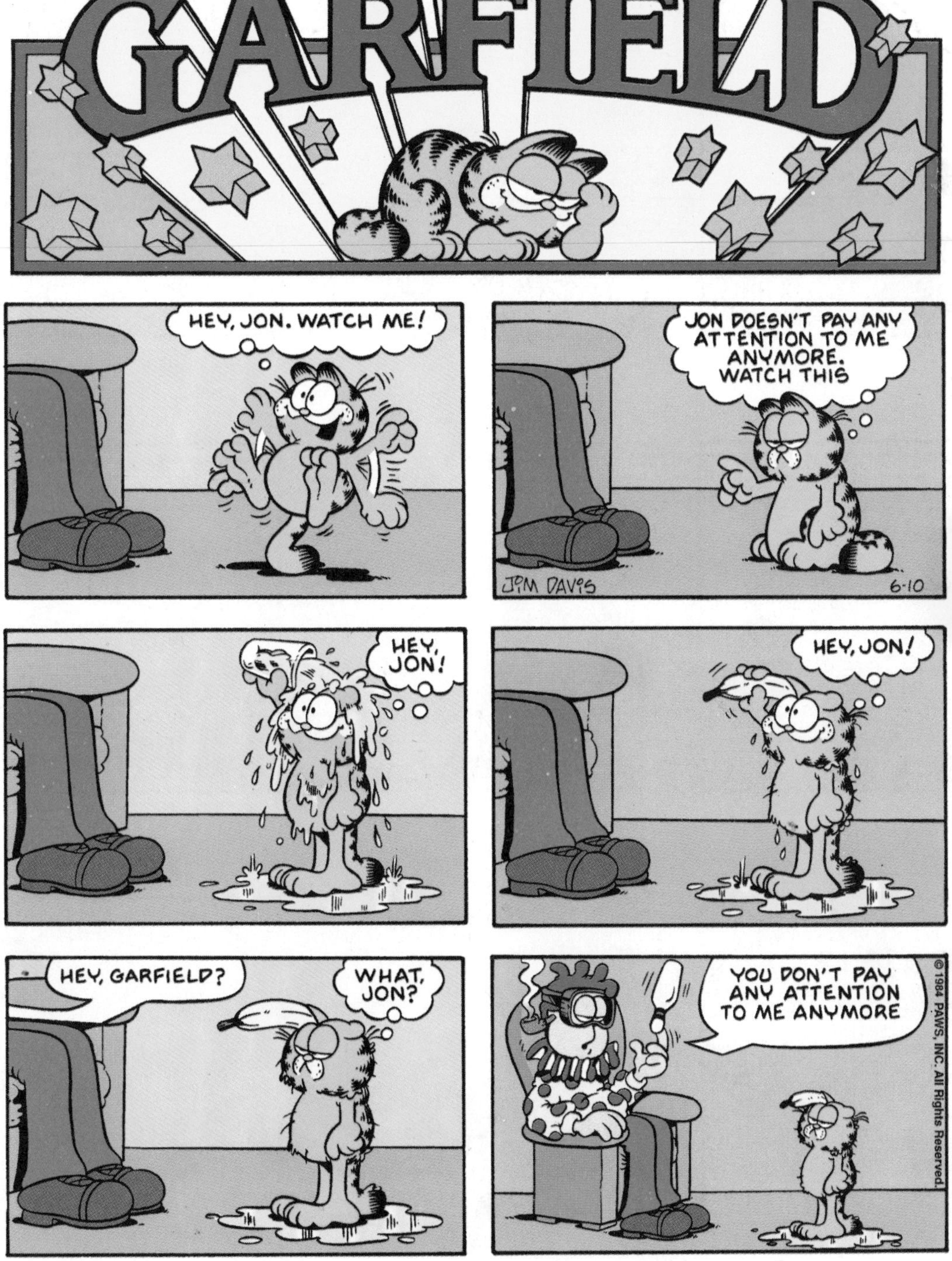
GARFIELD
HEY, JON. WATCH ME!
JON DOESN'T PAY ANY ATTENTION TO ME ANYMORE. WATCH THIS
JIM DAVIS
6-10
HEY, JON!
HEY, JON!
HEY, GARFIELD?
WHAT, JON?
YOU DON'T PAY ANY ATTENTION TO ME ANYMORE
© 1984 PAWS, INC. All Rights Reserved.

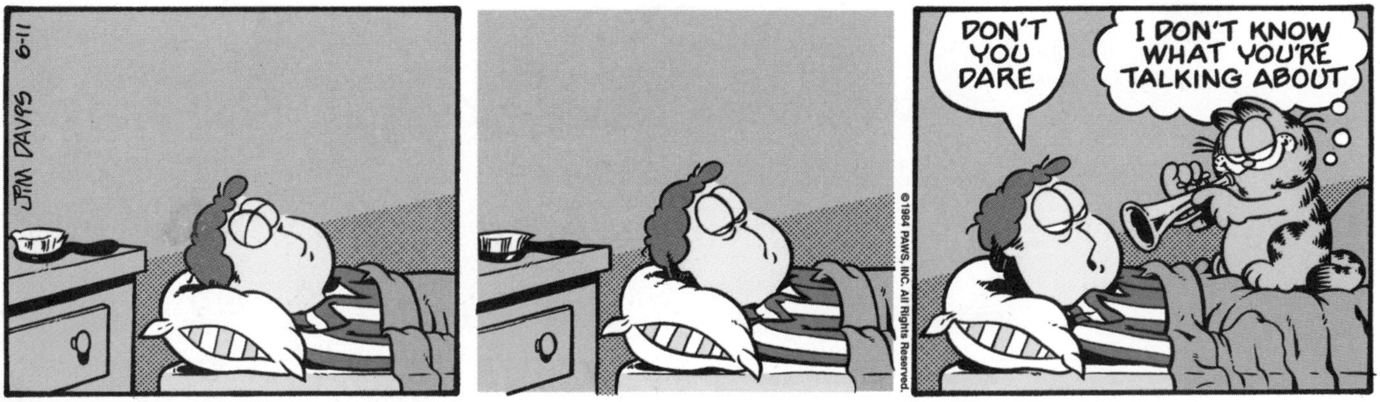
JIM DAVIS 6-11
© 1984 PAWS, INC. All Rights Reserved.
DON'T YOU DARE
I DON'T KNOW WHAT YOU'RE TALKING ABOUT

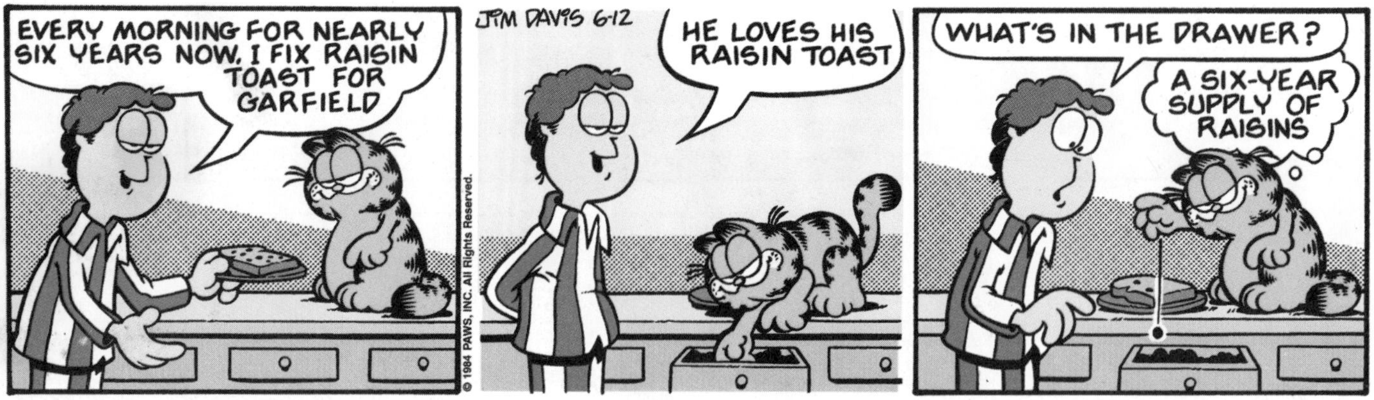
EVERY MORNING FOR NEARLY SIX YEARS NOW, I FIX RAISIN TOAST FOR GARFIELD
© 1984 PAWS, INC. All Rights Reserved.
JIM DAVIS 6-12
HE LOVES HIS RAISIN TOAST
WHAT'S IN THE DRAWER?
A SIX-YEAR SUPPLY OF RAISINS

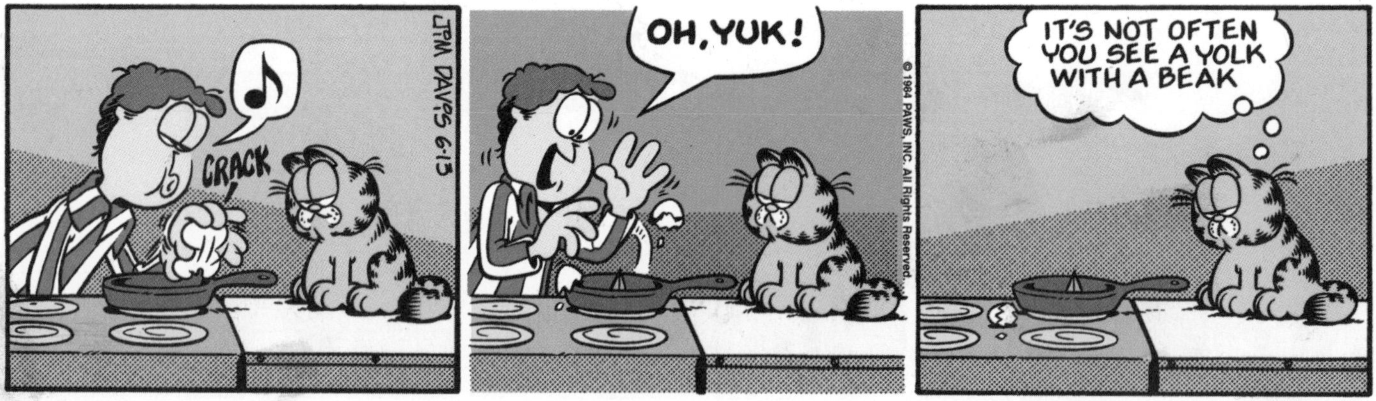
JIM DAVIS 6-13
♪
CRACK
OH, YUK!
© 1984 PAWS, INC. All Rights Reserved.
IT'S NOT OFTEN YOU SEE A YOLK WITH A BEAK

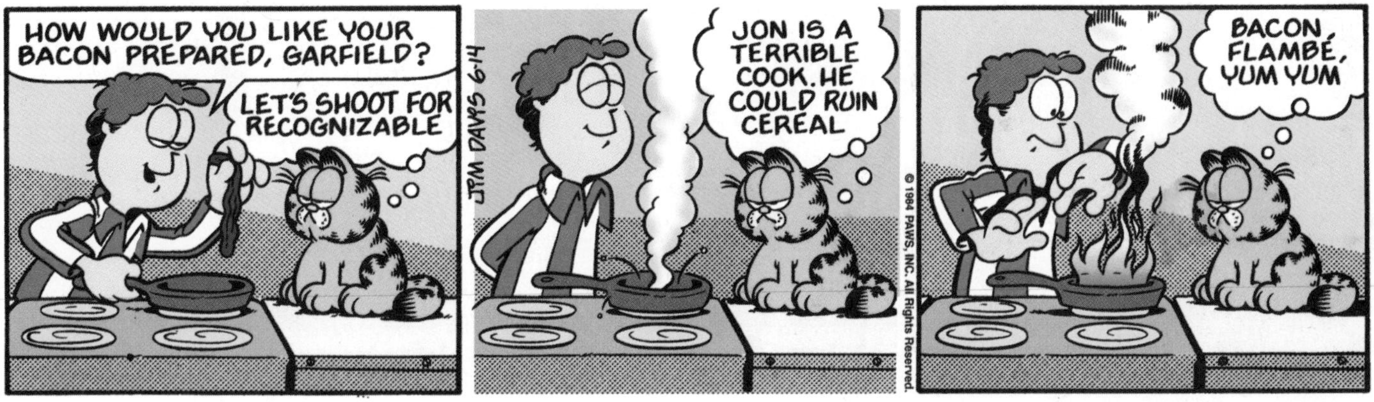
HOW WOULD YOU LIKE YOUR BACON PREPARED, GARFIELD?
LET'S SHOOT FOR RECOGNIZABLE
JIM DAVIS 6-14
JON IS A TERRIBLE COOK. HE COULD RUIN CEREAL
© 1984 PAWS, INC. All Rights Reserved.
BACON, FLAMBÉ, YUM YUM

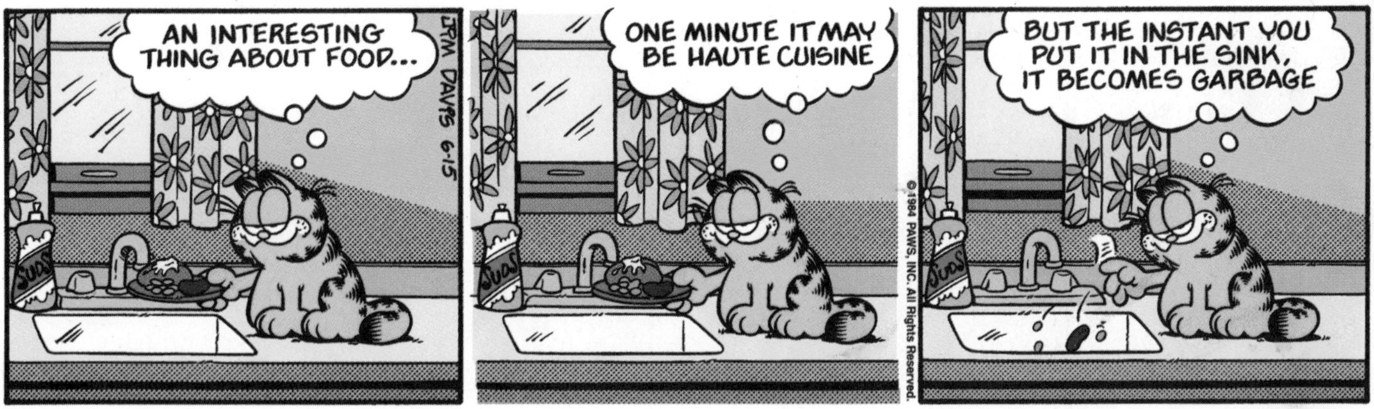
AN INTERESTING THING ABOUT FOOD...
JIM DAVIS 6-15
SUDS
ONE MINUTE IT MAY BE HAUTE CUISINE
© 1984 PAWS, INC. All Rights Reserved.
BUT THE INSTANT YOU PUT IT IN THE SINK, IT BECOMES GARBAGE

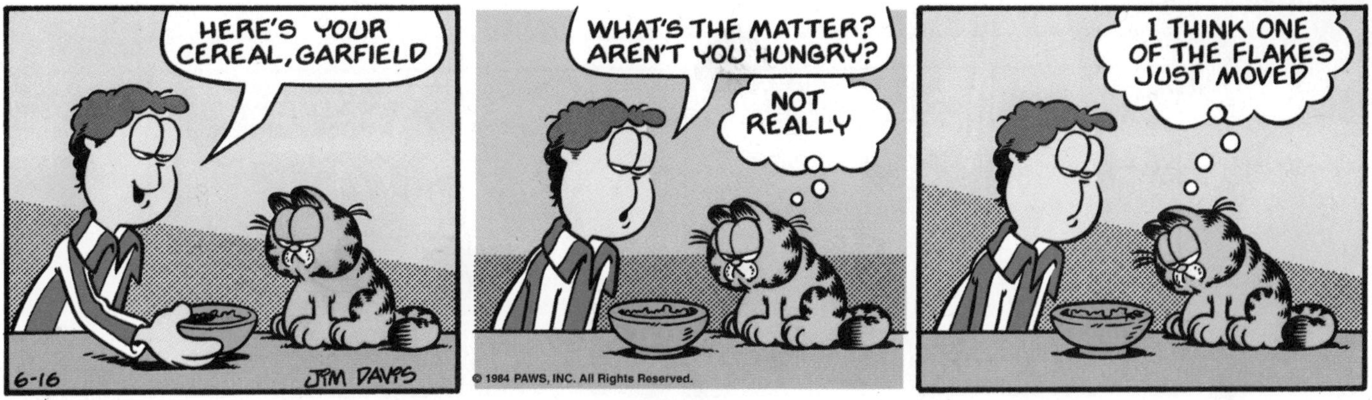
HERE'S YOUR CEREAL, GARFIELD
6-16
JIM DAVIS
WHAT'S THE MATTER? AREN'T YOU HUNGRY?
NOT REALLY
© 1984 PAWS, INC. All Rights Reserved.
I THINK ONE OF THE FLAKES JUST MOVED

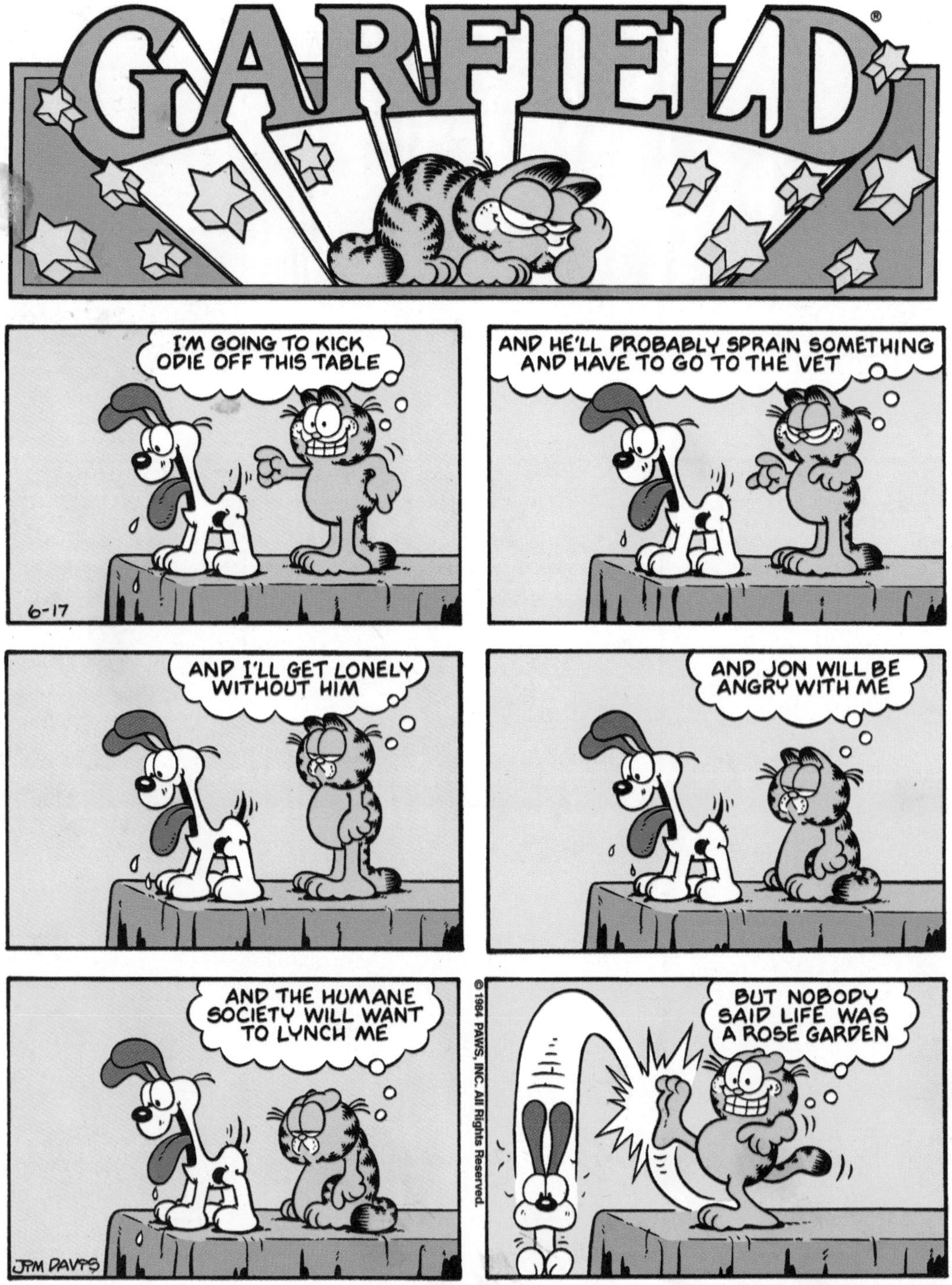
GARFIELD®
I'M GOING TO KICK ODIE OFF THIS TABLE
6-17
AND HE'LL PROBABLY SPRAIN SOMETHING AND HAVE TO GO TO THE VET
AND I'LL GET LONELY WITHOUT HIM
AND JON WILL BE ANGRY WITH ME
AND THE HUMANE SOCIETY WILL WANT TO LYNCH ME
JIM DAVIS
BUT NOBODY SAID LIFE WAS A ROSE GARDEN

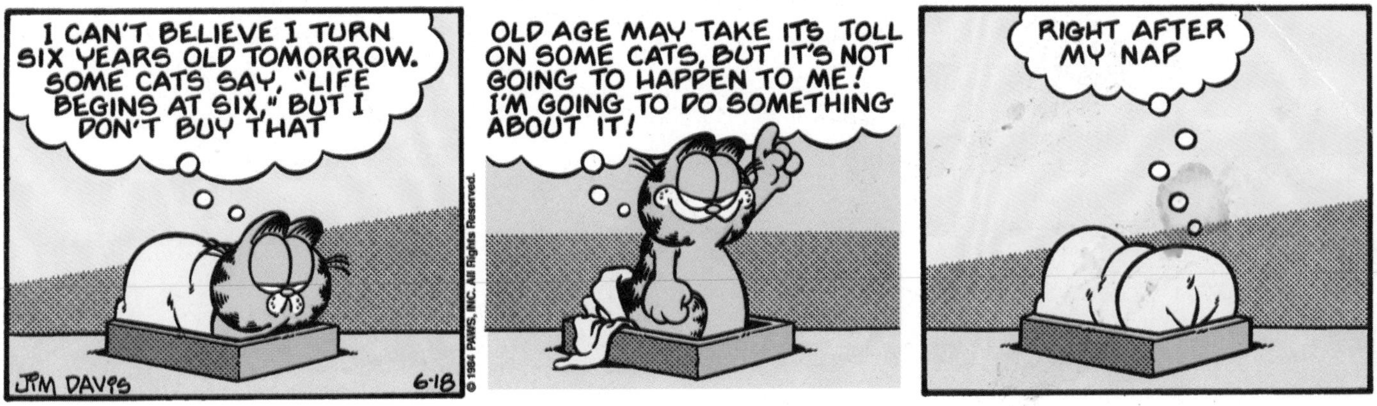
I CAN'T BELIEVE I TURN SIX YEARS OLD TOMORROW. SOME CATS SAY, "LIFE BEGINS AT SIX," BUT I DON'T BUY THAT
JIM DAVIS
6-18
© 1984 PAWS, INC. All Rights Reserved.
OLD AGE MAY TAKE ITS TOLL ON SOME CATS, BUT IT'S NOT GOING TO HAPPEN TO ME! I'M GOING TO DO SOMETHING ABOUT IT!
RIGHT AFTER MY NAP

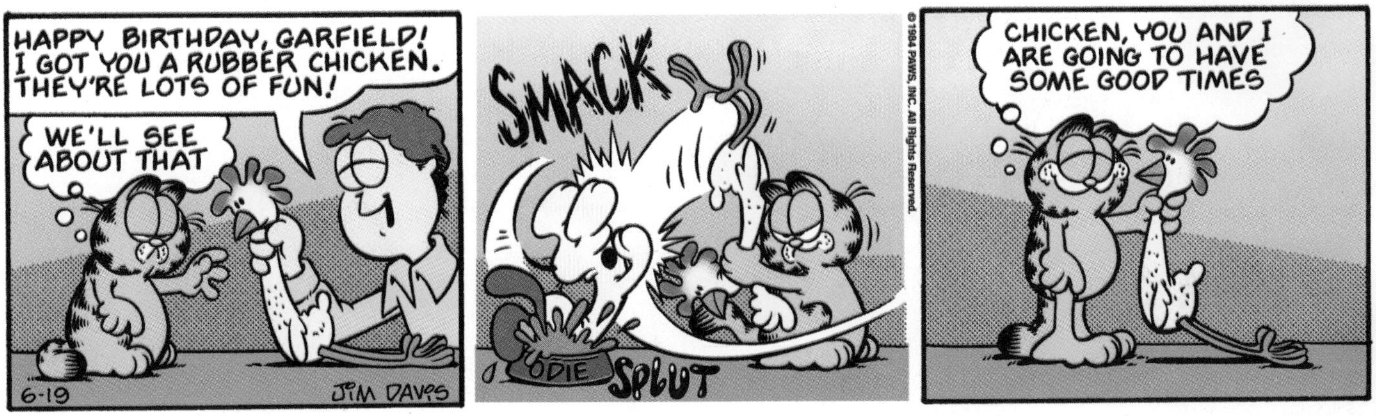
HAPPY BIRTHDAY, GARFIELD! I GOT YOU A RUBBER CHICKEN. THEY'RE LOTS OF FUN!
WE'LL SEE ABOUT THAT
6-19
JIM DAVIS
SMACK
ODIE
SPLUT
© 1984 PAWS, INC. All Rights Reserved.
CHICKEN, YOU AND I ARE GOING TO HAVE SOME GOOD TIMES

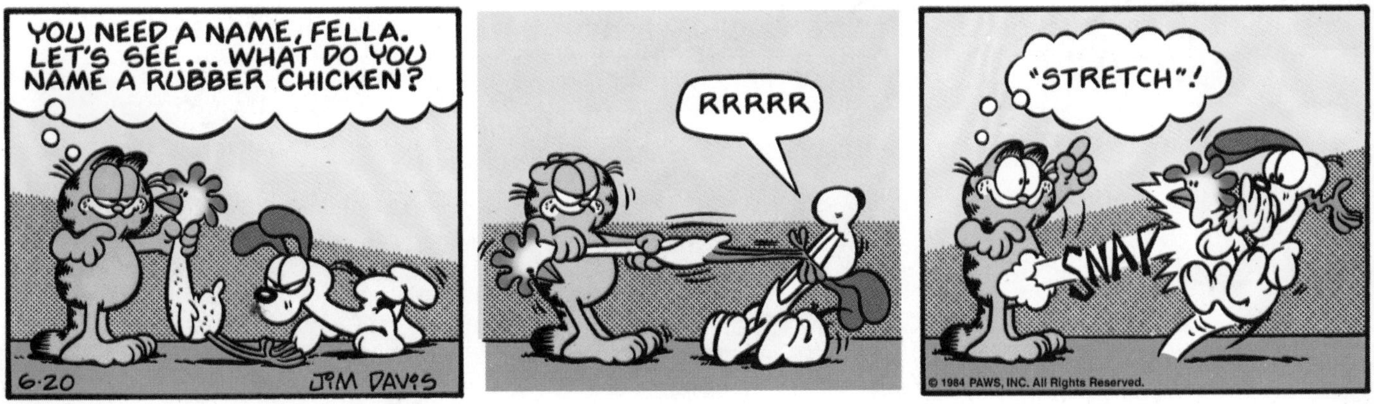
YOU NEED A NAME, FELLA. LET'S SEE... WHAT DO YOU NAME A RUBBER CHICKEN?
6-20
JIM DAVIS
RRRRR
"STRETCH"!
SNAP
© 1984 PAWS, INC. All Rights Reserved.

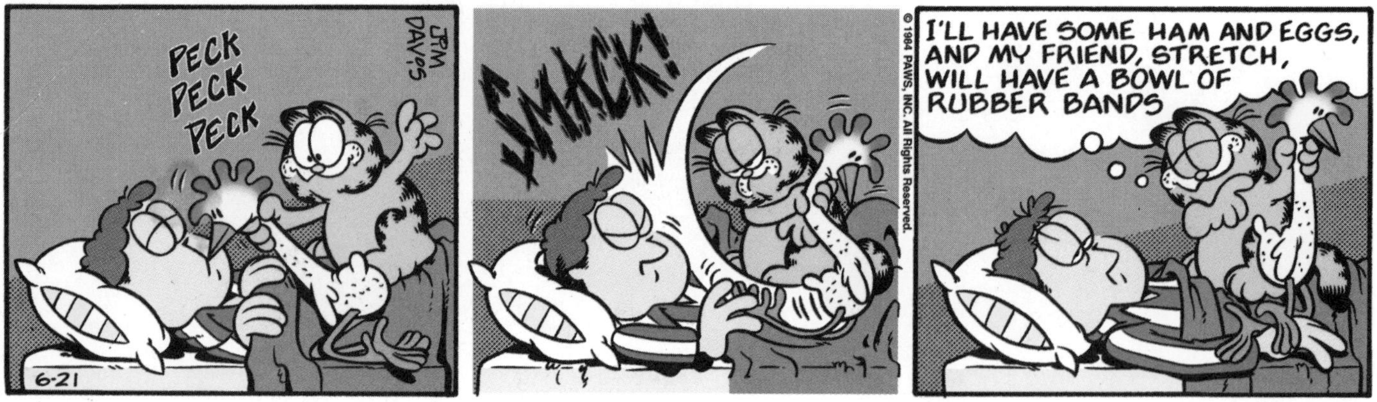
PECK
PECK
PECK
JIM DAVIS
6-21
SMACK!
© 1984 PAWS, INC. All Rights Reserved.
I'LL HAVE SOME HAM AND EGGS, AND MY FRIEND, STRETCH, WILL HAVE A BOWL OF RUBBER BANDS

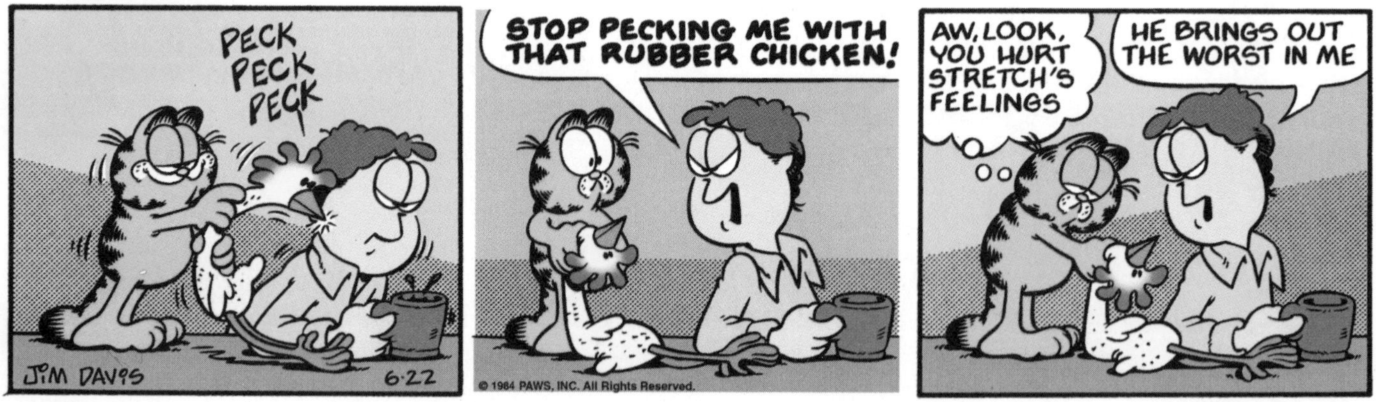
PECK
PECK
PECK
JIM DAVIS
6-22
STOP PECKING ME WITH THAT RUBBER CHICKEN!
© 1984 PAWS, INC. All Rights Reserved.
AW, LOOK, YOU HURT STRETCH'S FEELINGS
HE BRINGS OUT THE WORST IN ME

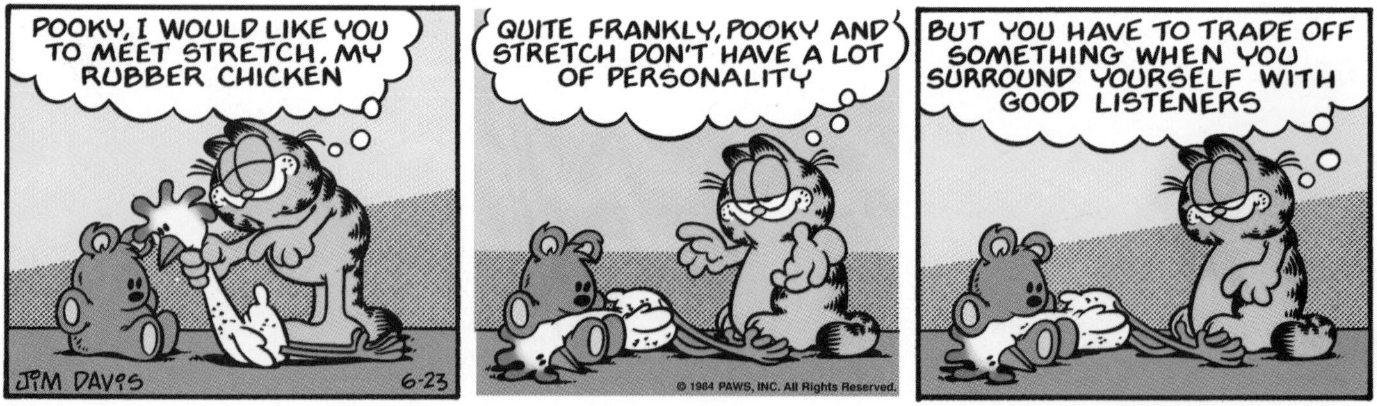
POOKY, I WOULD LIKE YOU TO MEET STRETCH, MY RUBBER CHICKEN
JIM DAVIS
6-23
QUITE FRANKLY, POOKY AND STRETCH DON'T HAVE A LOT OF PERSONALITY
© 1984 PAWS, INC. All Rights Reserved.
BUT YOU HAVE TO TRADE OFF SOMETHING WHEN YOU SURROUND YOURSELF WITH GOOD LISTENERS

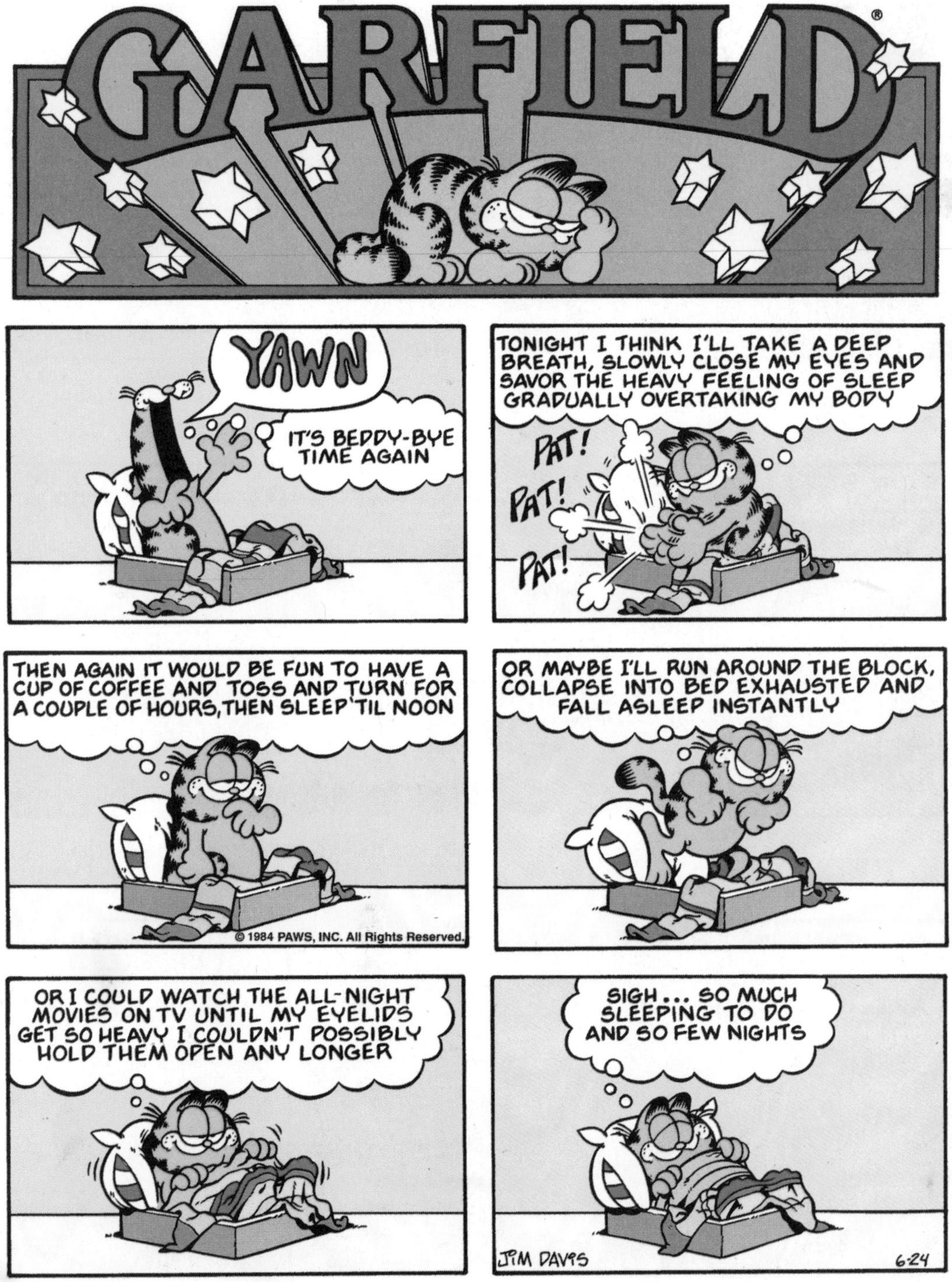
GARFIELD®
YAWN
IT'S BEDDY-BYE TIME AGAIN
TONIGHT I THINK I'LL TAKE A DEEP BREATH, SLOWLY CLOSE MY EYES AND SAVOR THE HEAVY FEELING OF SLEEP GRADUALLY OVERTAKING MY BODY
PAT!
PAT!
PAT!
THEN AGAIN IT WOULD BE FUN TO HAVE A CUP OF COFFEE AND TOSS AND TURN FOR A COUPLE OF HOURS, THEN SLEEP 'TIL NOON
© 1984 PAWS, INC. All Rights Reserved.
OR MAYBE I'LL RUN AROUND THE BLOCK, COLLAPSE INTO BED EXHAUSTED AND FALL ASLEEP INSTANTLY
OR I COULD WATCH THE ALL-NIGHT MOVIES ON TV UNTIL MY EYELIDS GET SO HEAVY I COULDN'T POSSIBLY HOLD THEM OPEN ANY LONGER
SIGH... SO MUCH SLEEPING TO DO AND SO FEW NIGHTS
JIM DAVIS
6-24

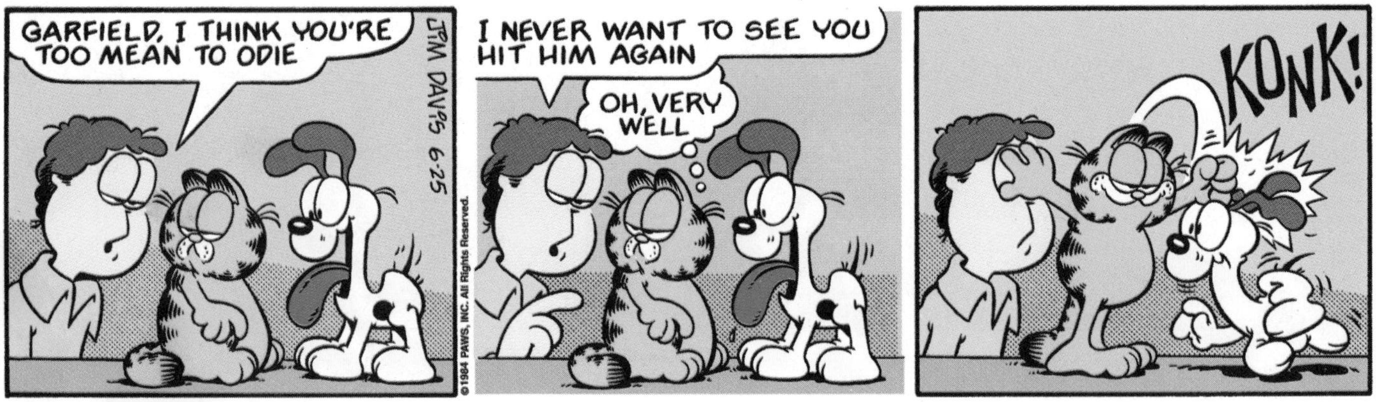
GARFIELD, I THINK YOU'RE TOO MEAN TO ODIE
JIM DAVIS 6-25
© 1984 PAWS, INC. All Rights Reserved.
I NEVER WANT TO SEE YOU HIT HIM AGAIN
OH, VERY WELL
KONK!

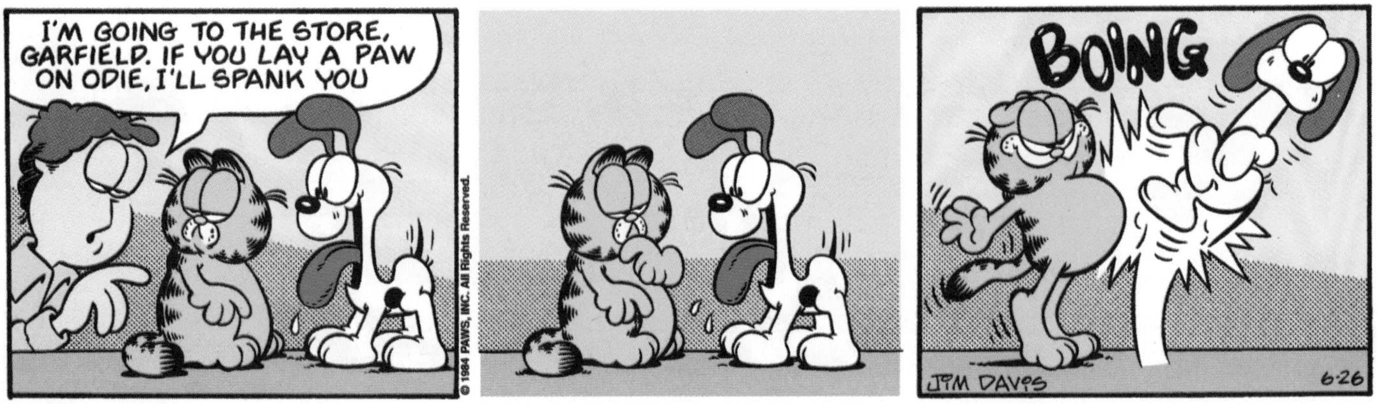
I'M GOING TO THE STORE, GARFIELD. IF YOU LAY A PAW ON ODIE, I'LL SPANK YOU
© 1984 PAWS, INC. All Rights Reserved.
BOING
JIM DAVIS
6-26

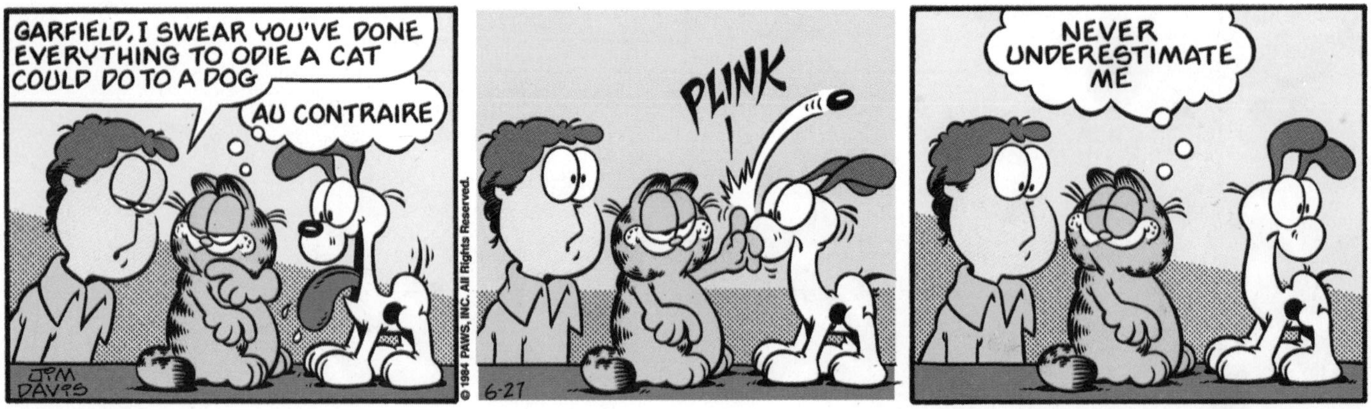
GARFIELD, I SWEAR YOU'VE DONE EVERYTHING TO ODIE A CAT COULD DO TO A DOG
AU CONTRAIRE
JIM DAVIS
© 1984 PAWS, INC. All Rights Reserved.
PLINK
6-27
NEVER UNDERESTIMATE ME

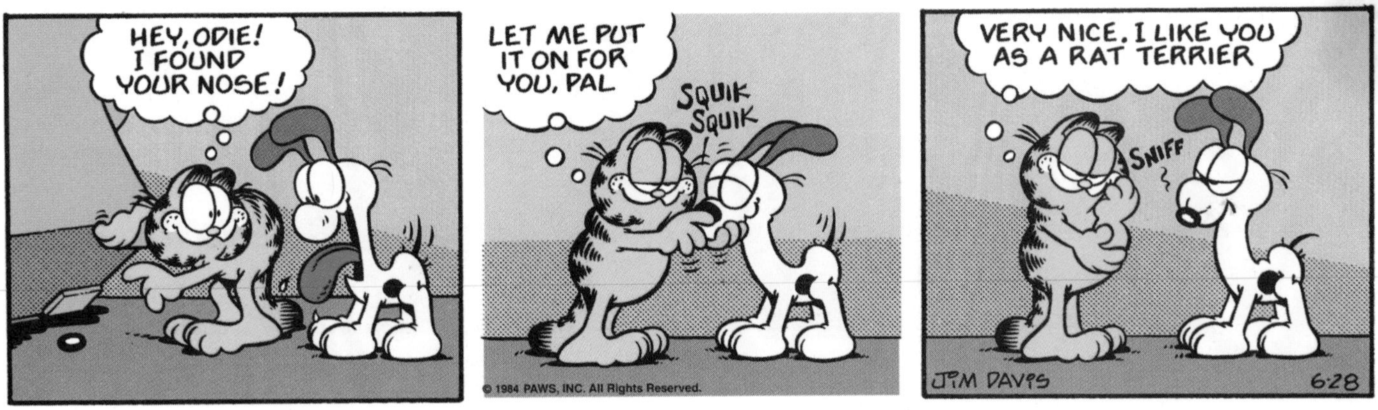
HEY, ODIE! I FOUND YOUR NOSE!
LET ME PUT IT ON FOR YOU, PAL
SQUIK SQUIK
© 1984 PAWS, INC. All Rights Reserved.
VERY NICE. I LIKE YOU AS A RAT TERRIER
SNIFF
JIM DAVIS 6-28

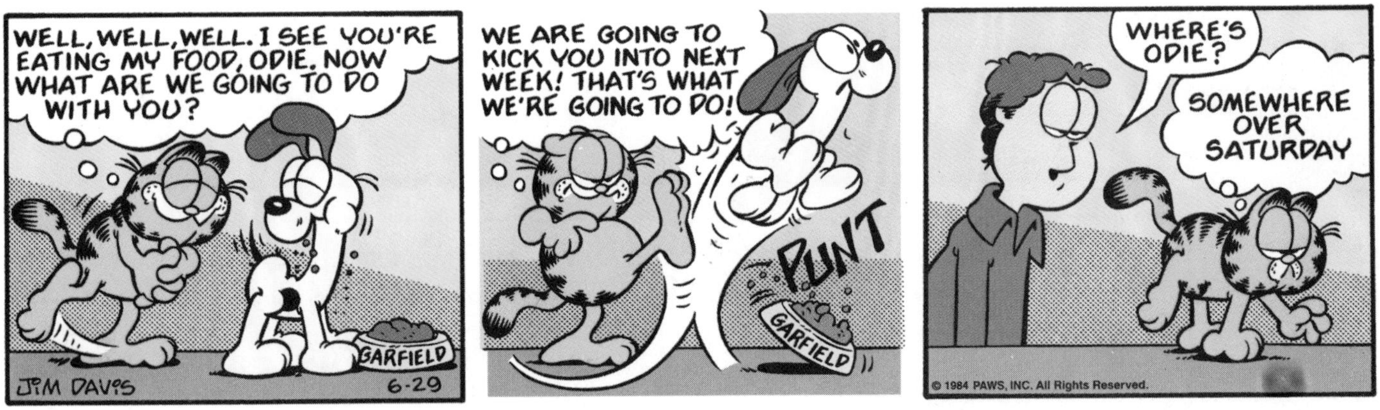
WELL, WELL, WELL. I SEE YOU'RE EATING MY FOOD, ODIE. NOW WHAT ARE WE GOING TO DO WITH YOU?
GARFIELD
JIM DAVIS 6-29
WE ARE GOING TO KICK YOU INTO NEXT WEEK! THAT'S WHAT WE'RE GOING TO DO!
PUNT
GARFIELD
WHERE'S ODIE?
SOMEWHERE OVER SATURDAY
© 1984 PAWS, INC. All Rights Reserved.

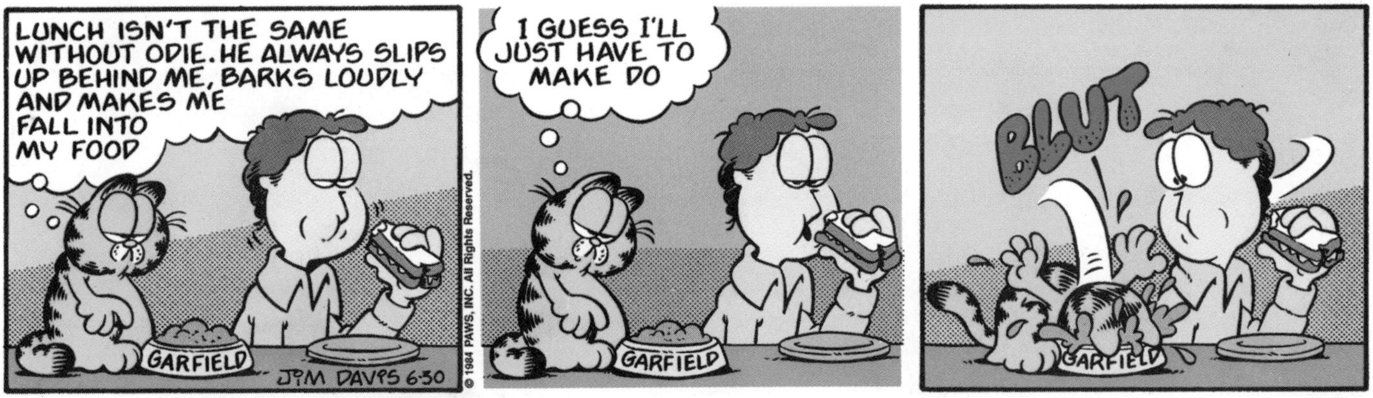
LUNCH ISN'T THE SAME WITHOUT ODIE. HE ALWAYS SLIPS UP BEHIND ME, BARKS LOUDLY AND MAKES ME FALL INTO MY FOOD
GARFIELD
JIM DAVIS 6-30
© 1984 PAWS, INC. All Rights Reserved.
I GUESS I'LL JUST HAVE TO MAKE DO
GARFIELD
BLUT
GARFIELD

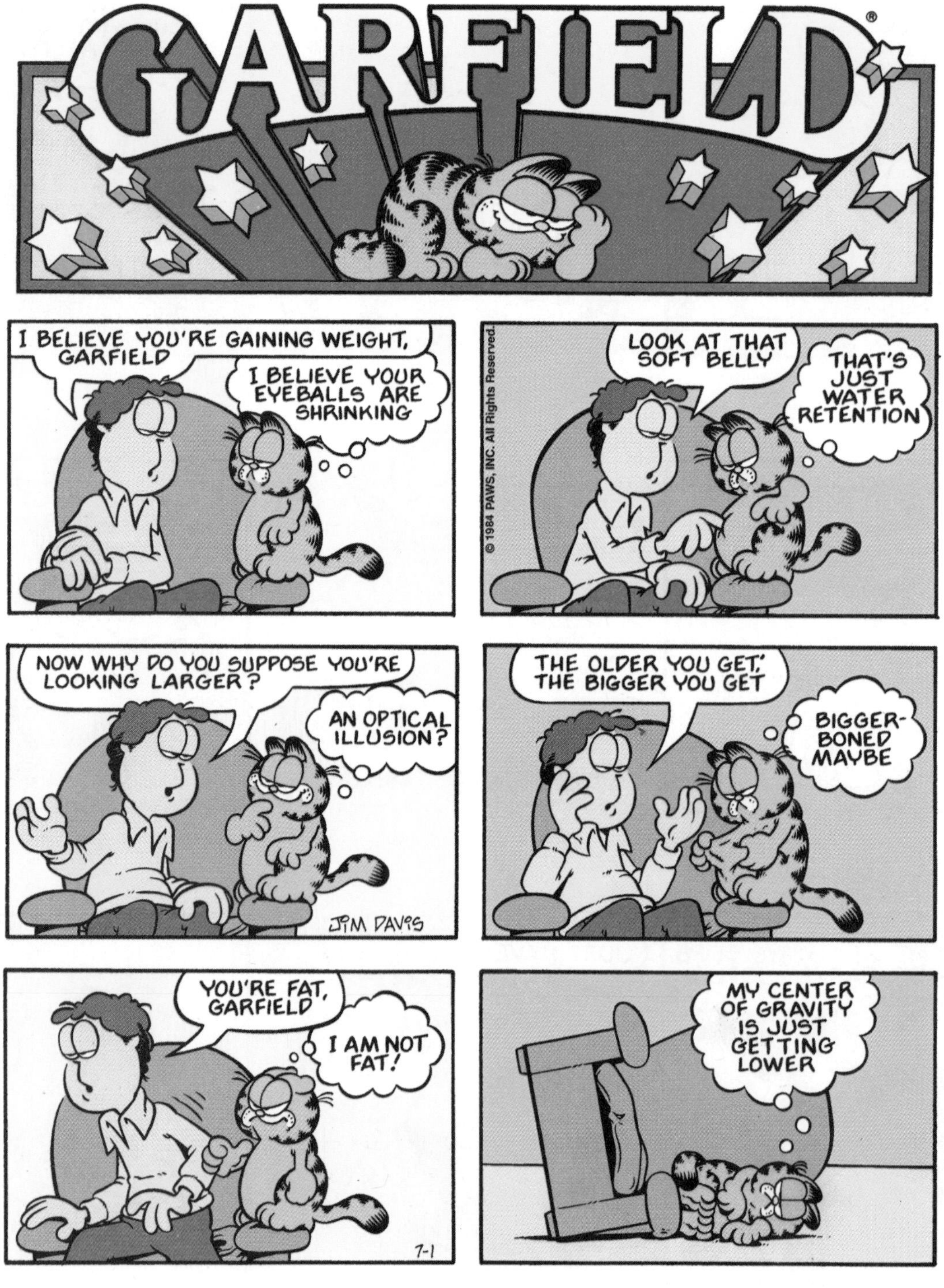
GARFIELD®
I BELIEVE YOU'RE GAINING WEIGHT, GARFIELD
I BELIEVE YOUR EYEBALLS ARE SHRINKING
© 1984 PAWS, INC. All Rights Reserved.
LOOK AT THAT SOFT BELLY
THAT'S JUST WATER RETENTION
NOW WHY DO YOU SUPPOSE YOU'RE LOOKING LARGER?
AN OPTICAL ILLUSION?
JIM DAVIS
THE OLDER YOU GET, THE BIGGER YOU GET
BIGGER-BONED MAYBE
YOU'RE FAT, GARFIELD
I AM NOT FAT!
7-1
MY CENTER OF GRAVITY IS JUST GETTING LOWER

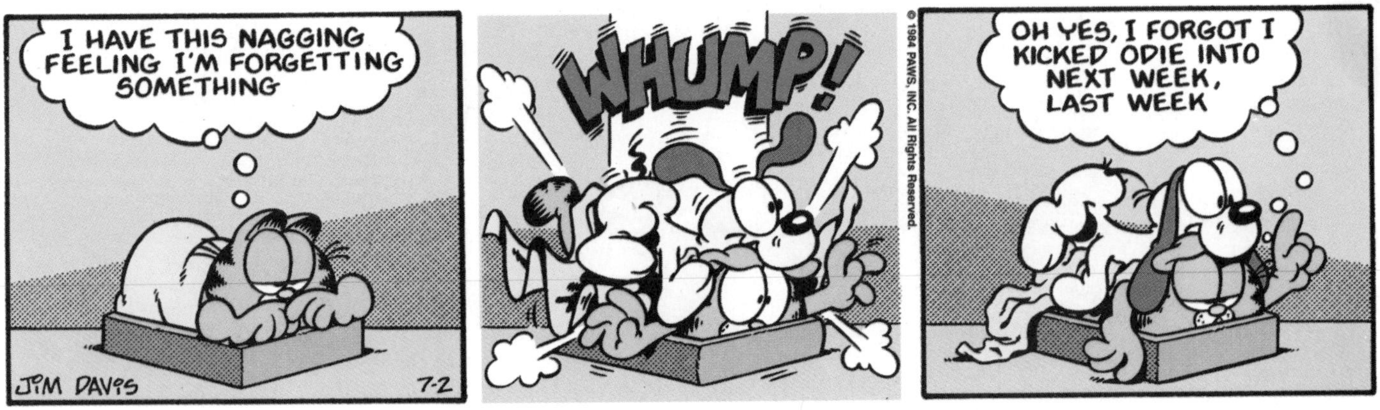
I HAVE THIS NAGGING FEELING I'M FORGETTING SOMETHING
JIM DAVIS
7-2
WHUMP!
© 1984 PAWS, INC. All Rights Reserved.
OH YES, I FORGOT I KICKED ODIE INTO NEXT WEEK, LAST WEEK

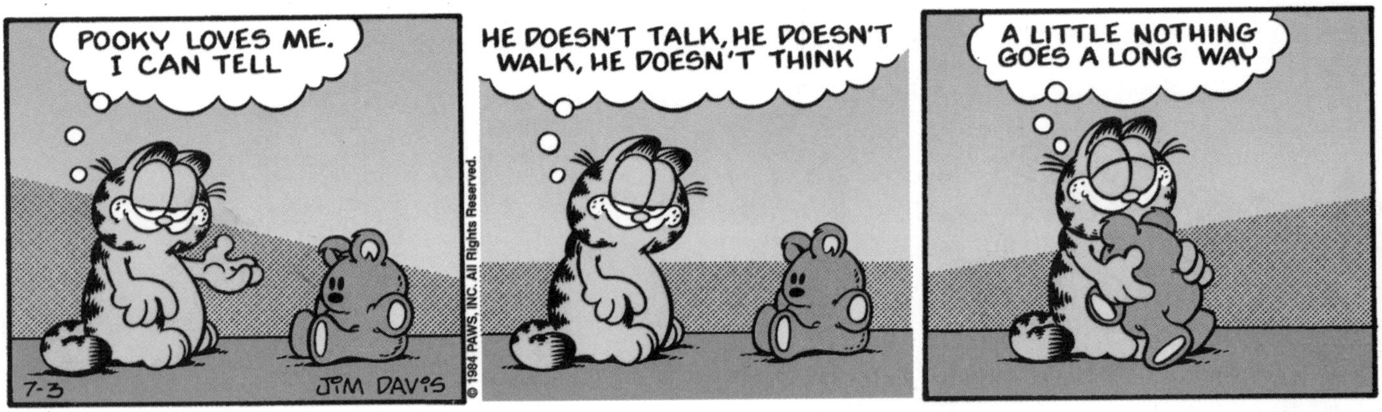
POOKY LOVES ME. I CAN TELL
7-3
JIM DAVIS
© 1984 PAWS, INC. All Rights Reserved.
HE DOESN'T TALK, HE DOESN'T WALK, HE DOESN'T THINK
A LITTLE NOTHING GOES A LONG WAY

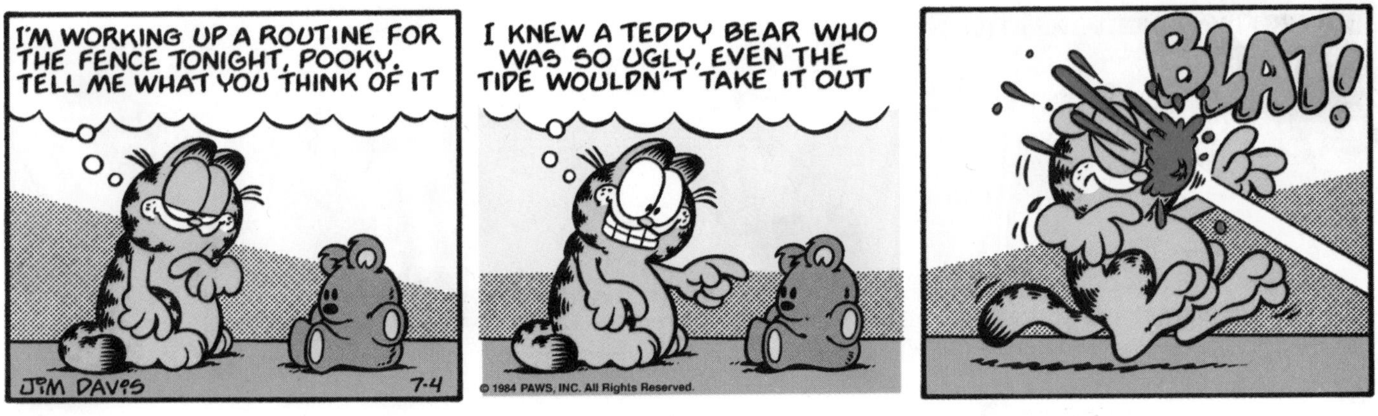
I'M WORKING UP A ROUTINE FOR THE FENCE TONIGHT, POOKY. TELL ME WHAT YOU THINK OF IT
JIM DAVIS
7-4
I KNEW A TEDDY BEAR WHO WAS SO UGLY, EVEN THE TIDE WOULDN'T TAKE IT OUT
© 1984 PAWS, INC. All Rights Reserved.
BLAT!

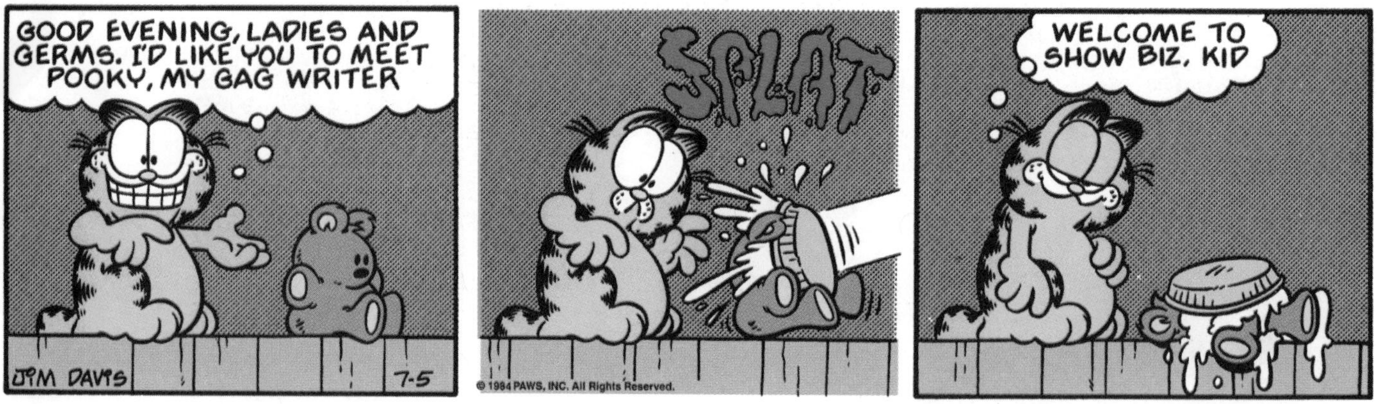
GOOD EVENING, LADIES AND GERMS. I'D LIKE YOU TO MEET POOKY, MY GAG WRITER
JIM DAVIS
7-5
SPLAT
© 1984 PAWS, INC. All Rights Reserved.
WELCOME TO SHOW BIZ, KID

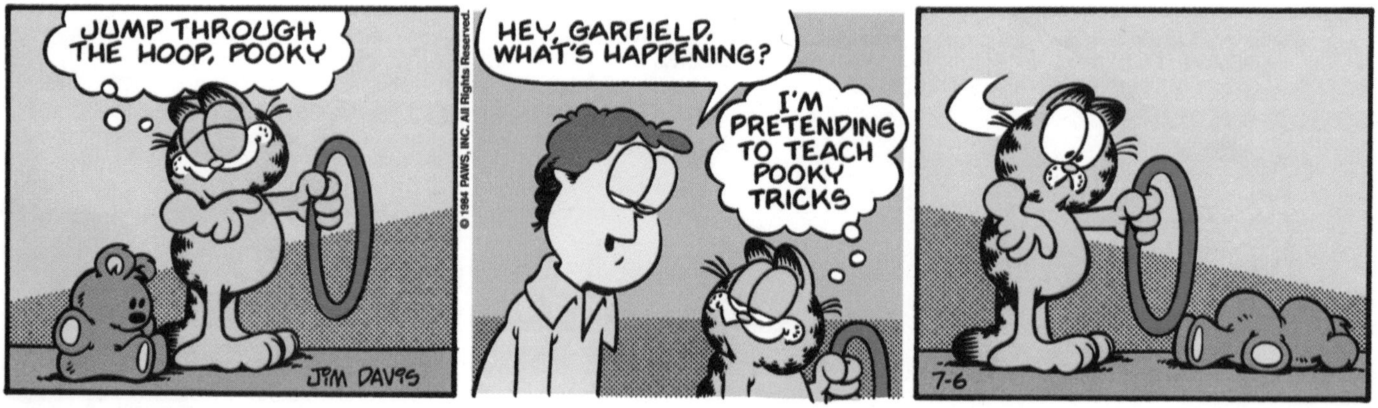
JUMP THROUGH THE HOOP, POOKY
JIM DAVIS
© 1984 PAWS, INC. All Rights Reserved.
HEY, GARFIELD. WHAT'S HAPPENING?
I'M PRETENDING TO TEACH POOKY TRICKS
7-6

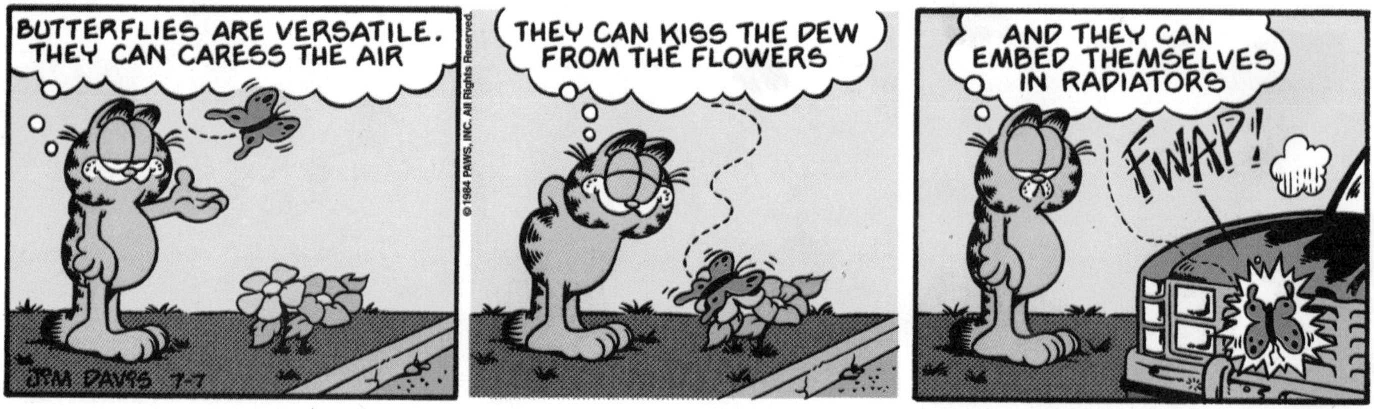
BUTTERFLIES ARE VERSATILE. THEY CAN CARESS THE AIR
JIM DAVIS 7-7
© 1984 PAWS, INC. All Rights Reserved.
THEY CAN KISS THE DEW FROM THE FLOWERS
AND THEY CAN EMBED THEMSELVES IN RADIATORS
FWAP!

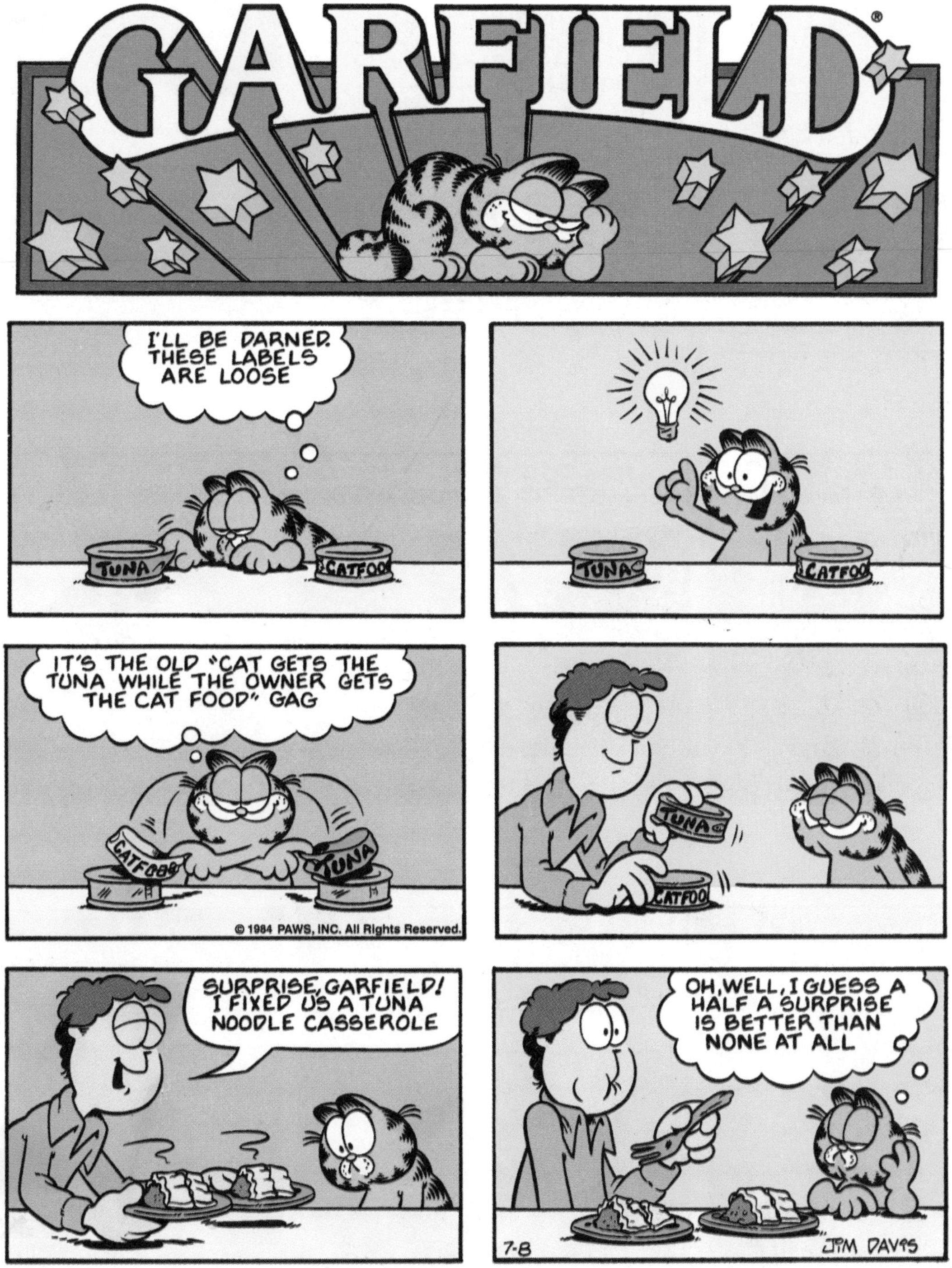
GARFIELD
I'LL BE DARNED. THESE LABELS ARE LOOSE
IT'S THE OLD "CAT GETS THE TUNA WHILE THE OWNER GETS THE CAT FOOD" GAG
© 1984 PAWS, INC. All Rights Reserved.
SURPRISE, GARFIELD! I FIXED US A TUNA NOODLE CASSEROLE
OH, WELL, I GUESS A HALF A SURPRISE IS BETTER THAN NONE AT ALL
7-8

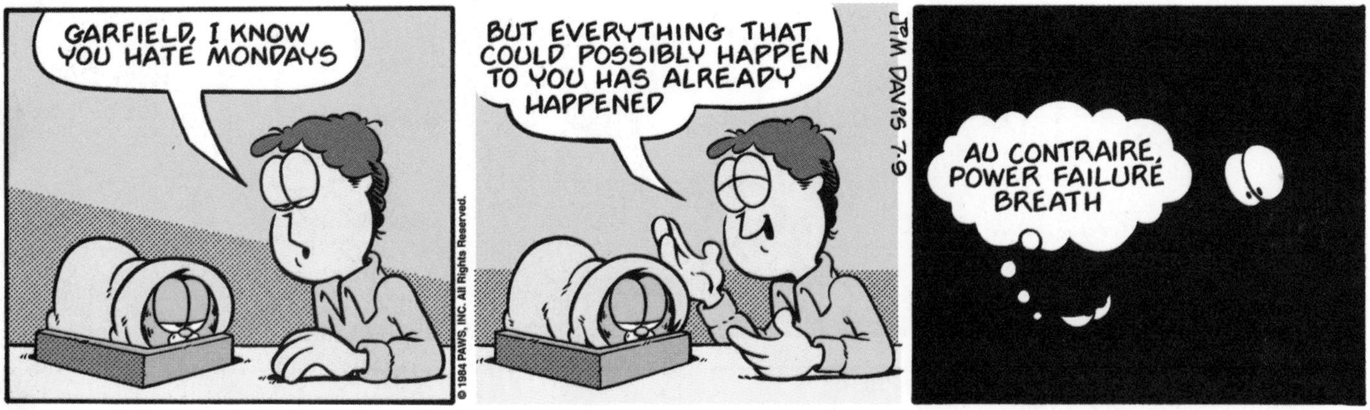
GARFIELD, I KNOW YOU HATE MONDAYS
© 1984 PAWS, INC. All Rights Reserved.
BUT EVERYTHING THAT COULD POSSIBLY HAPPEN TO YOU HAS ALREADY HAPPENED
JIM DAVIS 7-9
AU CONTRAIRE, POWER FAILURE BREATH

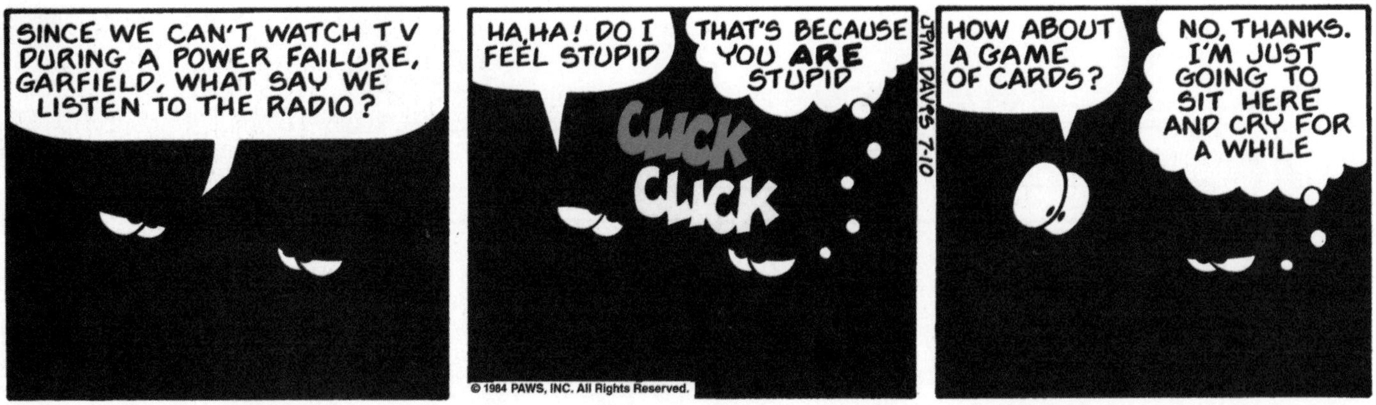
SINCE WE CAN'T WATCH T V DURING A POWER FAILURE, GARFIELD, WHAT SAY WE LISTEN TO THE RADIO?
HA,HA! DO I FEEL STUPID
THAT'S BECAUSE YOU **ARE** STUPID
CLICK
CLICK
© 1984 PAWS, INC. All Rights Reserved.
JIM DAVIS 7-10
HOW ABOUT A GAME OF CARDS?
NO, THANKS. I'M JUST GOING TO SIT HERE AND CRY FOR A WHILE

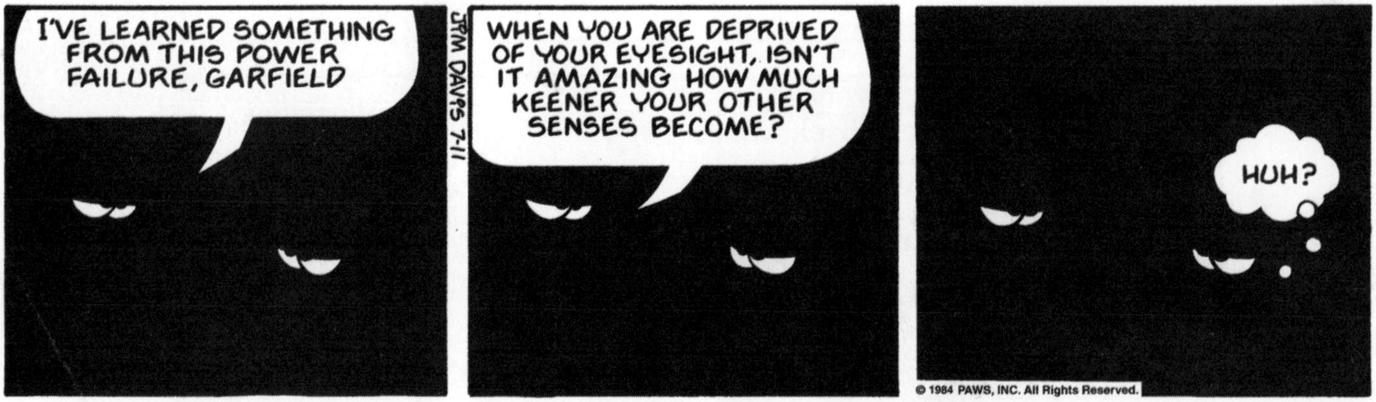
I'VE LEARNED SOMETHING FROM THIS POWER FAILURE, GARFIELD
JIM DAVIS 7-11
WHEN YOU ARE DEPRIVED OF YOUR EYESIGHT, ISN'T IT AMAZING HOW MUCH KEENER YOUR OTHER SENSES BECOME?
HUH?
© 1984 PAWS, INC. All Rights Reserved.

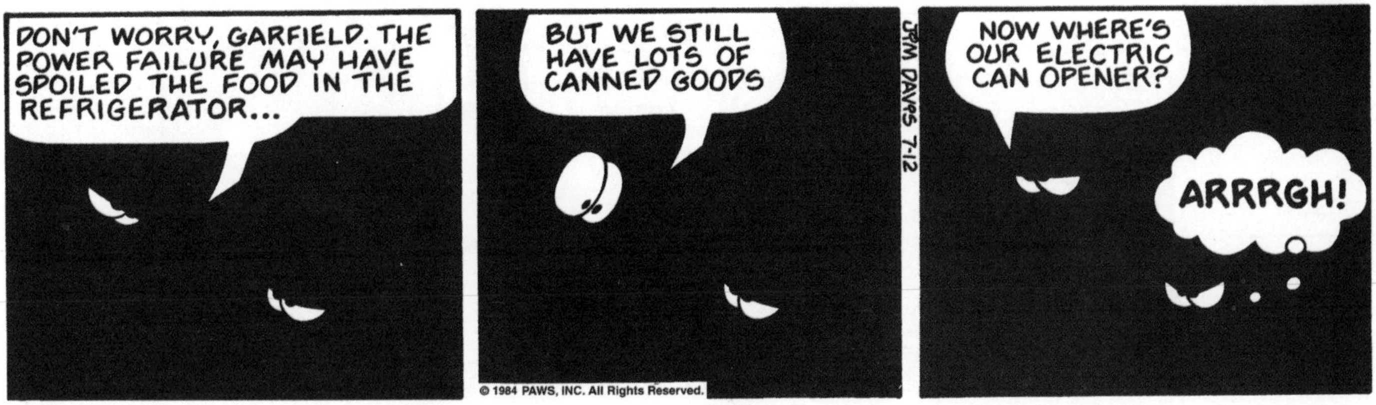
DON'T WORRY, GARFIELD. THE POWER FAILURE MAY HAVE SPOILED THE FOOD IN THE REFRIGERATOR...
BUT WE STILL HAVE LOTS OF CANNED GOODS
NOW WHERE'S OUR ELECTRIC CAN OPENER?
ARRRGH!
JIM DAVIS 7-12
© 1984 PAWS, INC. All Rights Reserved.

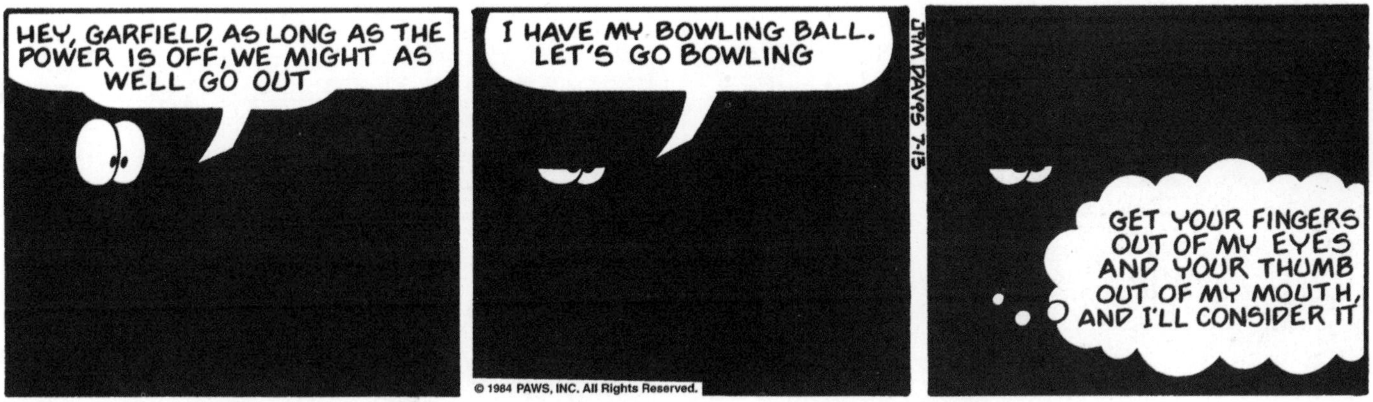
HEY, GARFIELD, AS LONG AS THE POWER IS OFF, WE MIGHT AS WELL GO OUT
I HAVE MY BOWLING BALL. LET'S GO BOWLING
GET YOUR FINGERS OUT OF MY EYES AND YOUR THUMB OUT OF MY MOUTH, AND I'LL CONSIDER IT
JIM DAVIS 7-13
© 1984 PAWS, INC. All Rights Reserved.

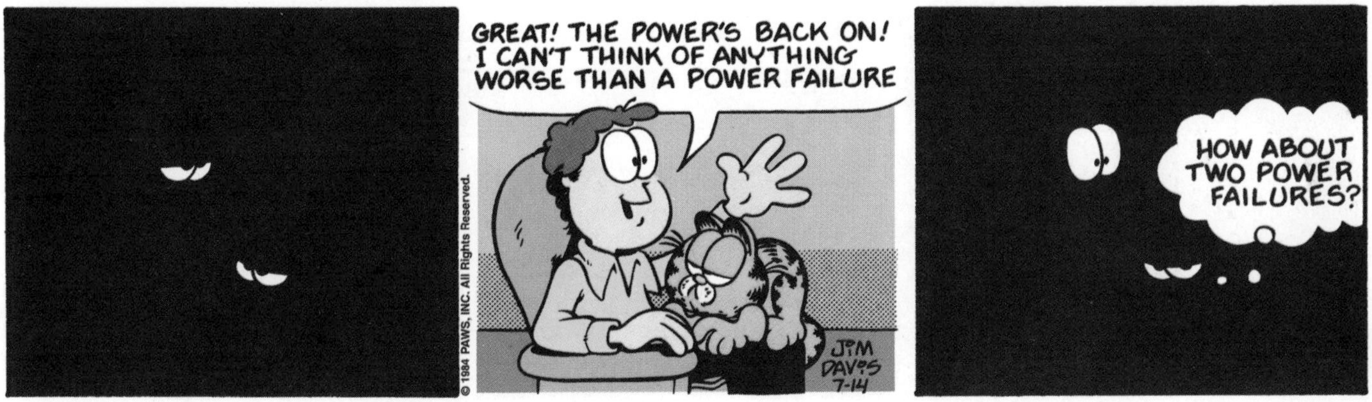
GREAT! THE POWER'S BACK ON! I CAN'T THINK OF ANYTHING WORSE THAN A POWER FAILURE
HOW ABOUT TWO POWER FAILURES?
JIM DAVIS 7-14
© 1984 PAWS, INC. All Rights Reserved.

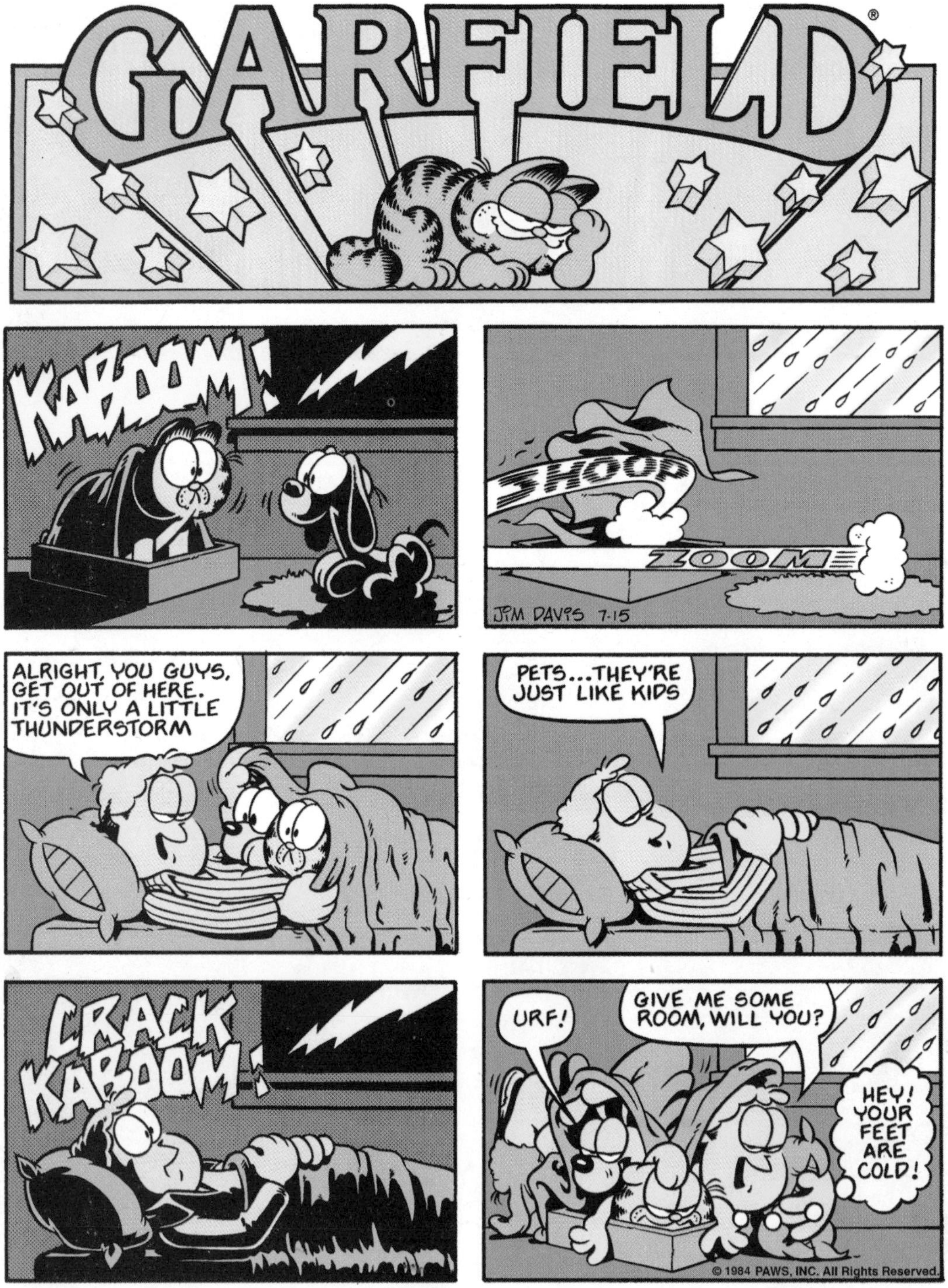
GARFIELD®
KABOOM!
SHOOP
ZOOM
JIM DAVIS 7-15
ALRIGHT, YOU GUYS, GET OUT OF HERE. IT'S ONLY A LITTLE THUNDERSTORM
PETS...THEY'RE JUST LIKE KIDS
CRACK KABOOM!
URF!
GIVE ME SOME ROOM, WILL YOU?
HEY! YOUR FEET ARE COLD!
© 1984 PAWS, INC. All Rights Reserved.

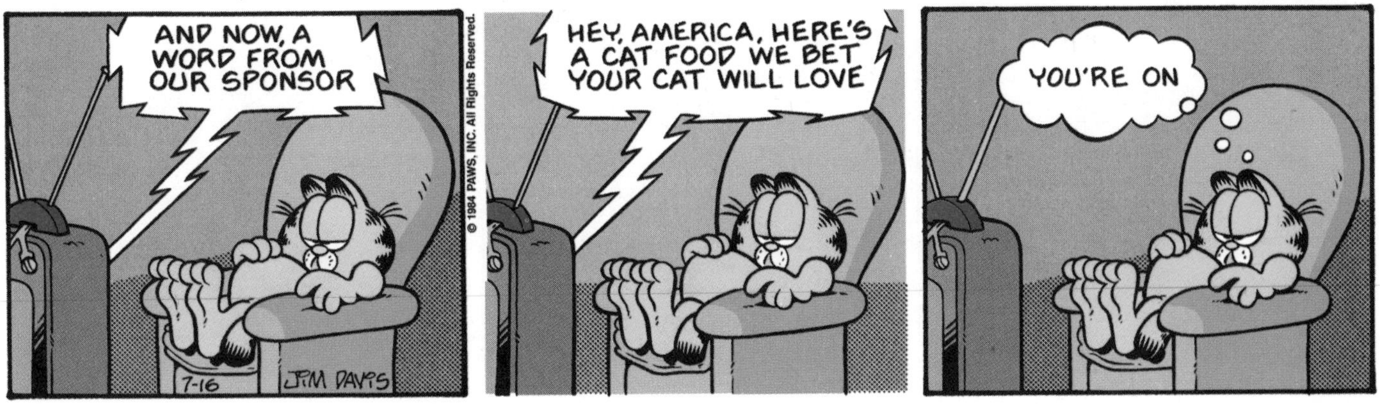
AND NOW, A WORD FROM OUR SPONSOR
7-16
JIM DAVIS
© 1984 PAWS, INC. All Rights Reserved.
HEY, AMERICA, HERE'S A CAT FOOD WE BET YOUR CAT WILL LOVE
YOU'RE ON

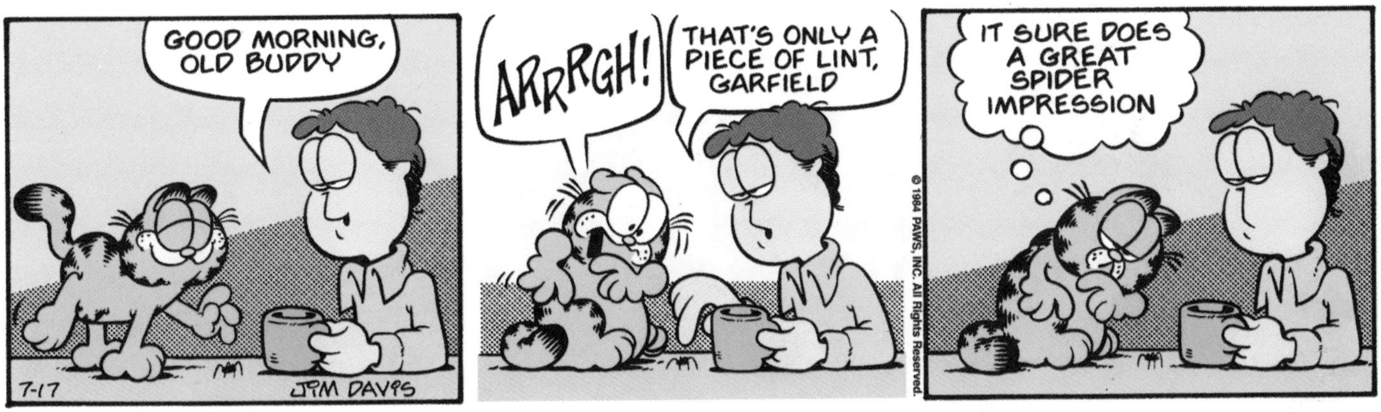
GOOD MORNING, OLD BUDDY
7-17
JIM DAVIS
ARRRGH!
THAT'S ONLY A PIECE OF LINT, GARFIELD
© 1984 PAWS, INC. All Rights Reserved.
IT SURE DOES A GREAT SPIDER IMPRESSION

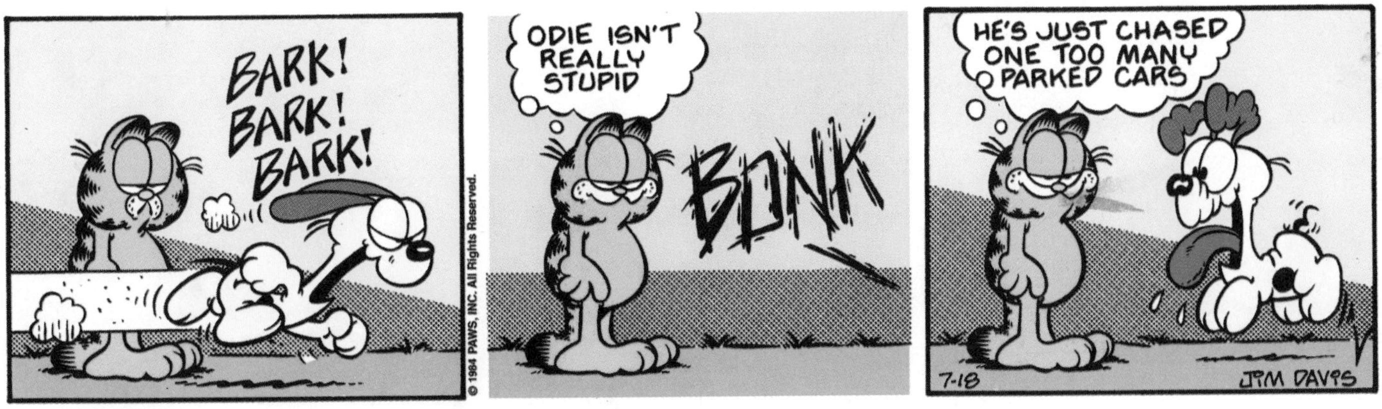
BARK! BARK! BARK!
© 1984 PAWS, INC. All Rights Reserved.
ODIE ISN'T REALLY STUPID
BONK
HE'S JUST CHASED ONE TOO MANY PARKED CARS
7-18
JIM DAVIS

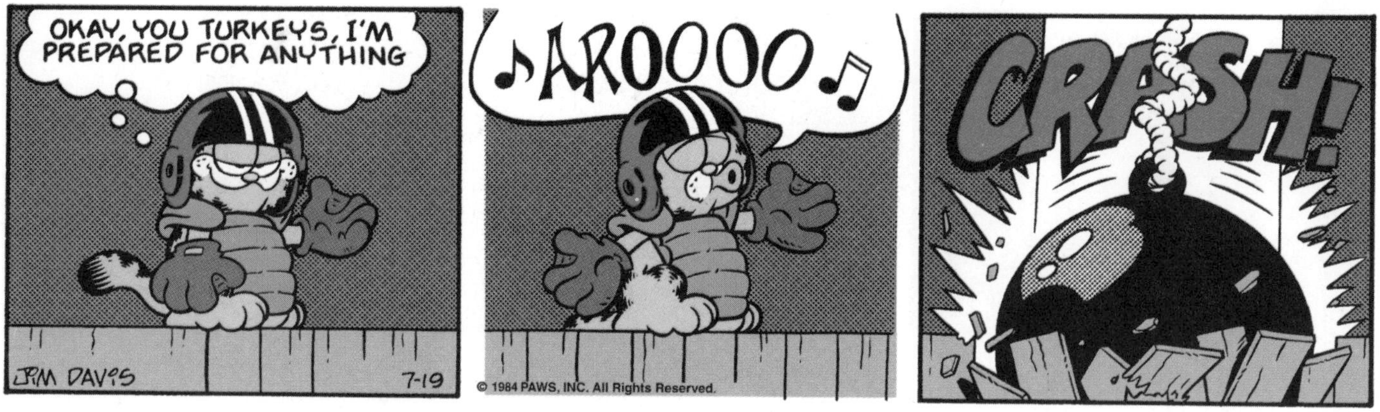
OKAY, YOU TURKEYS, I'M PREPARED FOR ANYTHING
JIM DAVIS
7-19
♪AROOOO♫
© 1984 PAWS, INC. All Rights Reserved.
CRASH!

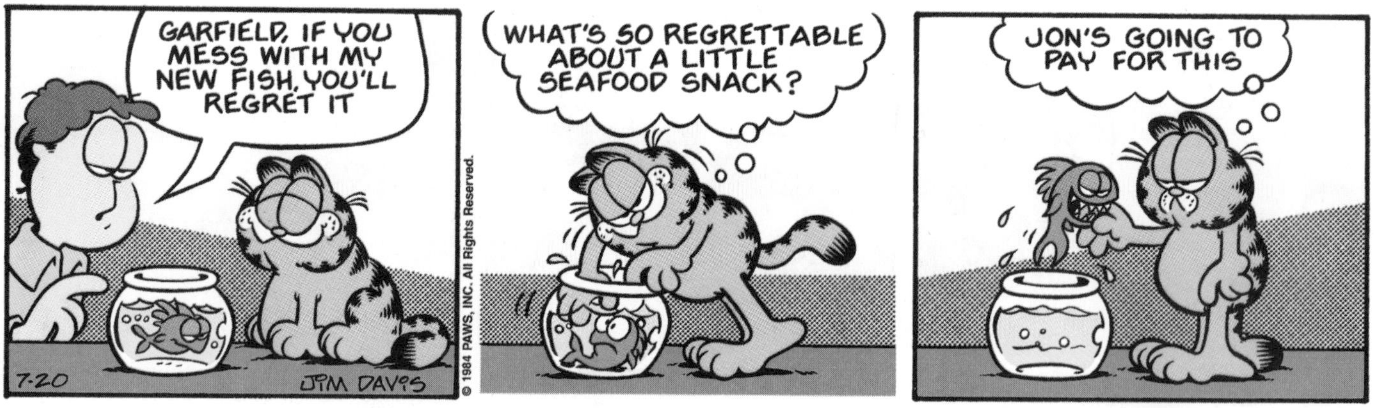
GARFIELD, IF YOU MESS WITH MY NEW FISH, YOU'LL REGRET IT
7-20
JIM DAVIS
© 1984 PAWS, INC. All Rights Reserved.
WHAT'S SO REGRETTABLE ABOUT A LITTLE SEAFOOD SNACK?
JON'S GOING TO PAY FOR THIS

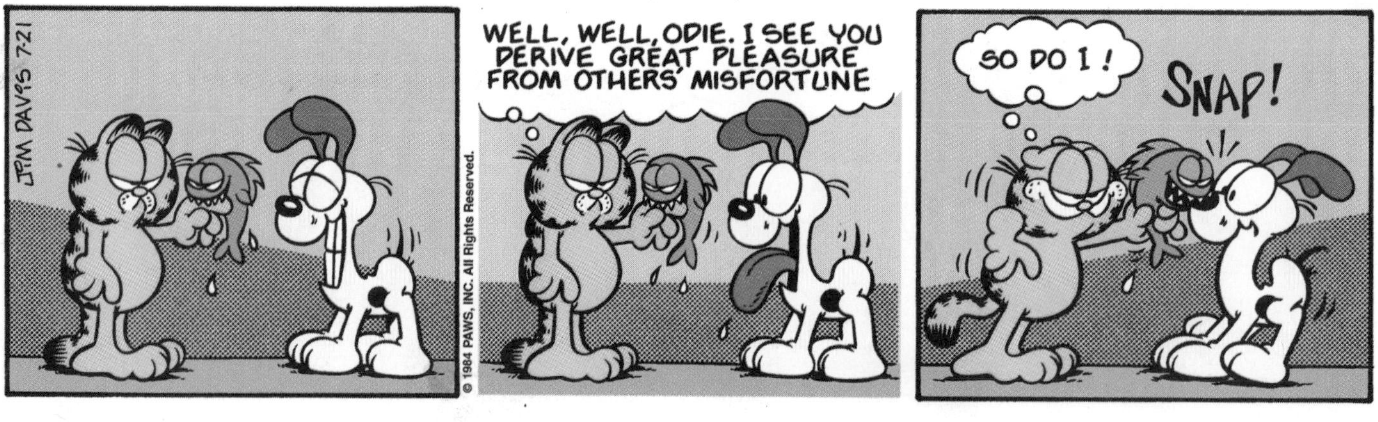
JIM DAVIS 7-21
© 1984 PAWS, INC. All Rights Reserved.
WELL, WELL, ODIE. I SEE YOU DERIVE GREAT PLEASURE FROM OTHERS' MISFORTUNE
SO DO I!
SNAP!

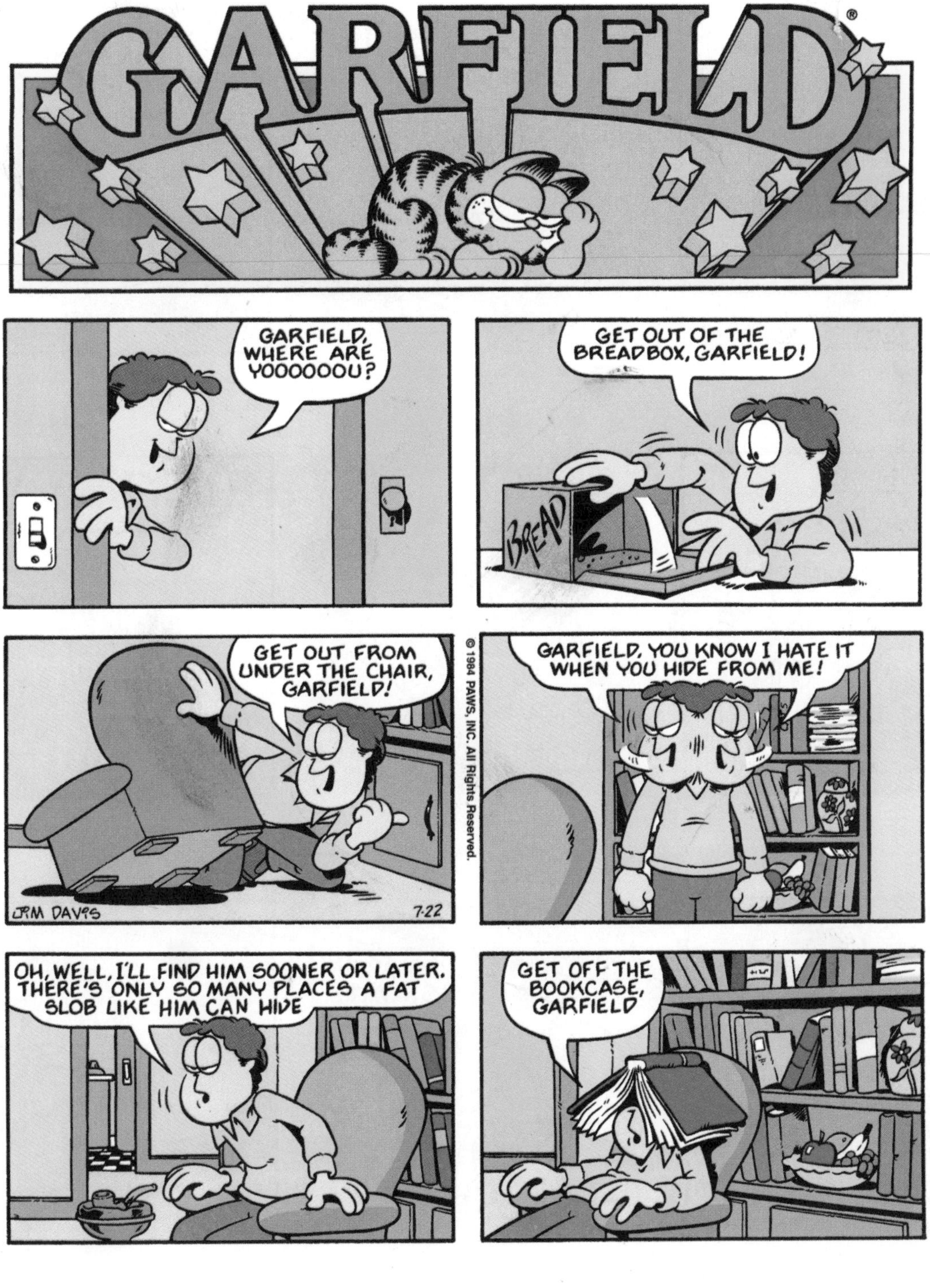
GARFIELD
GARFIELD, WHERE ARE YOOOOOOU?
GET OUT OF THE BREADBOX, GARFIELD!
BREAD
GET OUT FROM UNDER THE CHAIR, GARFIELD!
JIM DAVIS
7-22
GARFIELD, YOU KNOW I HATE IT WHEN YOU HIDE FROM ME!
OH, WELL, I'LL FIND HIM SOONER OR LATER. THERE'S ONLY SO MANY PLACES A FAT SLOB LIKE HIM CAN HIDE
GET OFF THE BOOKCASE, GARFIELD

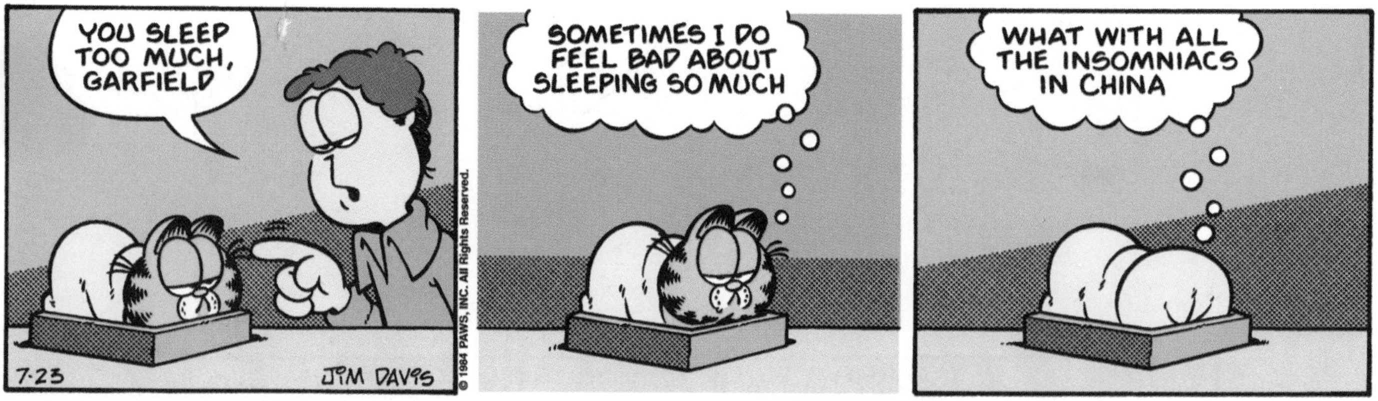
YOU SLEEP TOO MUCH, GARFIELD
7-23
JIM DAVIS
© 1984 PAWS, INC. All Rights Reserved.
SOMETIMES I DO FEEL BAD ABOUT SLEEPING SO MUCH
WHAT WITH ALL THE INSOMNIACS IN CHINA

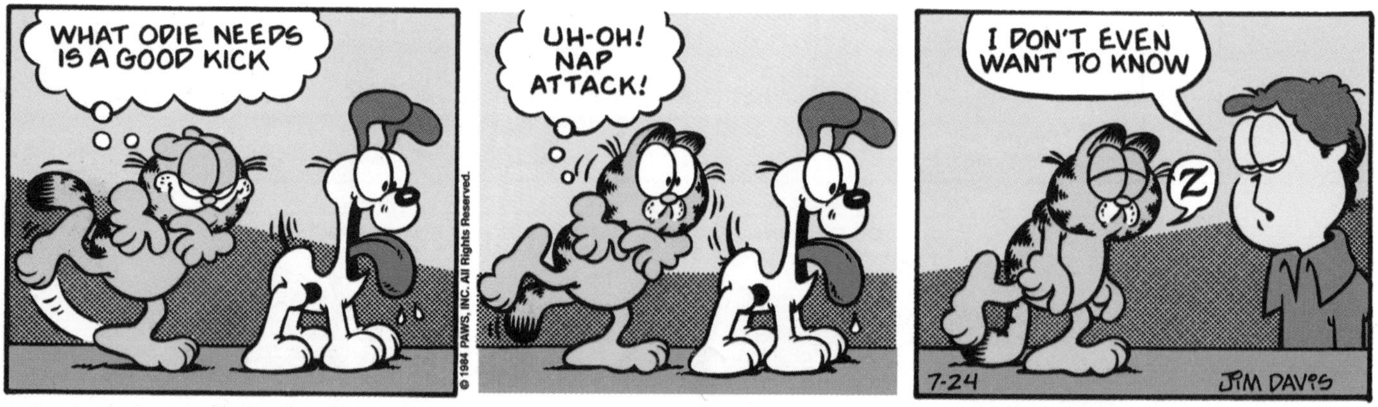
WHAT ODIE NEEDS IS A GOOD KICK
© 1984 PAWS, INC. All Rights Reserved.
UH-OH! NAP ATTACK!
I DON'T EVEN WANT TO KNOW
Z
7-24
JIM DAVIS

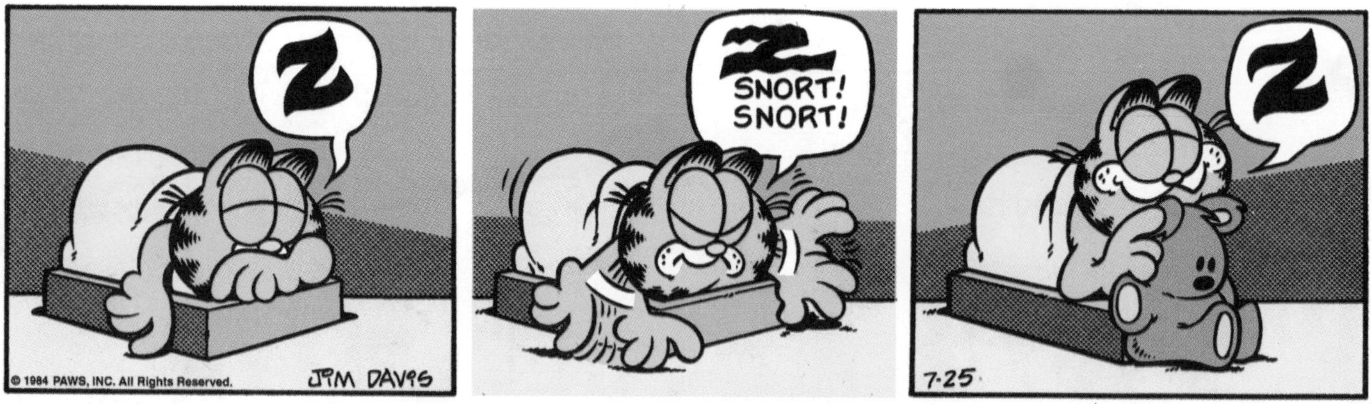
Z
© 1984 PAWS, INC. All Rights Reserved.
JIM DAVIS
Z
SNORT! SNORT!
Z
7-25

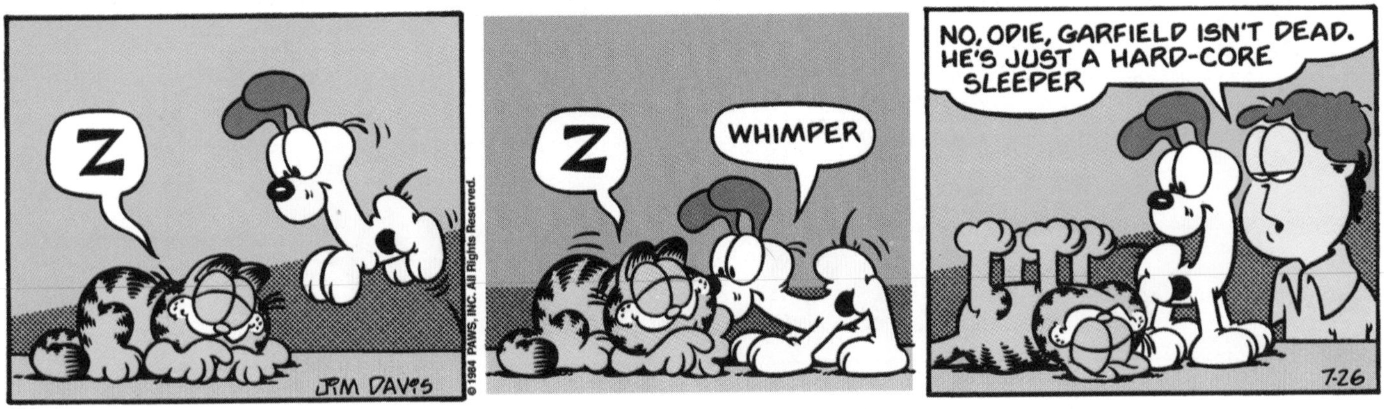
Z
JIM DAVIS
© 1984 PAWS, INC. All Rights Reserved.
Z
WHIMPER
NO, ODIE, GARFIELD ISN'T DEAD. HE'S JUST A HARD-CORE SLEEPER
7-26

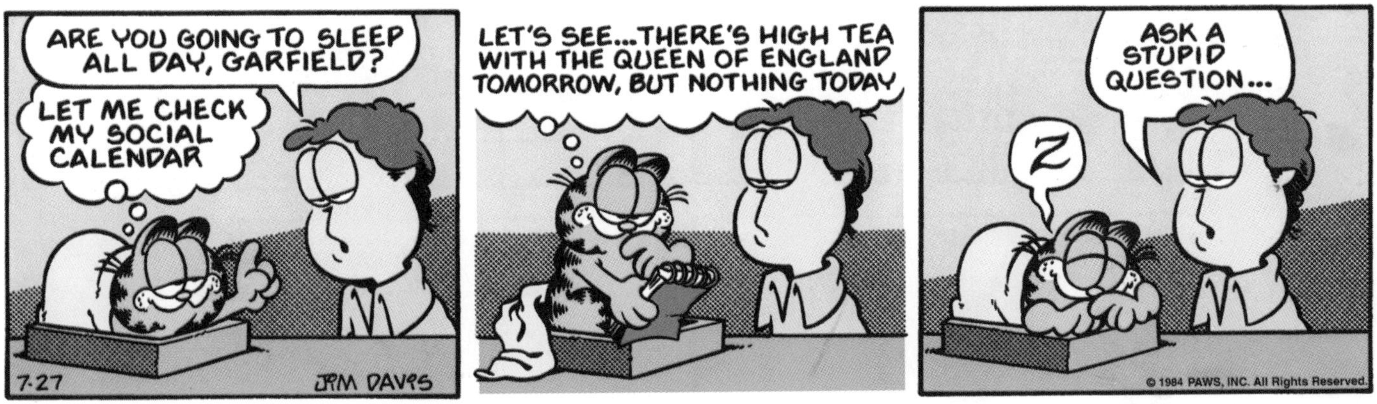
ARE YOU GOING TO SLEEP ALL DAY, GARFIELD?
LET ME CHECK MY SOCIAL CALENDAR
7-27
JIM DAVIS
LET'S SEE...THERE'S HIGH TEA WITH THE QUEEN OF ENGLAND TOMORROW, BUT NOTHING TODAY
ASK A STUPID QUESTION...
Z
© 1984 PAWS, INC. All Rights Reserved.

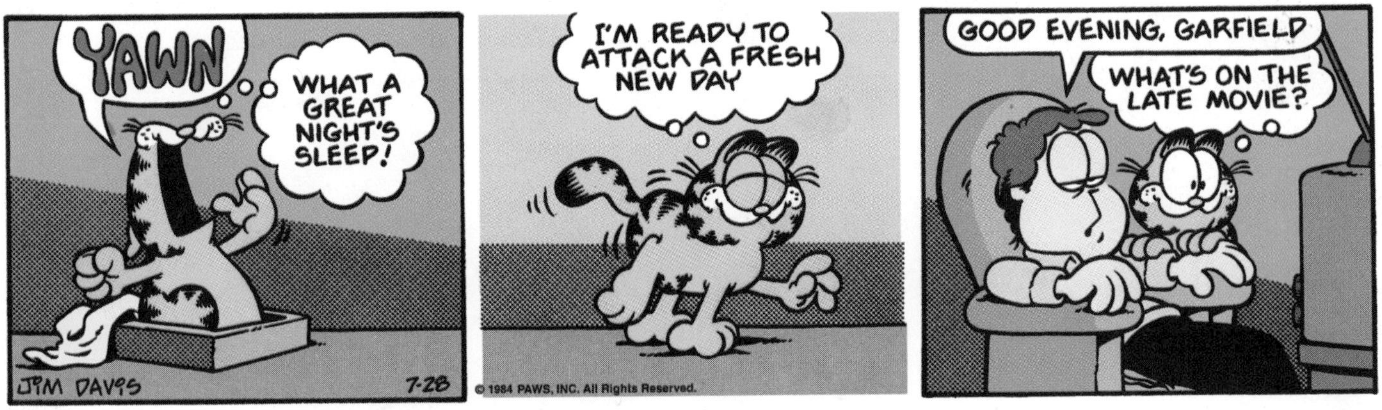
YAWN
WHAT A GREAT NIGHT'S SLEEP!
JIM DAVIS
7-28
I'M READY TO ATTACK A FRESH NEW DAY
© 1984 PAWS, INC. All Rights Reserved.
GOOD EVENING, GARFIELD
WHAT'S ON THE LATE MOVIE?

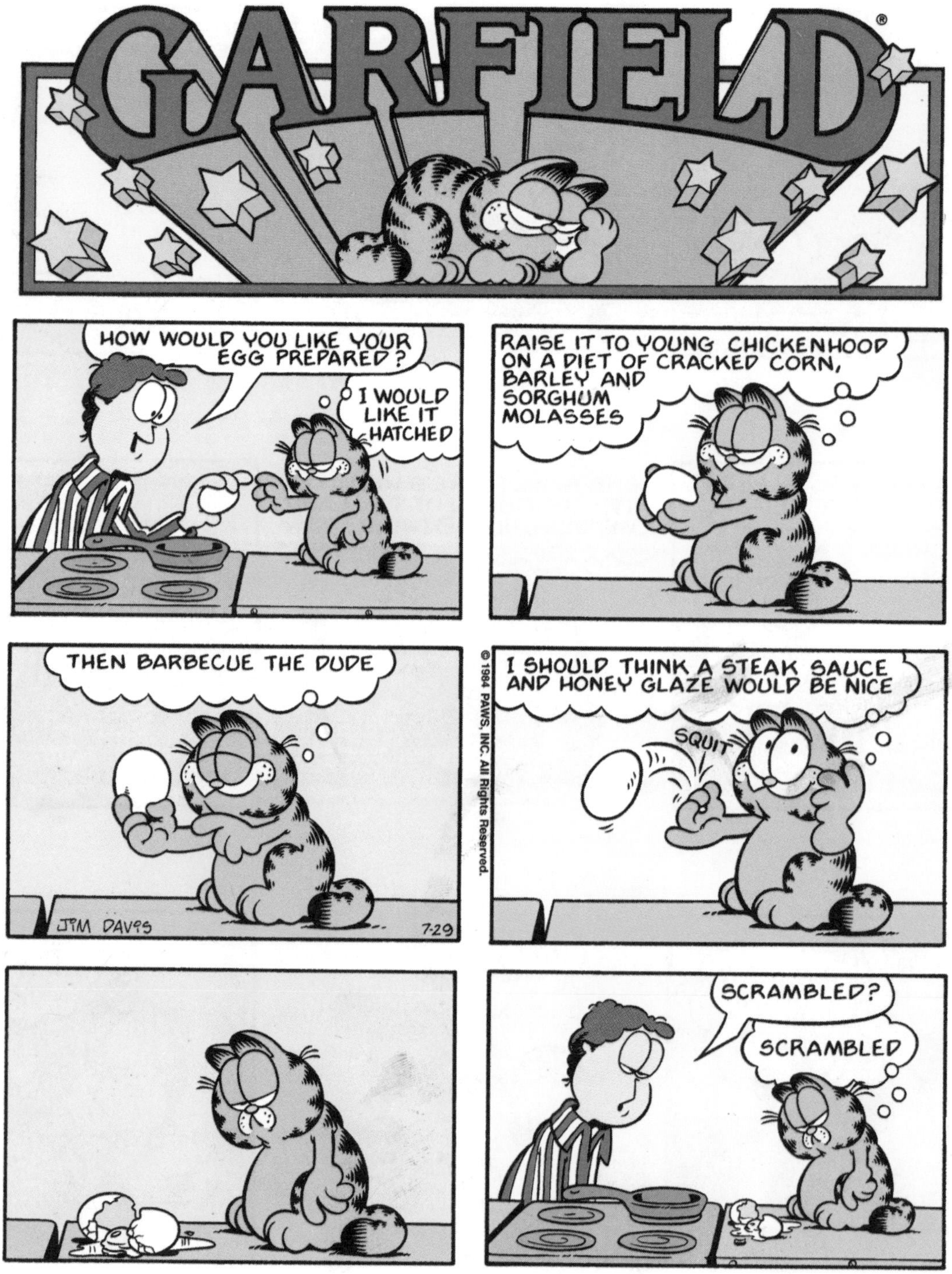
GARFIELD
HOW WOULD YOU LIKE YOUR EGG PREPARED?
I WOULD LIKE IT HATCHED
RAISE IT TO YOUNG CHICKENHOOD ON A DIET OF CRACKED CORN, BARLEY AND SORGHUM MOLASSES
THEN BARBECUE THE DUDE
JIM DAVIS
7-29
© 1984 PAWS, INC. All Rights Reserved.
I SHOULD THINK A STEAK SAUCE AND HONEY GLAZE WOULD BE NICE
SQUIT
SCRAMBLED?
SCRAMBLED

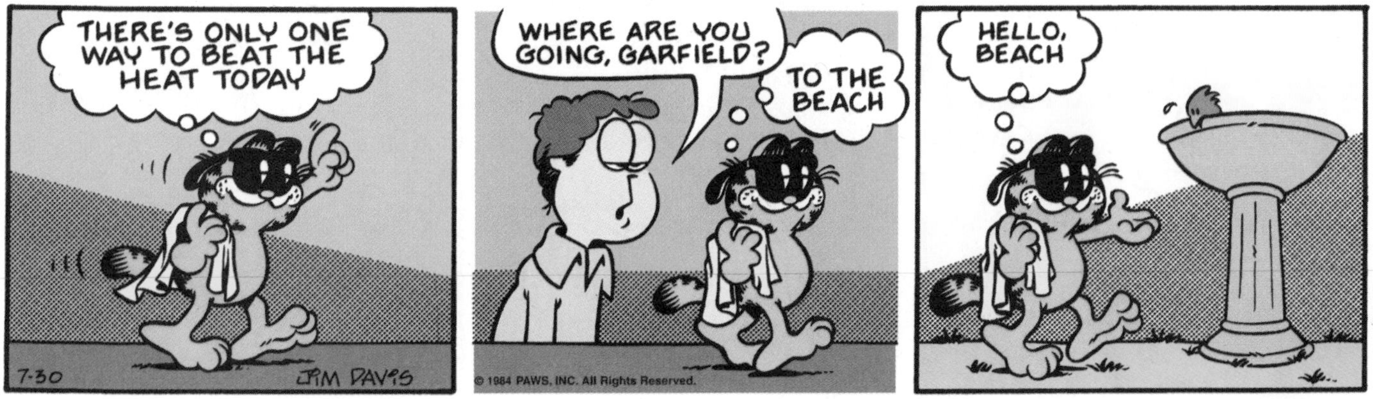
THERE'S ONLY ONE WAY TO BEAT THE HEAT TODAY
7-30
JIM DAVIS
WHERE ARE YOU GOING, GARFIELD?
TO THE BEACH
© 1984 PAWS, INC. All Rights Reserved.
HELLO, BEACH

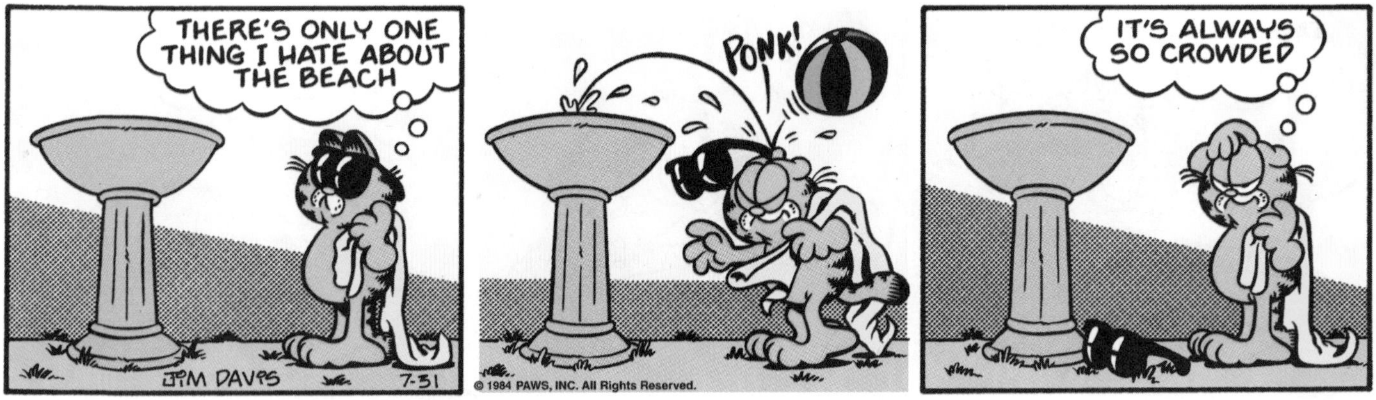
THERE'S ONLY ONE THING I HATE ABOUT THE BEACH
JIM DAVIS
7-31
PONK!
© 1984 PAWS, INC. All Rights Reserved.
IT'S ALWAYS SO CROWDED

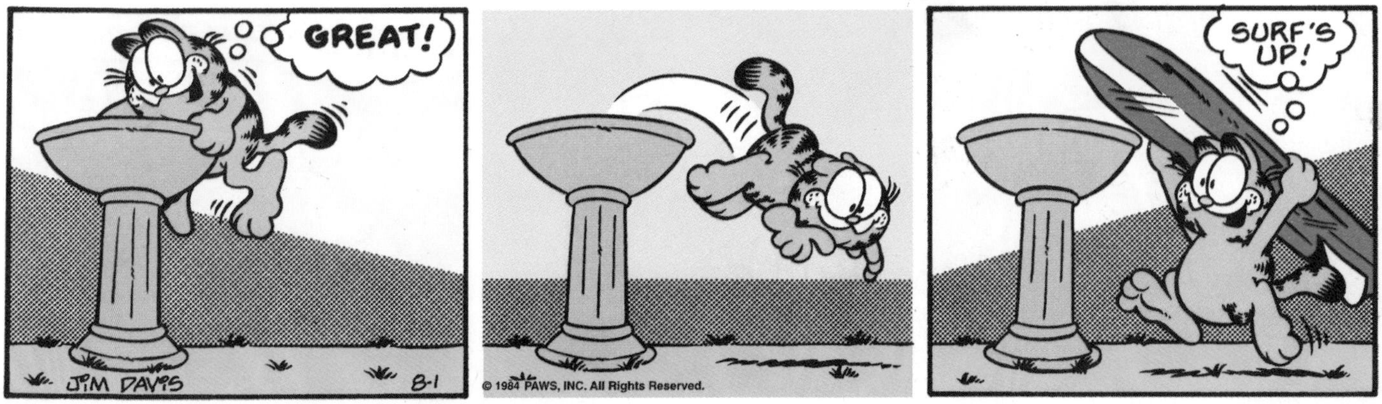
GREAT!
JIM DAVIS
8-1
© 1984 PAWS, INC. All Rights Reserved.
SURF'S UP!

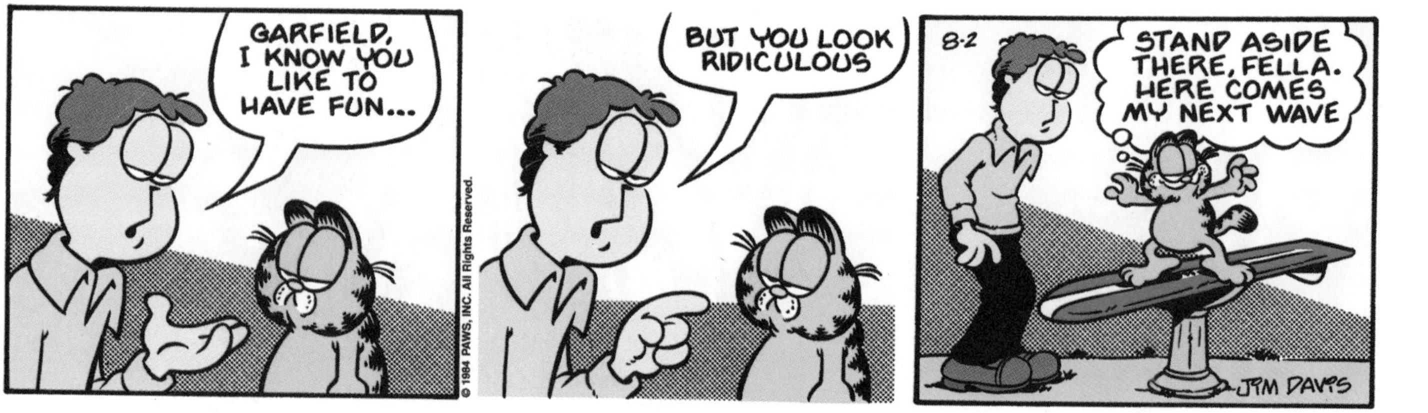
GARFIELD, I KNOW YOU LIKE TO HAVE FUN...
BUT YOU LOOK RIDICULOUS
8-2
STAND ASIDE THERE, FELLA. HERE COMES MY NEXT WAVE
JIM DAVIS
© 1984 PAWS, INC. All Rights Reserved.

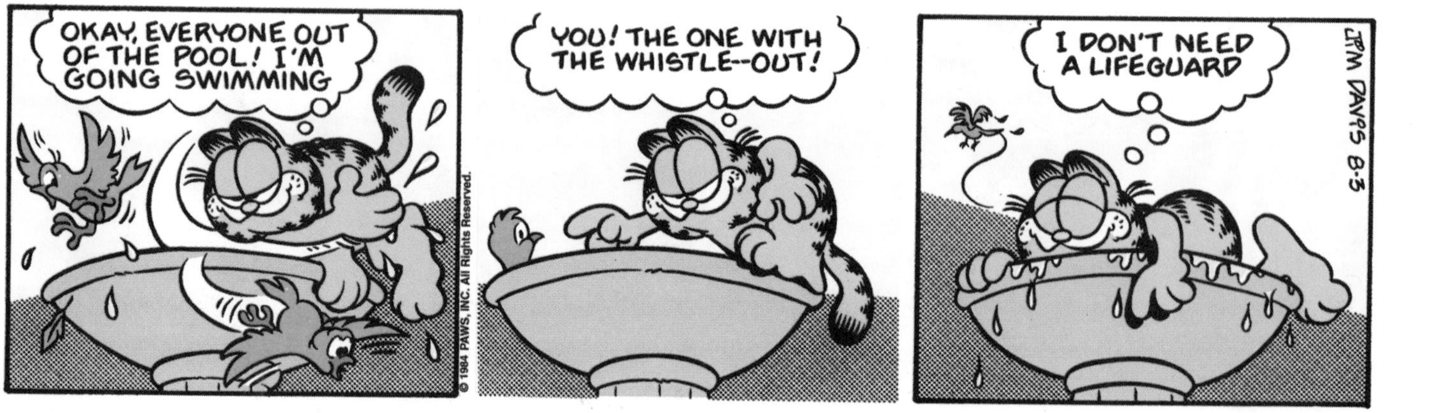
OKAY, EVERYONE OUT OF THE POOL! I'M GOING SWIMMING
YOU! THE ONE WITH THE WHISTLE--OUT!
I DON'T NEED A LIFEGUARD
JIM DAVIS 8-3
© 1984 PAWS, INC. All Rights Reserved.

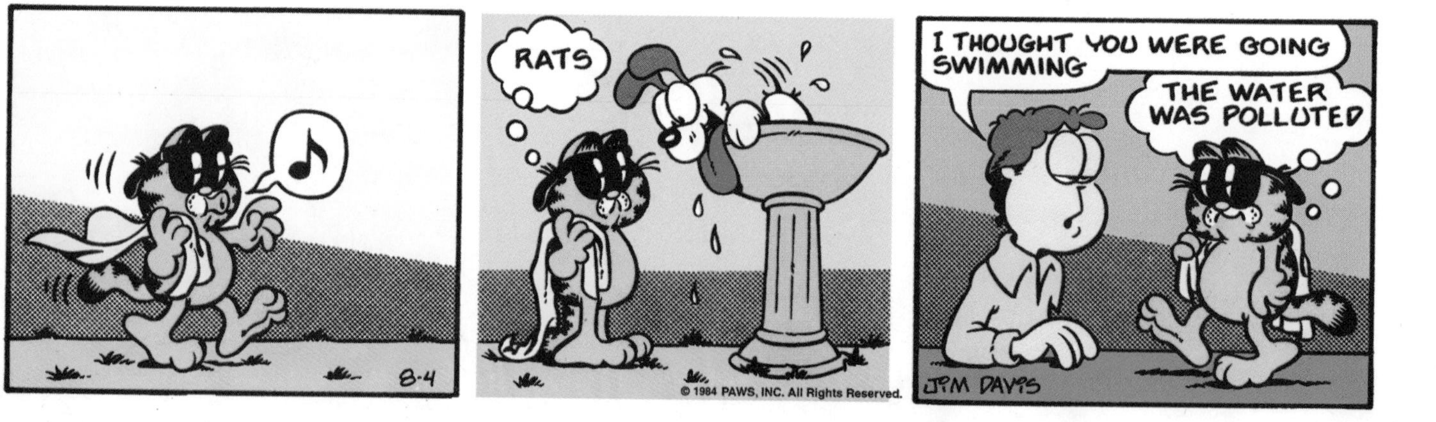
♪
8-4
RATS
I THOUGHT YOU WERE GOING SWIMMING
THE WATER WAS POLLUTED
JIM DAVIS
© 1984 PAWS, INC. All Rights Reserved.

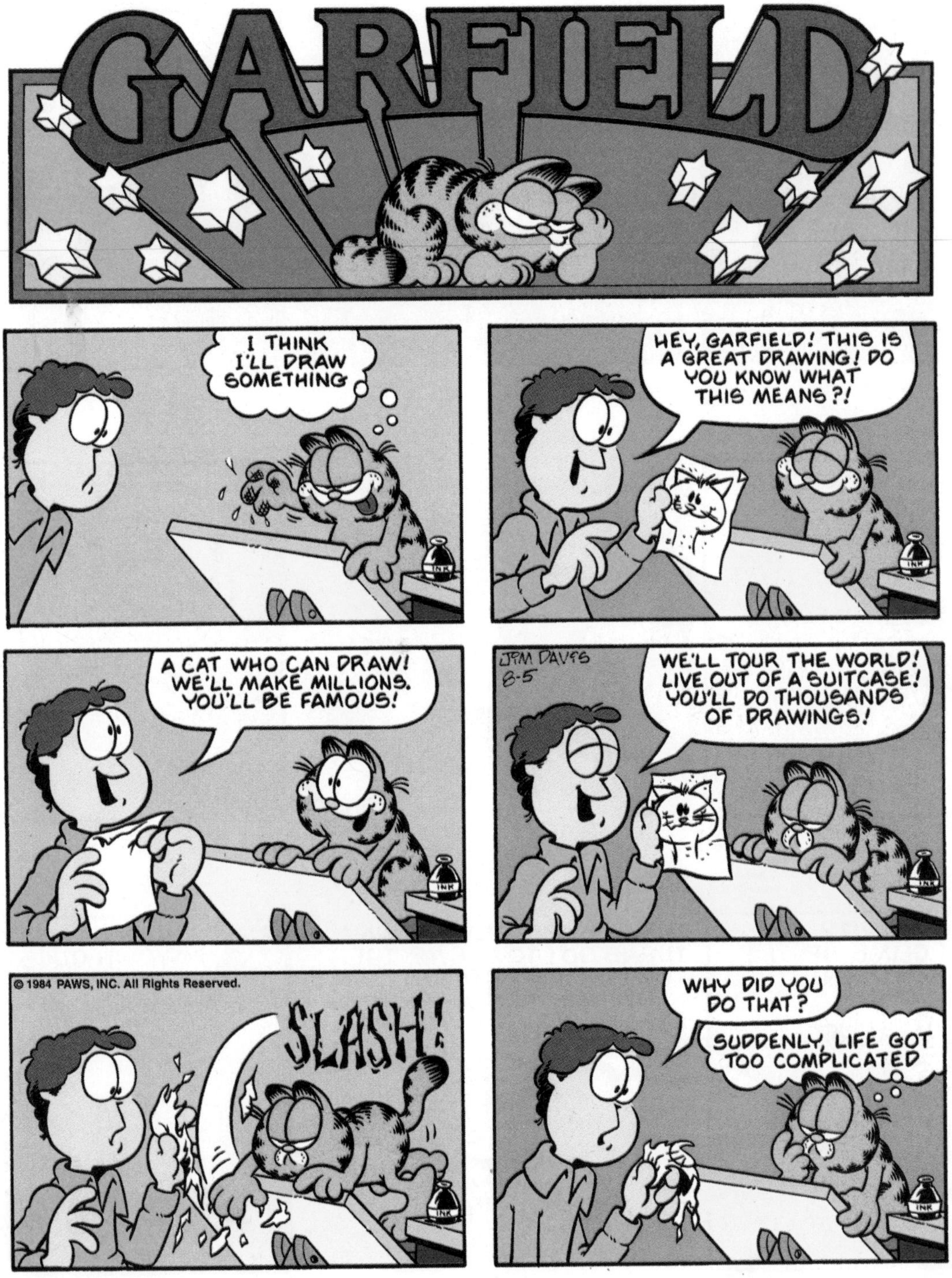
GARFIELD
I THINK I'LL DRAW SOMETHING
HEY, GARFIELD! THIS IS A GREAT DRAWING! DO YOU KNOW WHAT THIS MEANS?!
A CAT WHO CAN DRAW! WE'LL MAKE MILLIONS. YOU'LL BE FAMOUS!
JIM DAVIS 8-5
WE'LL TOUR THE WORLD! LIVE OUT OF A SUITCASE! YOU'LL DO THOUSANDS OF DRAWINGS!
© 1984 PAWS, INC. All Rights Reserved.
SLASH!
WHY DID YOU DO THAT?
SUDDENLY, LIFE GOT TOO COMPLICATED

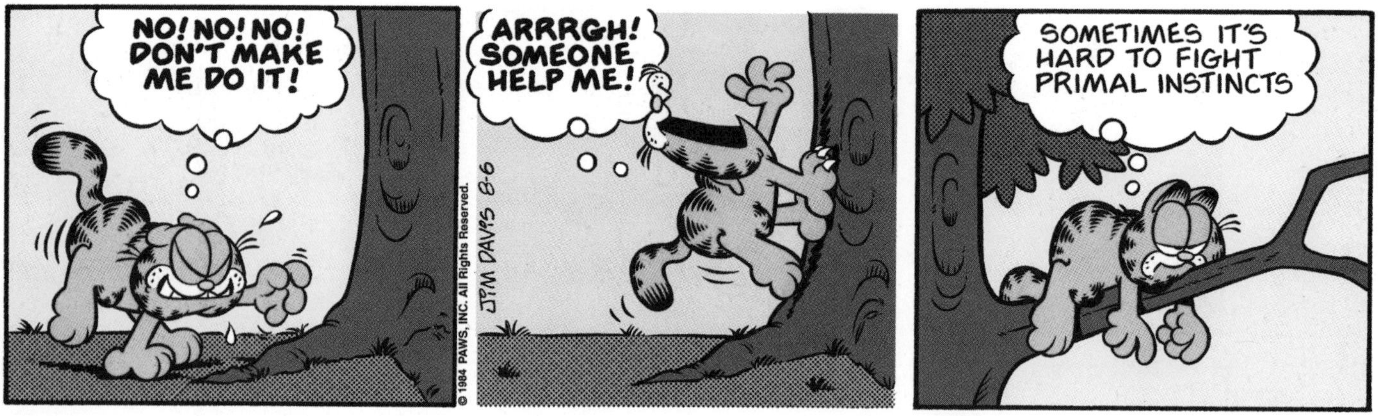
NO! NO! NO! DON'T MAKE ME DO IT!
© 1984 PAWS, INC. All Rights Reserved.
JIM DAVIS 8-6
ARRRGH! SOMEONE HELP ME!
SOMETIMES IT'S HARD TO FIGHT PRIMAL INSTINCTS

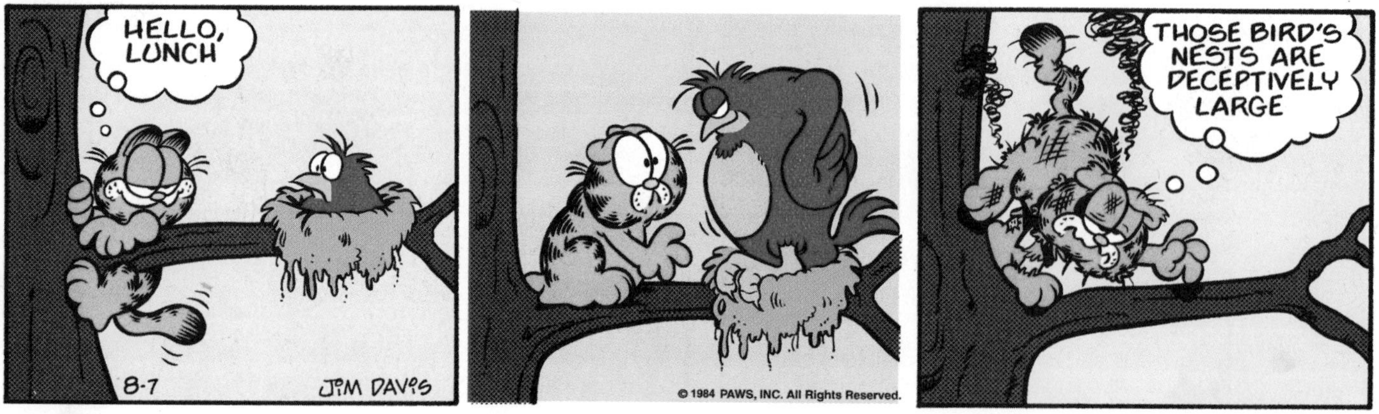
HELLO, LUNCH
8-7
JIM DAVIS
© 1984 PAWS, INC. All Rights Reserved.
THOSE BIRD'S NESTS ARE DECEPTIVELY LARGE

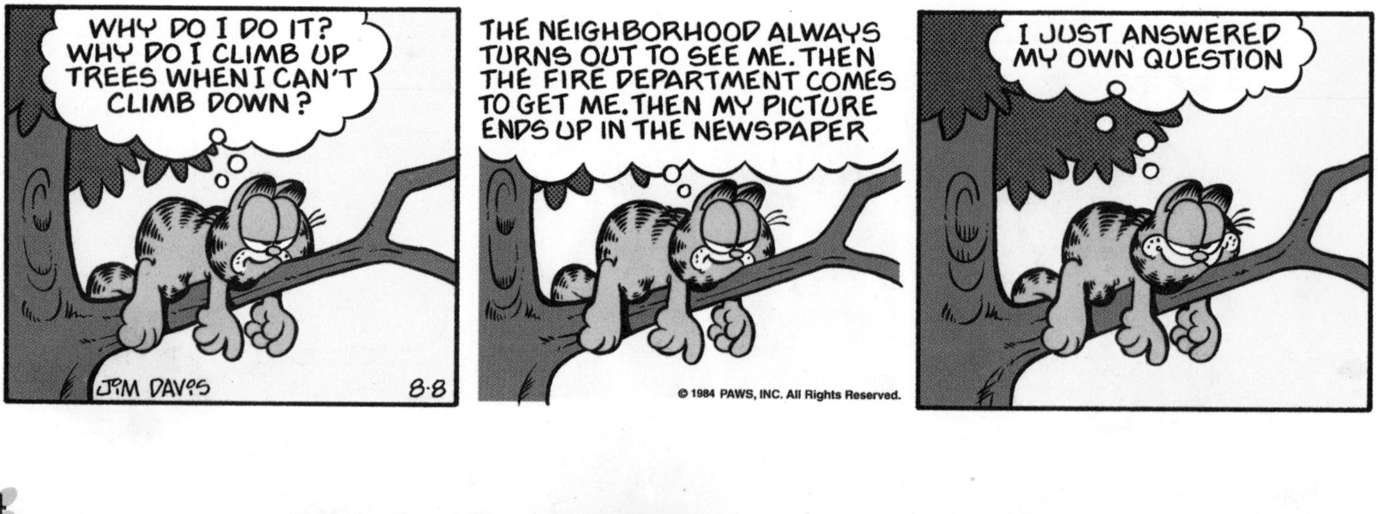
WHY DO I DO IT? WHY DO I CLIMB UP TREES WHEN I CAN'T CLIMB DOWN?
JIM DAVIS
8-8
THE NEIGHBORHOOD ALWAYS TURNS OUT TO SEE ME. THEN THE FIRE DEPARTMENT COMES TO GET ME. THEN MY PICTURE ENDS UP IN THE NEWSPAPER
© 1984 PAWS, INC. All Rights Reserved.
I JUST ANSWERED MY OWN QUESTION

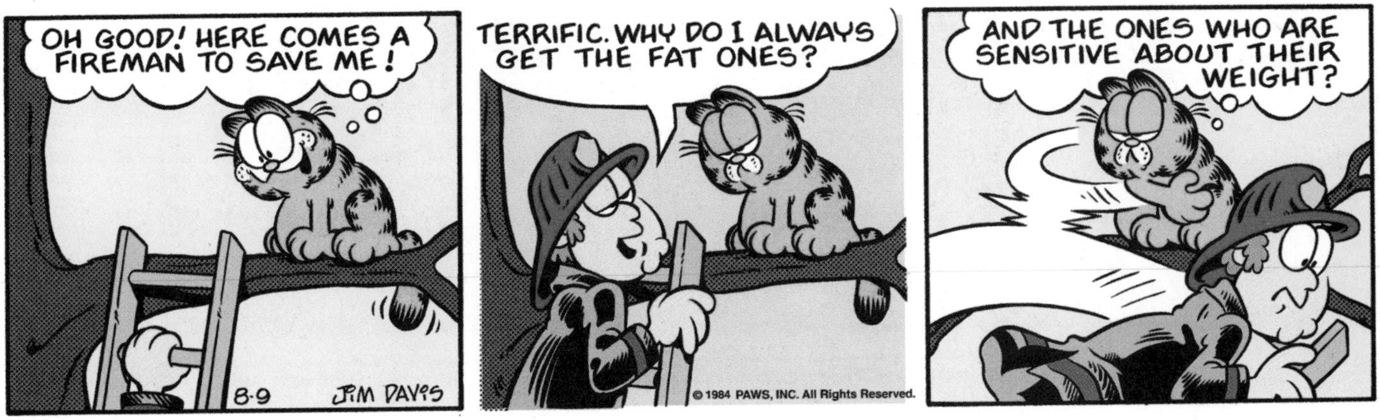
OH GOOD! HERE COMES A FIREMAN TO SAVE ME!
8-9
JIM DAVIS
TERRIFIC. WHY DO I ALWAYS GET THE FAT ONES?
© 1984 PAWS, INC. All Rights Reserved.
AND THE ONES WHO ARE SENSITIVE ABOUT THEIR WEIGHT?

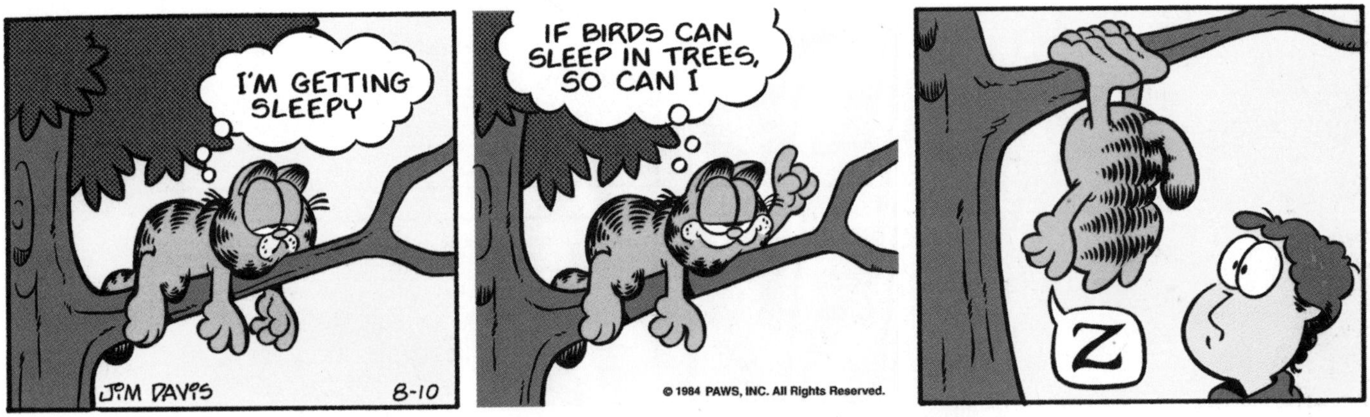
I'M GETTING SLEEPY
JIM DAVIS
8-10
IF BIRDS CAN SLEEP IN TREES, SO CAN I
© 1984 PAWS, INC. All Rights Reserved.
Z

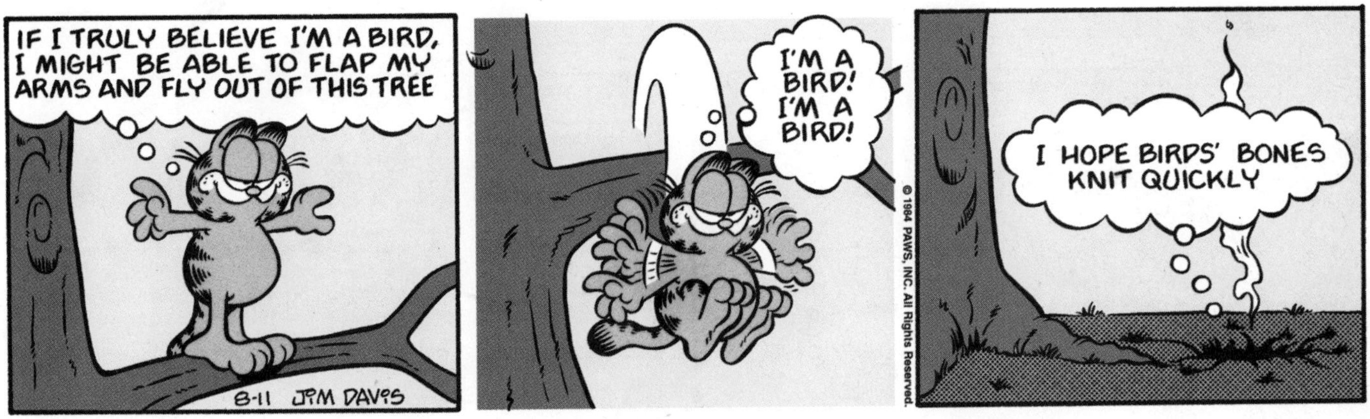
IF I TRULY BELIEVE I'M A BIRD, I MIGHT BE ABLE TO FLAP MY ARMS AND FLY OUT OF THIS TREE
8-11
JIM DAVIS
I'M A BIRD! I'M A BIRD!
© 1984 PAWS, INC. All Rights Reserved.
I HOPE BIRDS' BONES KNIT QUICKLY

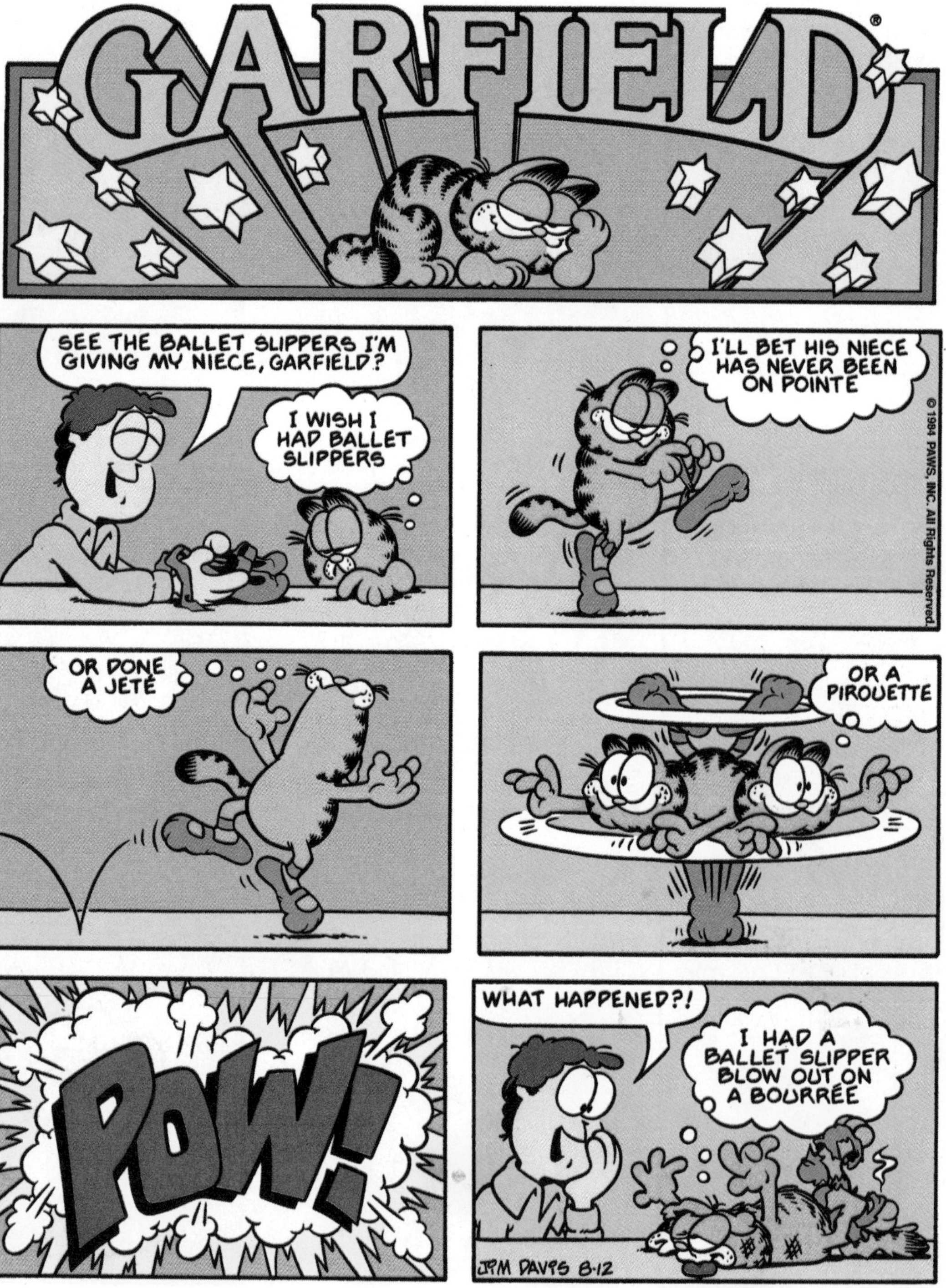
GARFIELD
SEE THE BALLET SLIPPERS I'M GIVING MY NIECE, GARFIELD?
I WISH I HAD BALLET SLIPPERS
I'LL BET HIS NIECE HAS NEVER BEEN ON POINTE
© 1984 PAWS, INC. All Rights Reserved.
OR DONE A JETÉ
OR A PIROUETTE
POW!
WHAT HAPPENED?!
I HAD A BALLET SLIPPER BLOW OUT ON A BOURRÉE
JIM DAVIS 8-12

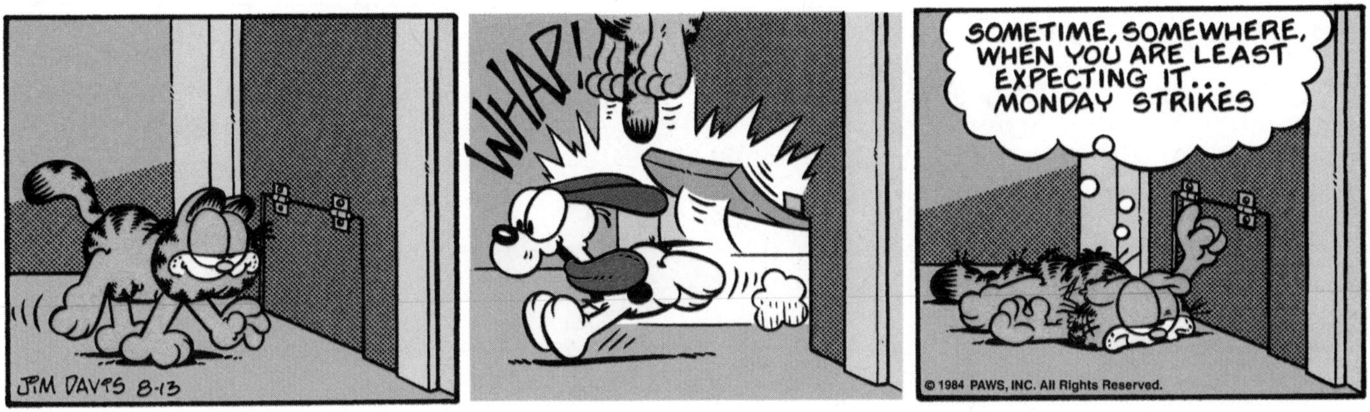
JIM DAVIS 8-13
WHAP!
SOMETIME, SOMEWHERE, WHEN YOU ARE LEAST EXPECTING IT... MONDAY STRIKES
© 1984 PAWS, INC. All Rights Reserved.

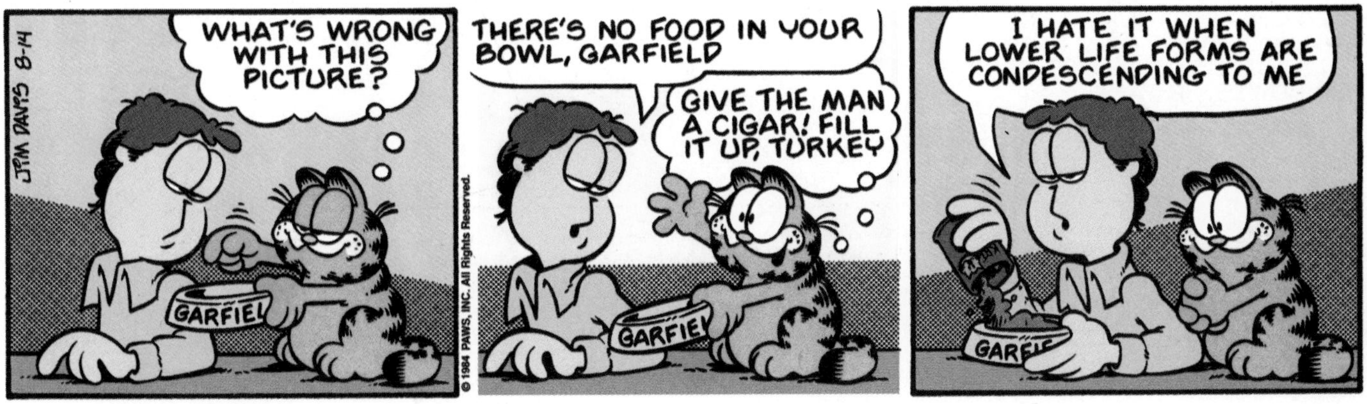
JIM DAVIS 8-14
WHAT'S WRONG WITH THIS PICTURE?
GARFIEL
© 1984 PAWS, INC. All Rights Reserved.
THERE'S NO FOOD IN YOUR BOWL, GARFIELD
GIVE THE MAN A CIGAR! FILL IT UP, TURKEY
GARFIEL
I HATE IT WHEN LOWER LIFE FORMS ARE CONDESCENDING TO ME
GARFIE

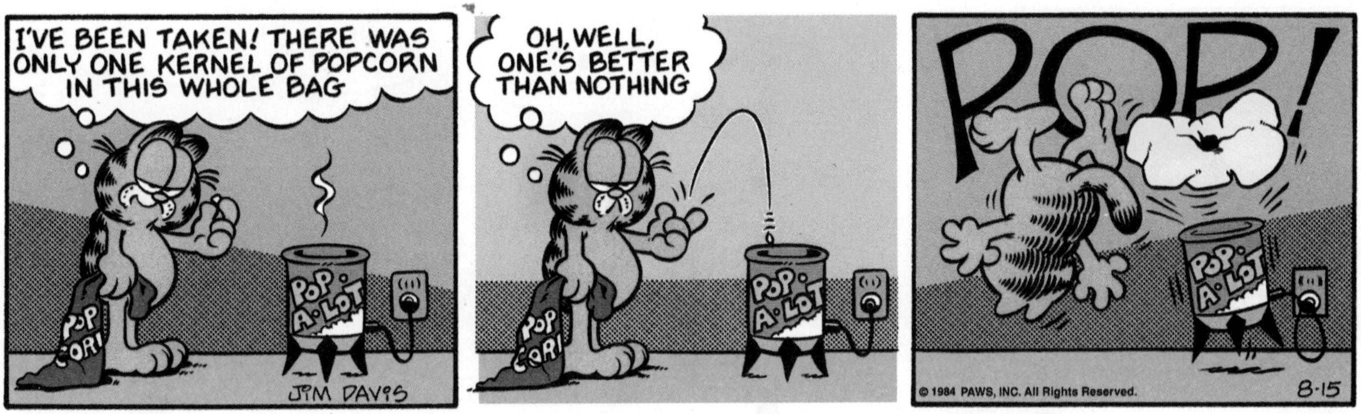
I'VE BEEN TAKEN! THERE WAS ONLY ONE KERNEL OF POPCORN IN THIS WHOLE BAG
POP-A-LOT
JIM DAVIS
OH, WELL, ONE'S BETTER THAN NOTHING
POP-A-LOT
POP!
POP-A-LOT
© 1984 PAWS, INC. All Rights Reserved.
8-15

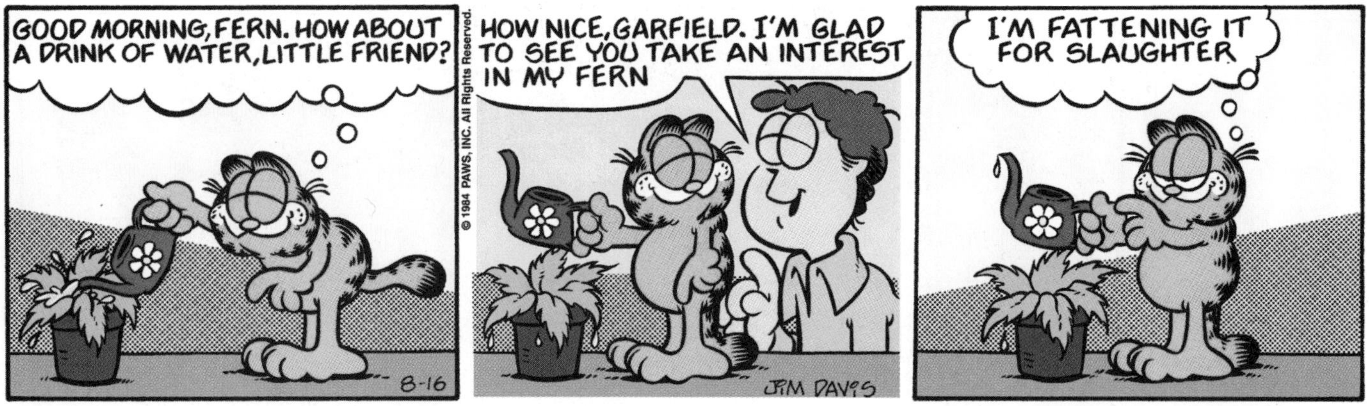
GOOD MORNING, FERN. HOW ABOUT A DRINK OF WATER, LITTLE FRIEND?
HOW NICE, GARFIELD. I'M GLAD TO SEE YOU TAKE AN INTEREST IN MY FERN
I'M FATTENING IT FOR SLAUGHTER
© 1984 PAWS, INC. All Rights Reserved.

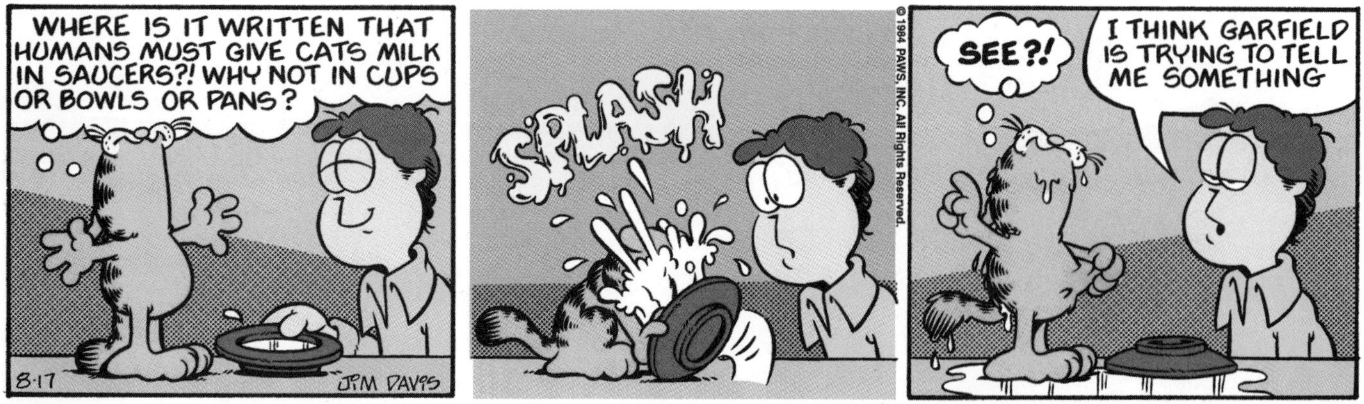
WHERE IS IT WRITTEN THAT HUMANS MUST GIVE CATS MILK IN SAUCERS?! WHY NOT IN CUPS OR BOWLS OR PANS?
SPLASH
SEE?!
I THINK GARFIELD IS TRYING TO TELL ME SOMETHING
© 1984 PAWS, INC. All Rights Reserved.

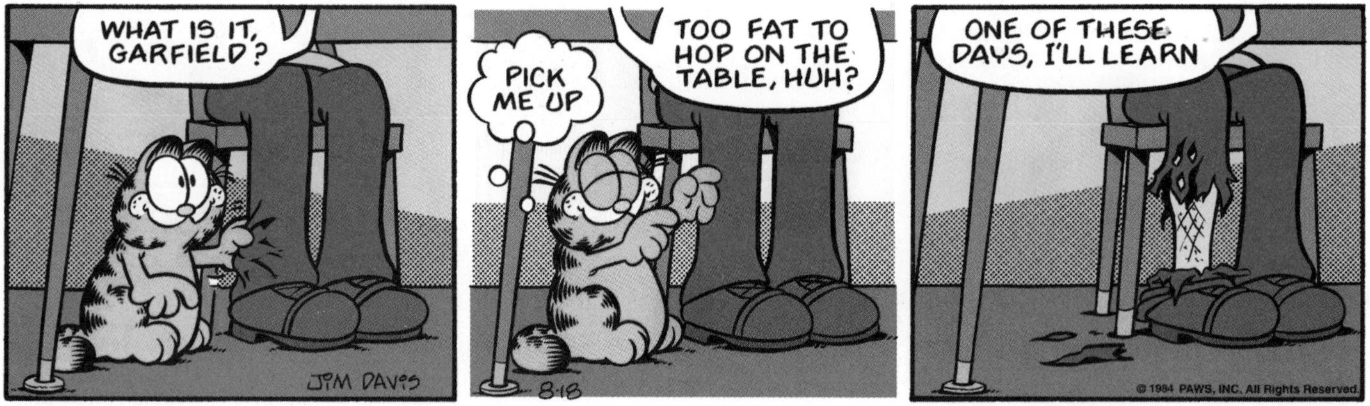
WHAT IS IT, GARFIELD?
PICK ME UP
TOO FAT TO HOP ON THE TABLE, HUH?
ONE OF THESE DAYS, I'LL LEARN
© 1984 PAWS, INC. All Rights Reserved.

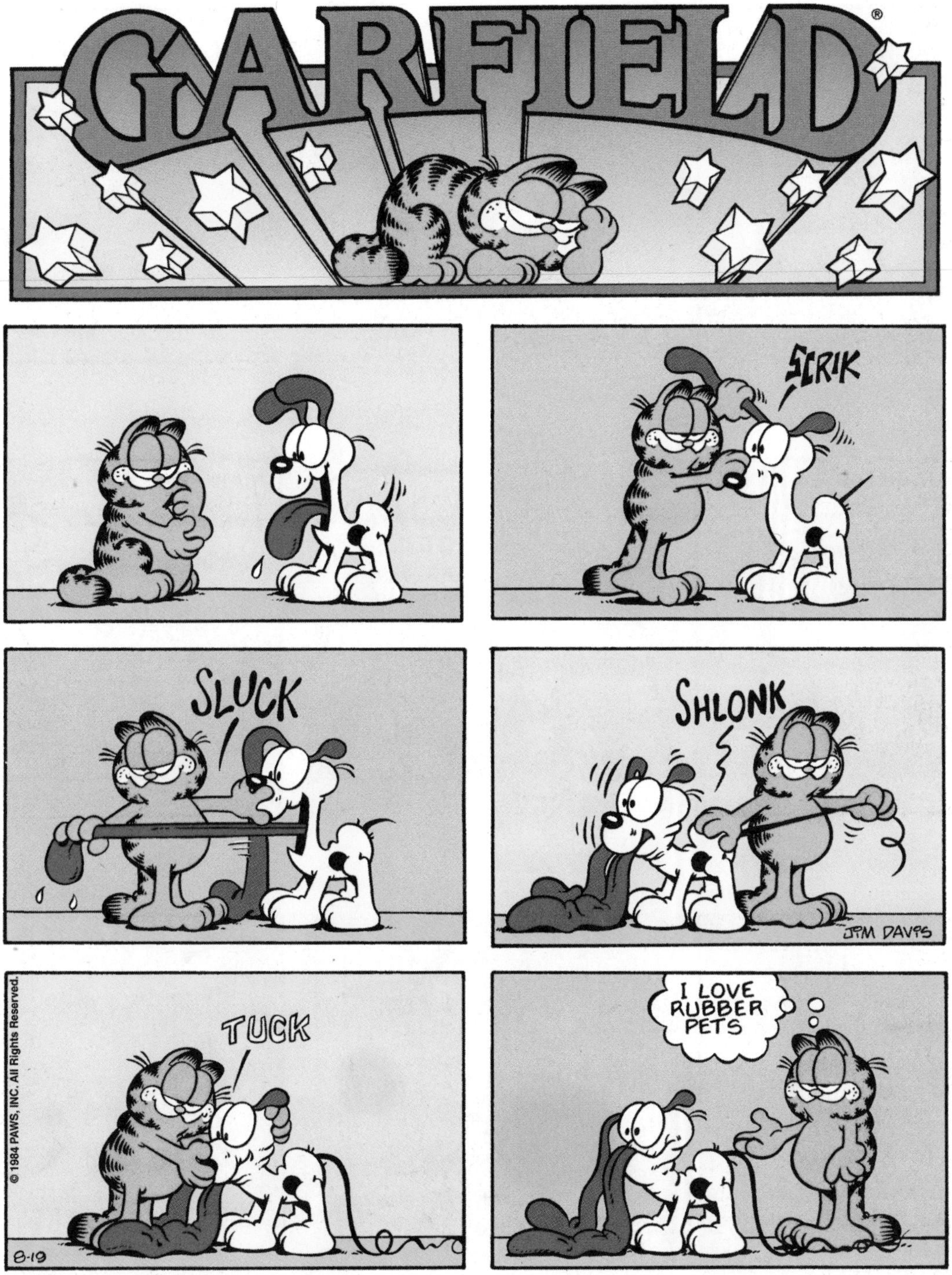
GARFIELD®
SCRIK
SLUCK
SHLONK
JIM DAVIS
© 1984 PAWS, INC. All Rights Reserved.
TUCK
8-19
I LOVE RUBBER PETS

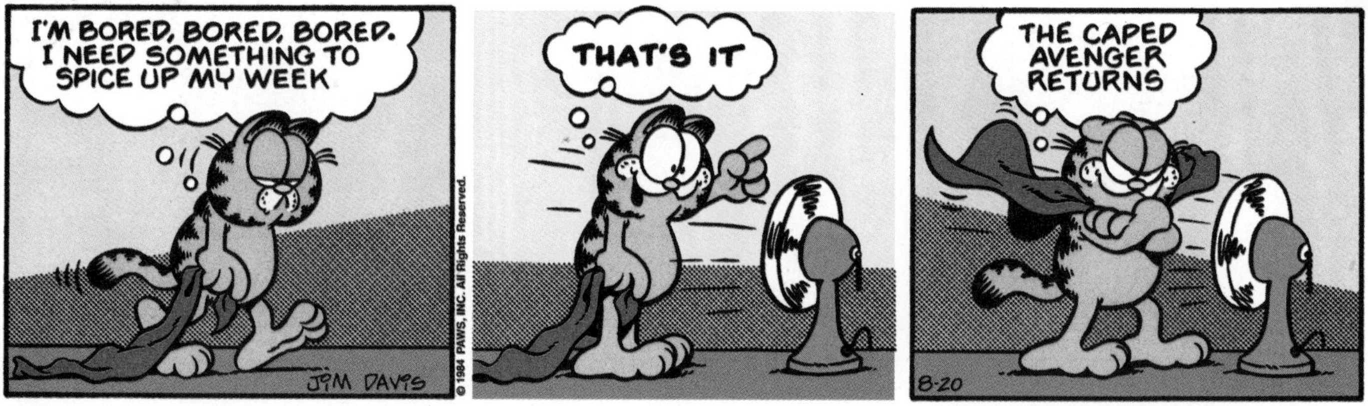
I'M BORED, BORED, BORED. I NEED SOMETHING TO SPICE UP MY WEEK
JIM DAVIS
© 1984 PAWS, INC. All Rights Reserved.
THAT'S IT
THE CAPED AVENGER RETURNS
8-20

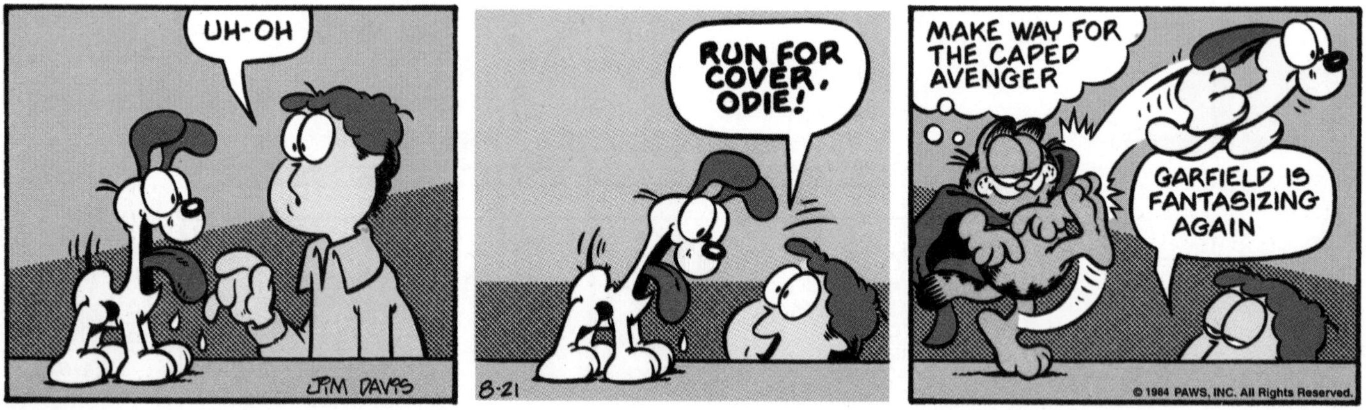
UH-OH
JIM DAVIS
RUN FOR COVER, ODIE!
8-21
MAKE WAY FOR THE CAPED AVENGER
GARFIELD IS FANTASIZING AGAIN
© 1984 PAWS, INC. All Rights Reserved.

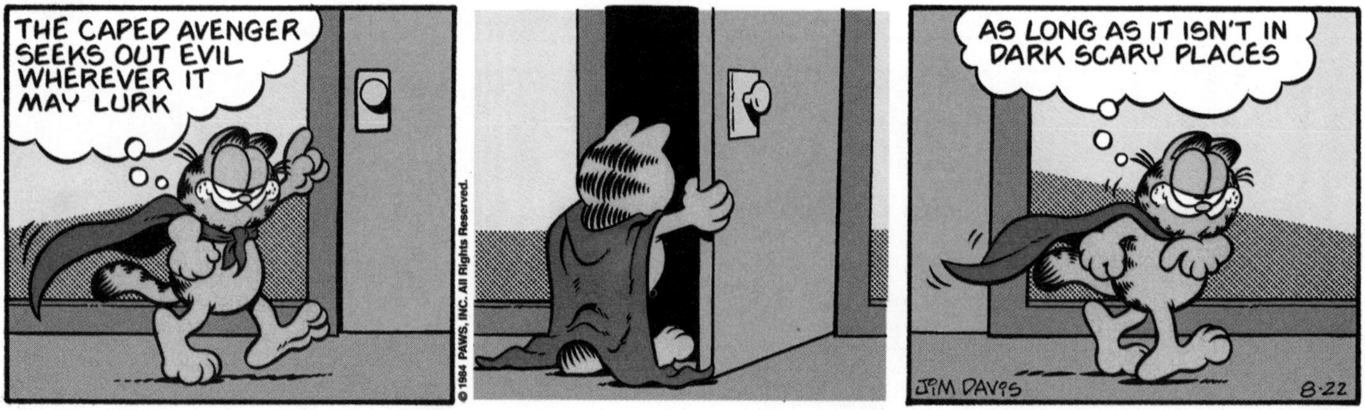
THE CAPED AVENGER SEEKS OUT EVIL WHEREVER IT MAY LURK
© 1984 PAWS, INC. All Rights Reserved.
AS LONG AS IT ISN'T IN DARK SCARY PLACES
JIM DAVIS
8-22

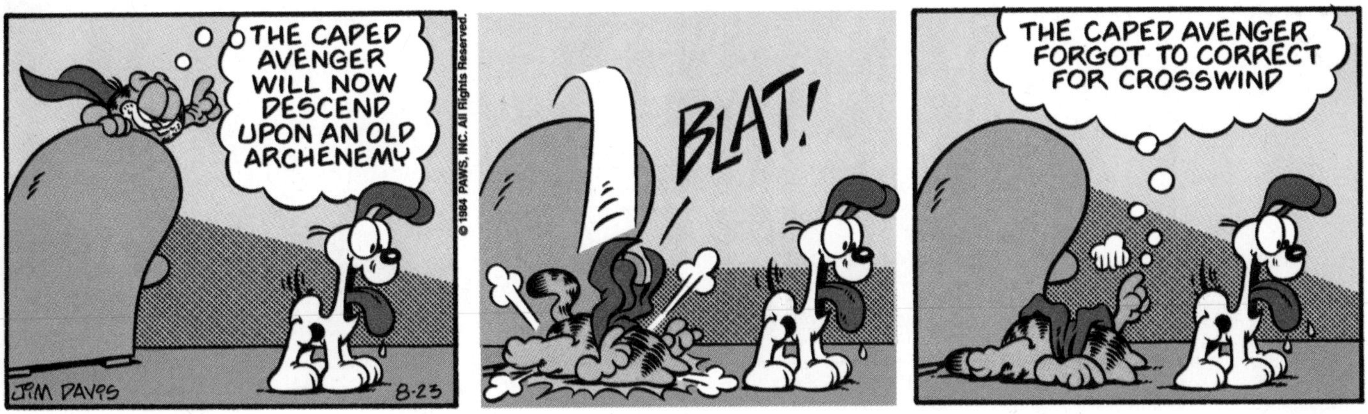
THE CAPED AVENGER WILL NOW DESCEND UPON AN OLD ARCHENEMY
BLAT!
THE CAPED AVENGER FORGOT TO CORRECT FOR CROSSWIND
JIM DAVIS
8-23
© 1984 PAWS, INC. All Rights Reserved.

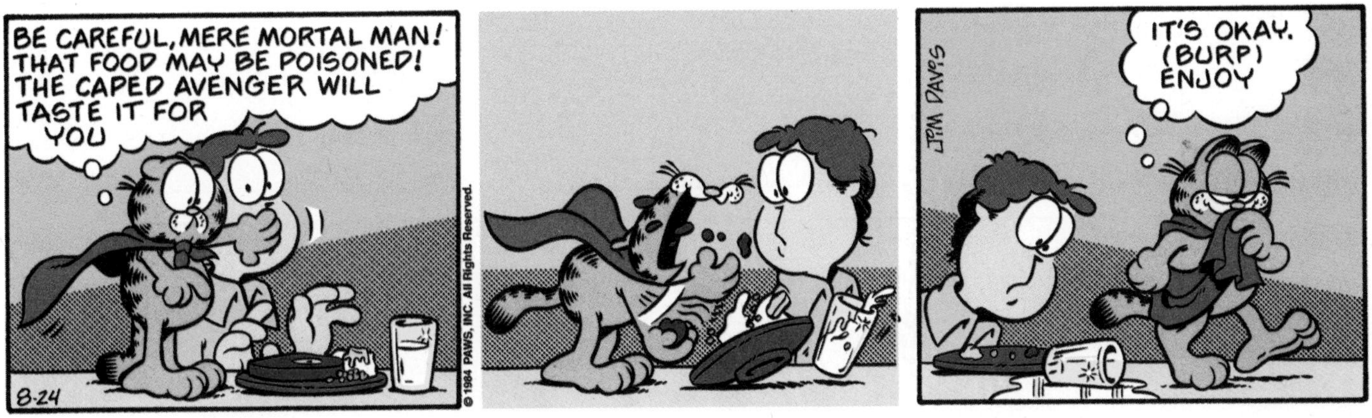
BE CAREFUL, MERE MORTAL MAN! THAT FOOD MAY BE POISONED! THE CAPED AVENGER WILL TASTE IT FOR YOU
IT'S OKAY. (BURP) ENJOY
JIM DAVIS
8-24
© 1984 PAWS, INC. All Rights Reserved.

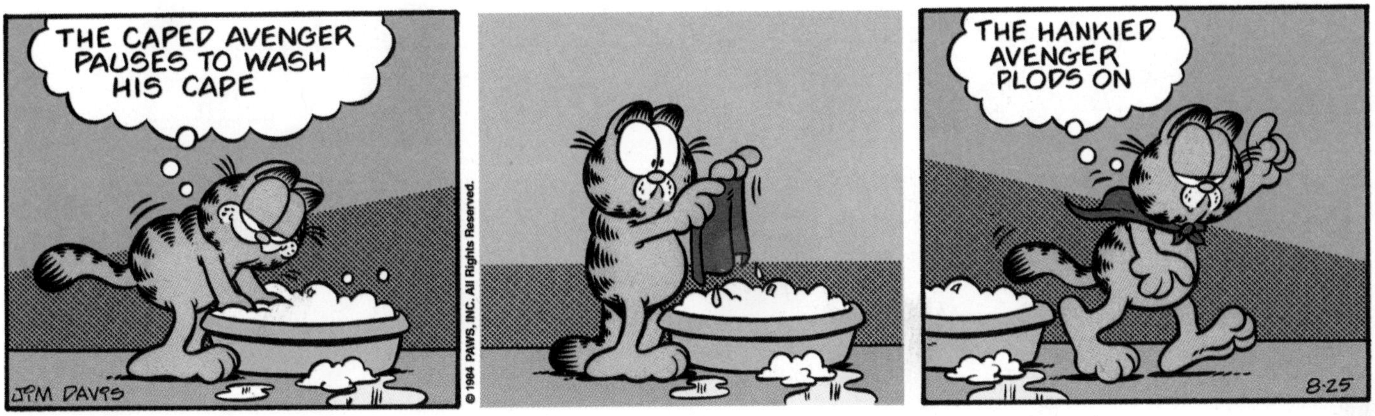
THE CAPED AVENGER PAUSES TO WASH HIS CAPE
THE HANKIED AVENGER PLODS ON
JIM DAVIS
8-25
© 1984 PAWS, INC. All Rights Reserved.

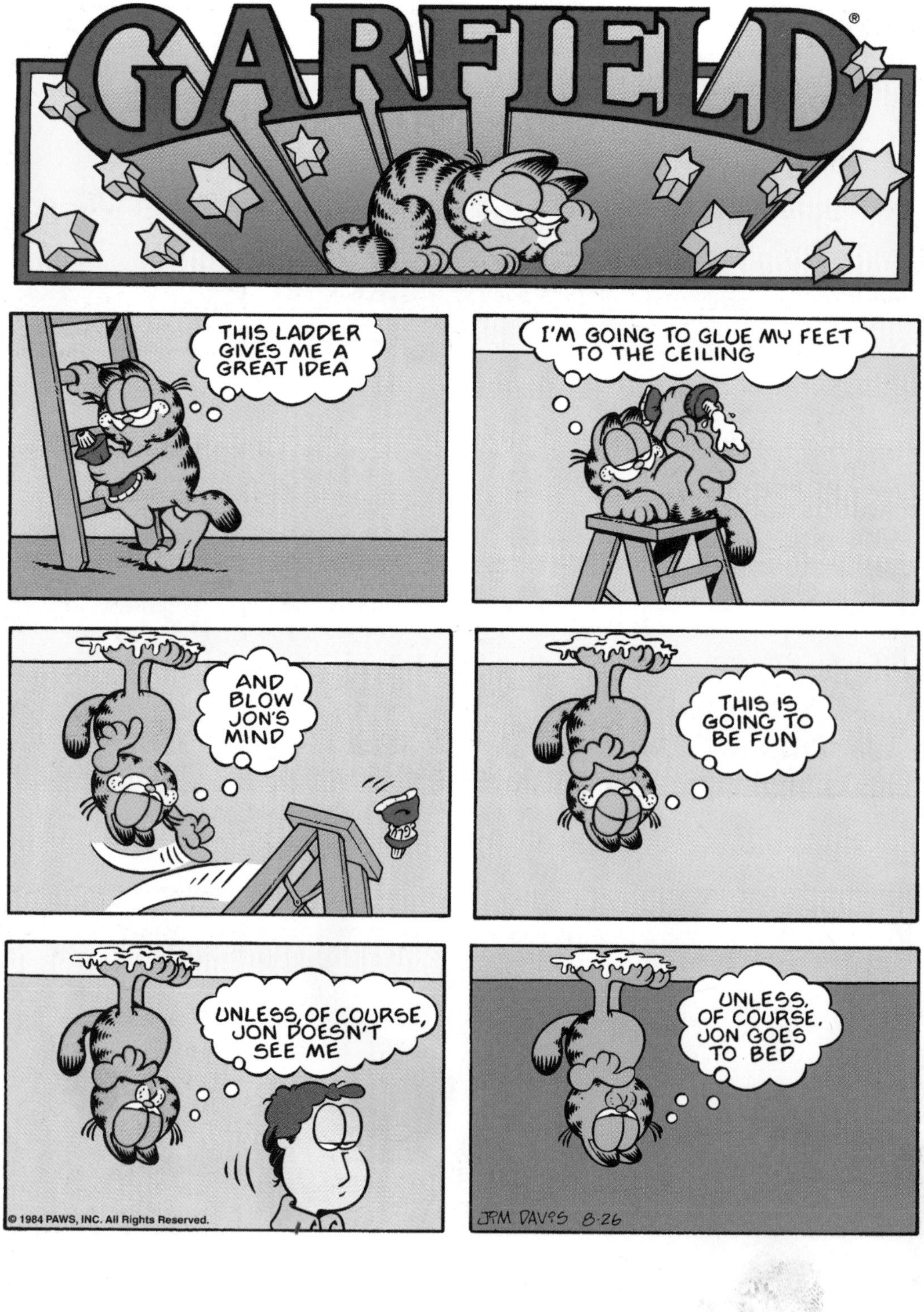
GARFIELD®
THIS LADDER GIVES ME A GREAT IDEA
I'M GOING TO GLUE MY FEET TO THE CEILING
AND BLOW JON'S MIND
THIS IS GOING TO BE FUN
UNLESS, OF COURSE, JON DOESN'T SEE ME
UNLESS, OF COURSE, JON GOES TO BED
JIM DAVIS 8-26

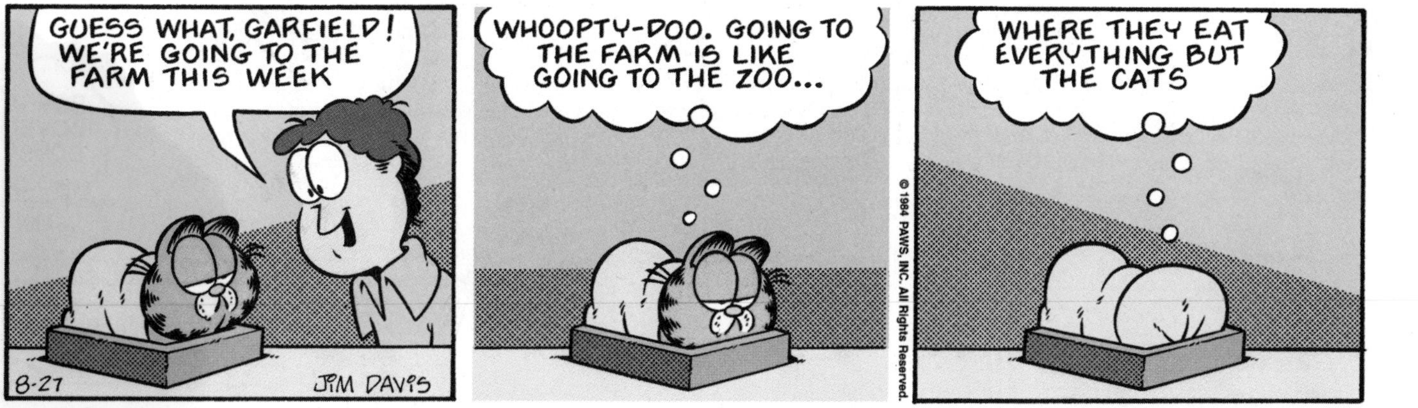
GUESS WHAT, GARFIELD! WE'RE GOING TO THE FARM THIS WEEK
8-27
JIM DAVIS
WHOOPTY-DOO. GOING TO THE FARM IS LIKE GOING TO THE ZOO...
© 1984 PAWS, INC. All Rights Reserved.
WHERE THEY EAT EVERYTHING BUT THE CATS

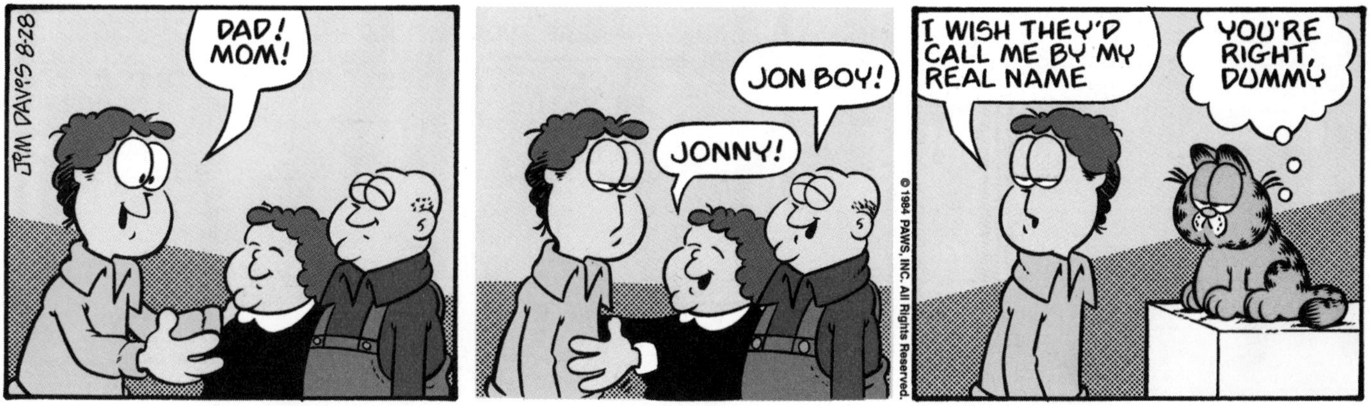
JIM DAVIS 8-28
DAD! MOM!
JON BOY!
JONNY!
© 1984 PAWS, INC. All Rights Reserved.
I WISH THEY'D CALL ME BY MY REAL NAME
YOU'RE RIGHT, DUMMY

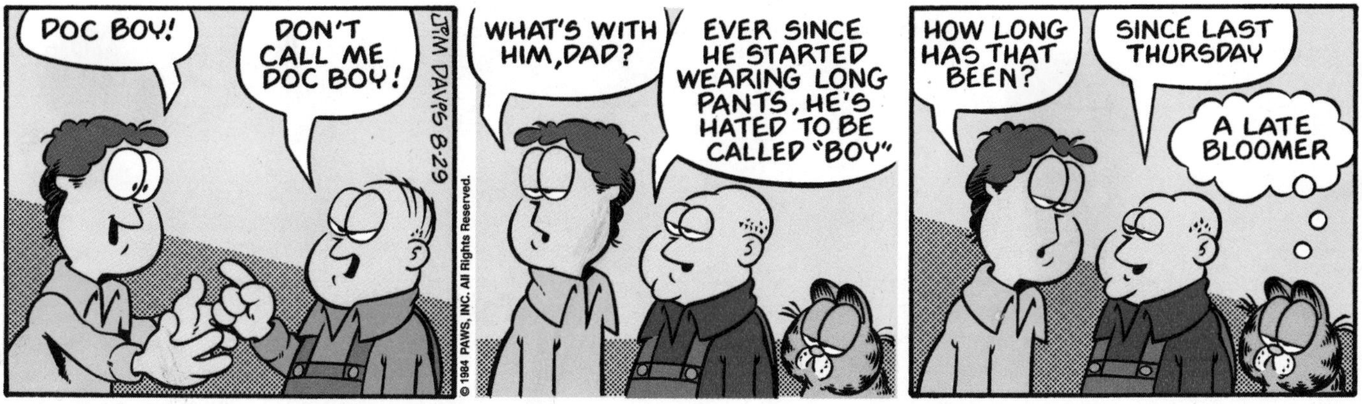
DOC BOY!
DON'T CALL ME DOC BOY!
JIM DAVIS 8-29
© 1984 PAWS, INC. All Rights Reserved.
WHAT'S WITH HIM, DAD?
EVER SINCE HE STARTED WEARING LONG PANTS, HE'S HATED TO BE CALLED "BOY"
HOW LONG HAS THAT BEEN?
SINCE LAST THURSDAY
A LATE BLOOMER

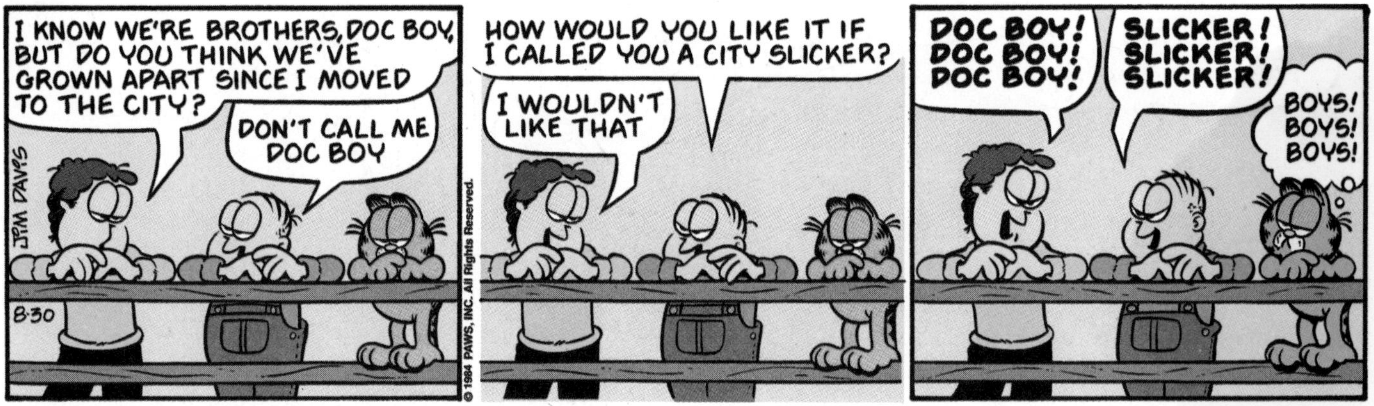
I KNOW WE'RE BROTHERS, DOC BOY, BUT DO YOU THINK WE'VE GROWN APART SINCE I MOVED TO THE CITY?
DON'T CALL ME DOC BOY
JIM DAVIS
8-30
© 1984 PAWS, INC. All Rights Reserved.
HOW WOULD YOU LIKE IT IF I CALLED YOU A CITY SLICKER?
I WOULDN'T LIKE THAT
DOC BOY! DOC BOY! DOC BOY!
SLICKER! SLICKER! SLICKER!
BOYS! BOYS! BOYS!

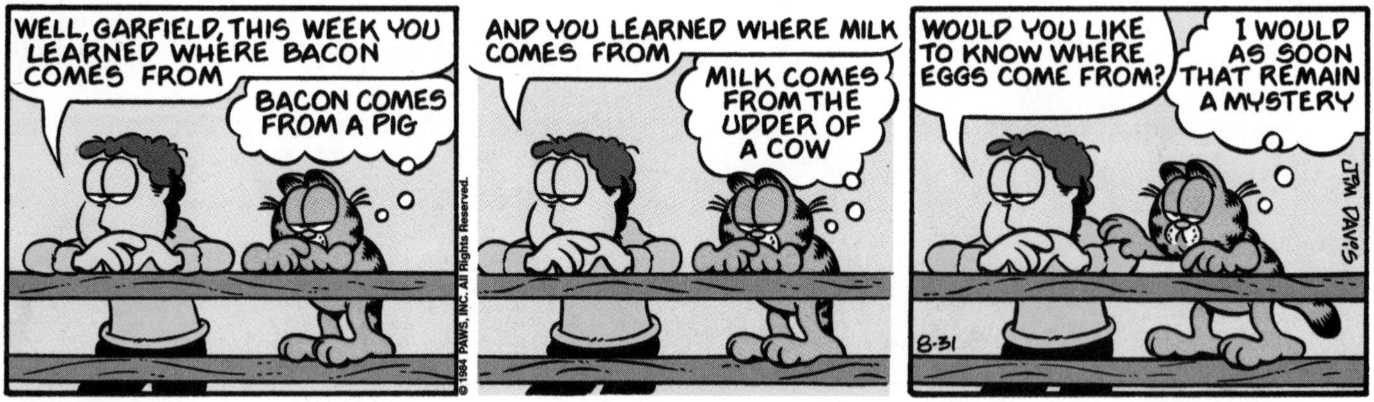
WELL, GARFIELD, THIS WEEK YOU LEARNED WHERE BACON COMES FROM
BACON COMES FROM A PIG
© 1984 PAWS, INC. All Rights Reserved.
AND YOU LEARNED WHERE MILK COMES FROM
MILK COMES FROM THE UDDER OF A COW
WOULD YOU LIKE TO KNOW WHERE EGGS COME FROM?
I WOULD AS SOON THAT REMAIN A MYSTERY
JIM DAVIS
8-31

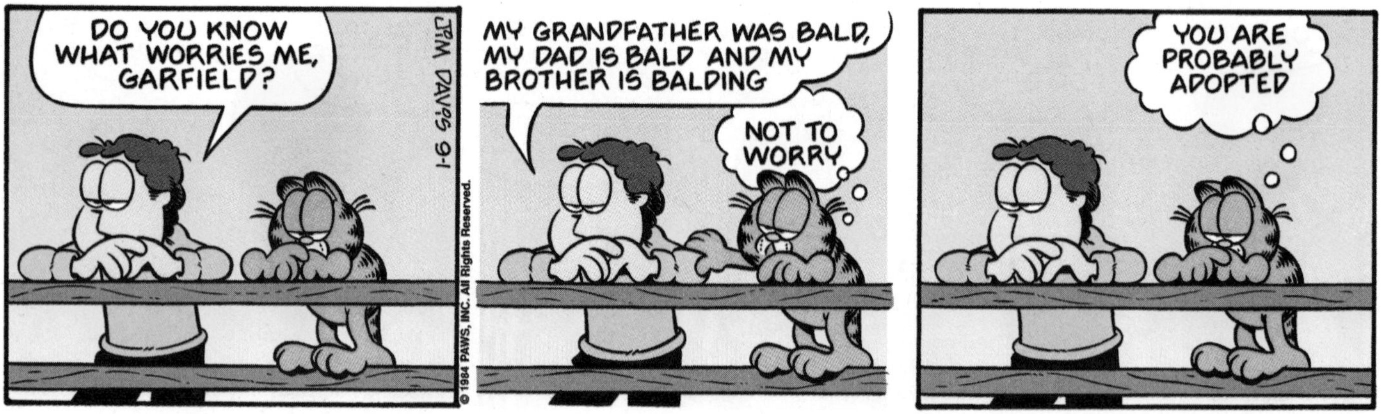
DO YOU KNOW WHAT WORRIES ME, GARFIELD?
JIM DAVIS 9-1
© 1984 PAWS, INC. All Rights Reserved.
MY GRANDFATHER WAS BALD, MY DAD IS BALD AND MY BROTHER IS BALDING
NOT TO WORRY
YOU ARE PROBABLY ADOPTED

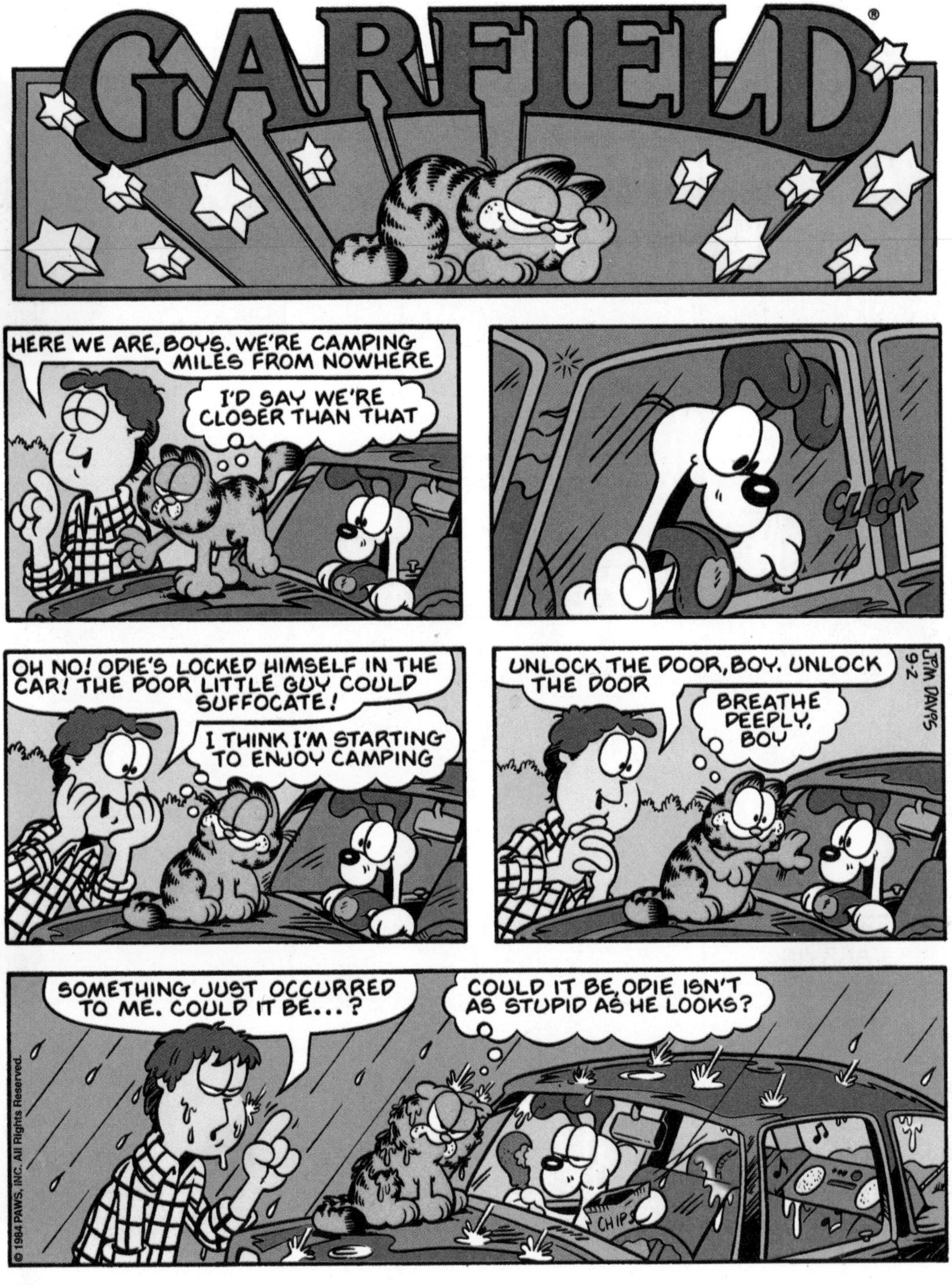
GARFIELD®
HERE WE ARE, BOYS. WE'RE CAMPING MILES FROM NOWHERE
I'D SAY WE'RE CLOSER THAN THAT
CLICK
OH NO! ODIE'S LOCKED HIMSELF IN THE CAR! THE POOR LITTLE GUY COULD SUFFOCATE!
I THINK I'M STARTING TO ENJOY CAMPING
UNLOCK THE DOOR, BOY. UNLOCK THE DOOR
BREATHE DEEPLY, BOY
JIM DAVIS 9-2
SOMETHING JUST OCCURRED TO ME. COULD IT BE...?
COULD IT BE, ODIE ISN'T AS STUPID AS HE LOOKS?
CHIPS

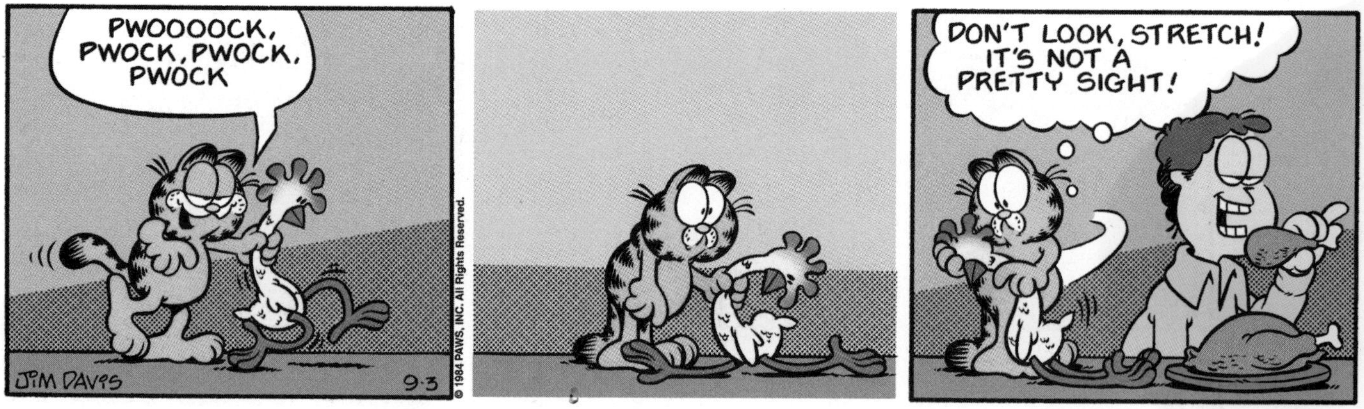
PWOOOOCK, PWOCK, PWOCK, PWOCK
JIM DAVIS 9-3
DON'T LOOK, STRETCH! IT'S NOT A PRETTY SIGHT!

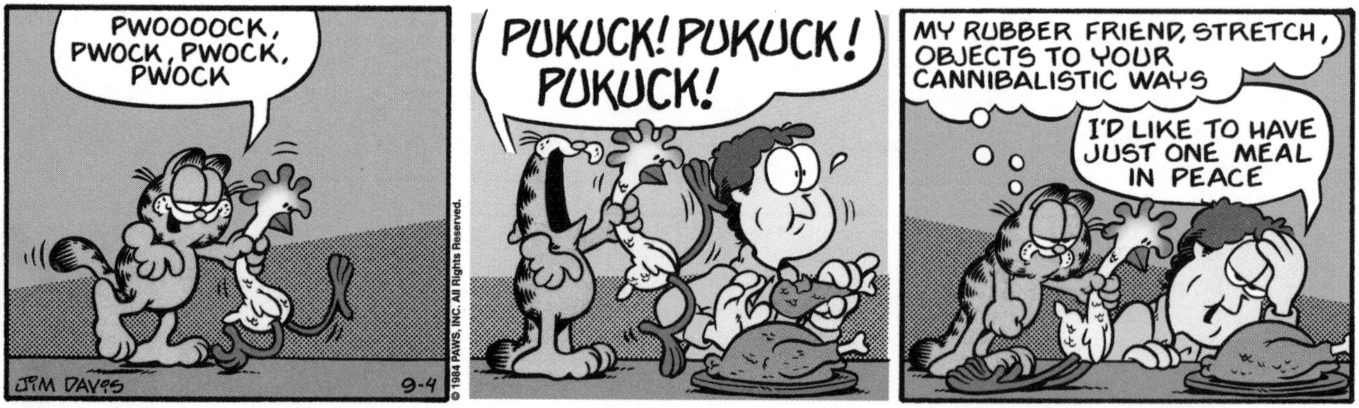
PWOOOOCK, PWOCK, PWOCK, PWOCK
JIM DAVIS 9-4
PUKUCK! PUKUCK! PUKUCK!
MY RUBBER FRIEND, STRETCH, OBJECTS TO YOUR CANNIBALISTIC WAYS
I'D LIKE TO HAVE JUST ONE MEAL IN PEACE

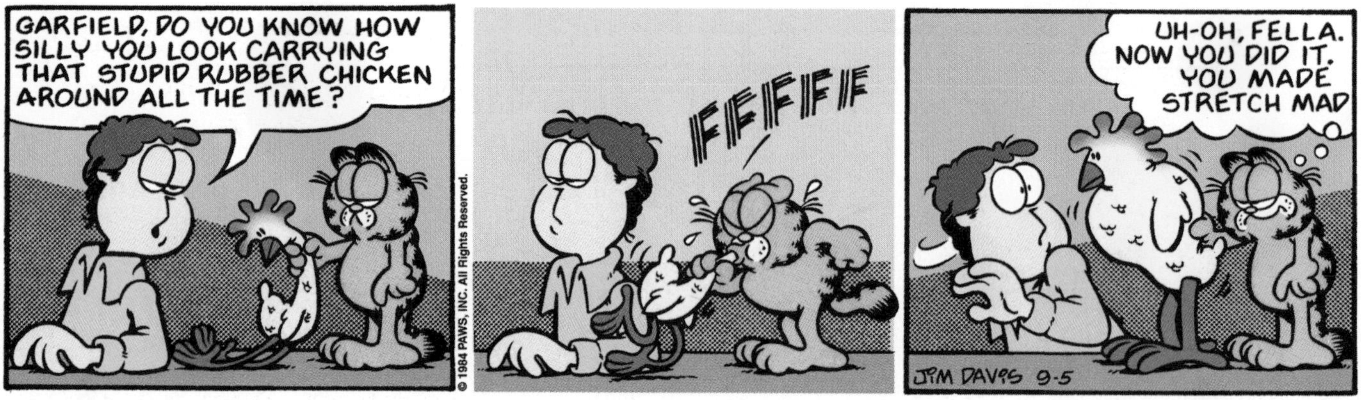
GARFIELD, DO YOU KNOW HOW SILLY YOU LOOK CARRYING THAT STUPID RUBBER CHICKEN AROUND ALL THE TIME?
FFFFFF
UH-OH, FELLA. NOW YOU DID IT. YOU MADE STRETCH MAD
JIM DAVIS 9-5

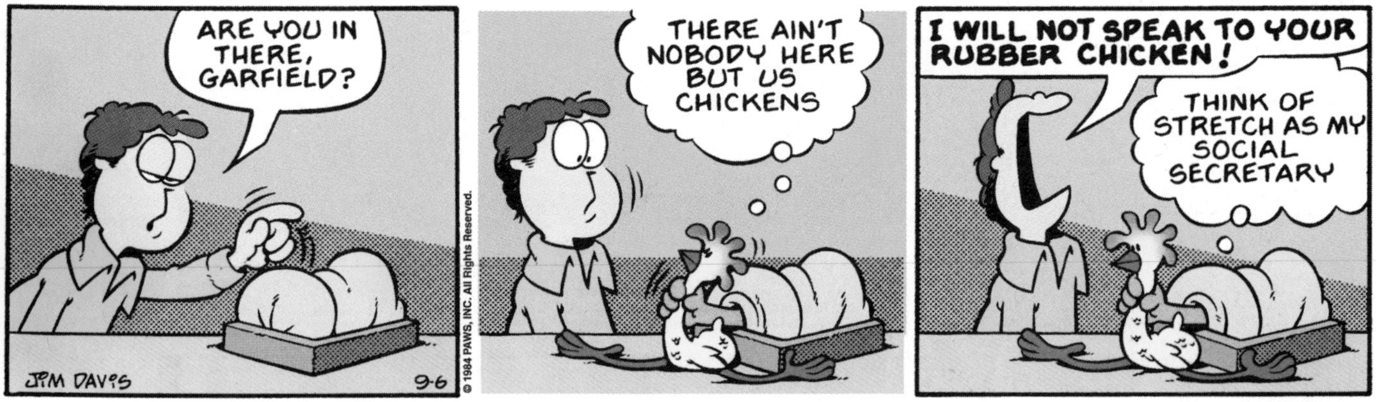
ARE YOU IN THERE, GARFIELD?
THERE AIN'T NOBODY HERE BUT US CHICKENS
I WILL NOT SPEAK TO YOUR RUBBER CHICKEN!
THINK OF STRETCH AS MY SOCIAL SECRETARY
JIM DAVIS
9-6

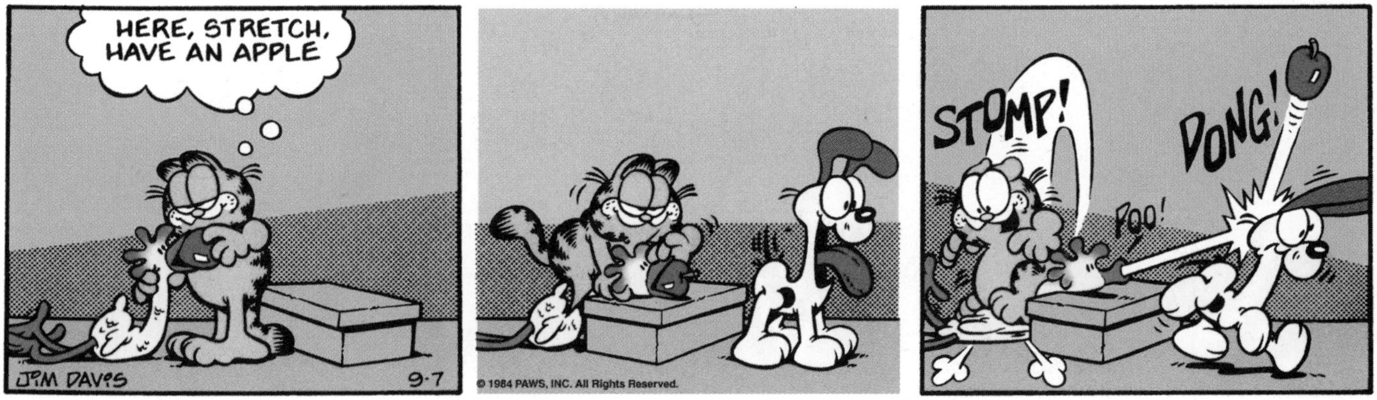
HERE, STRETCH, HAVE AN APPLE
STOMP!
POO!
DONG!
JIM DAVIS
9-7

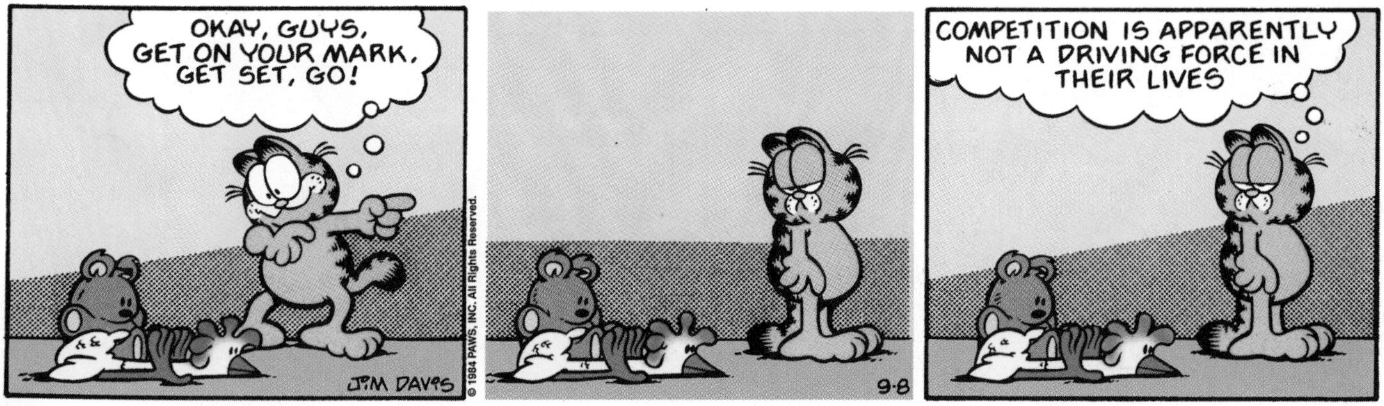
OKAY, GUYS, GET ON YOUR MARK, GET SET, GO!
COMPETITION IS APPARENTLY NOT A DRIVING FORCE IN THEIR LIVES
JIM DAVIS
9-8

GARFIELD
WHY, HELLO, NERMAL. AREN'T YOU CUTE
I WANT SOME ATTENTION, TOO
BONK
AW, POOR LITTLE GUY!
WELL, TWO CAN PLAY THE SYMPATHY GAME
CRASH!
JIM DAVIS 9-9
© 1984 PAWS, INC. All Rights Reserved.
THAT WAS ONE OF MY BEST PLATES
THAT WAS ONE OF MY BEST HEADS

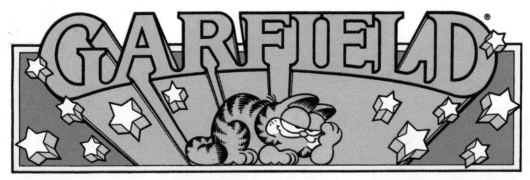

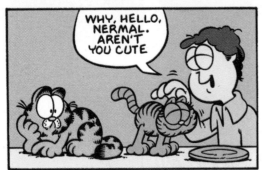

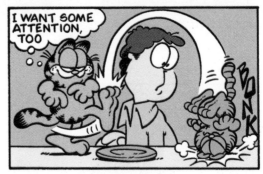

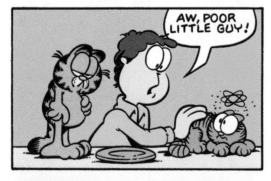

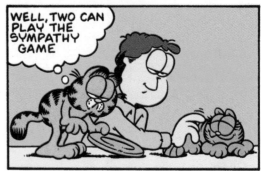

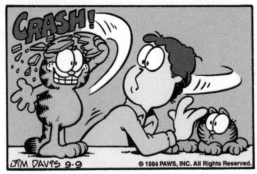

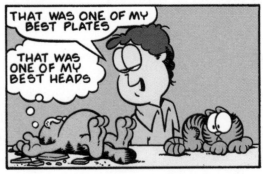

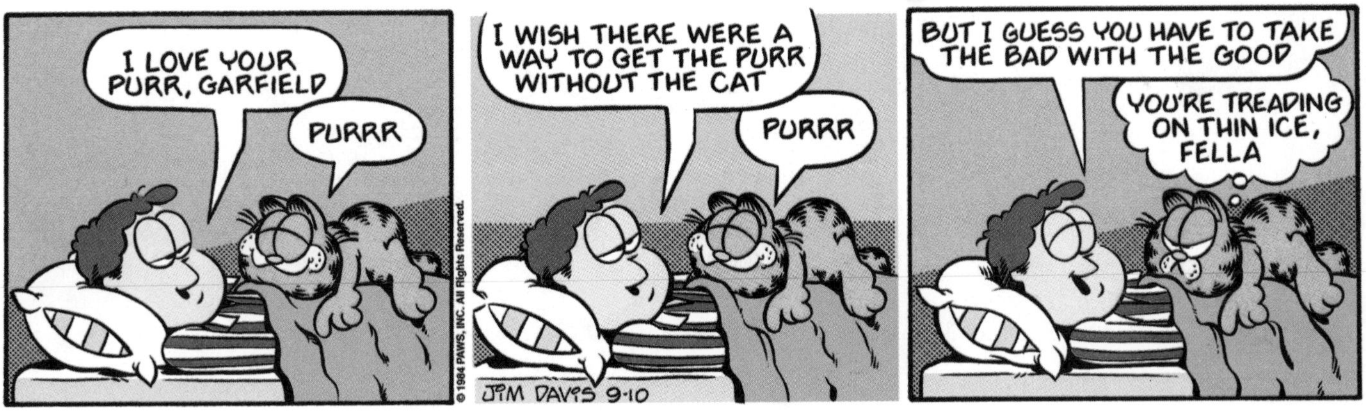
I LOVE YOUR PURR, GARFIELD
PURRR
I WISH THERE WERE A WAY TO GET THE PURR WITHOUT THE CAT
PURRR
BUT I GUESS YOU HAVE TO TAKE THE BAD WITH THE GOOD
YOU'RE TREADING ON THIN ICE, FELLA
© 1984 PAWS, INC. All Rights Reserved.
JIM DAVIS 9-10

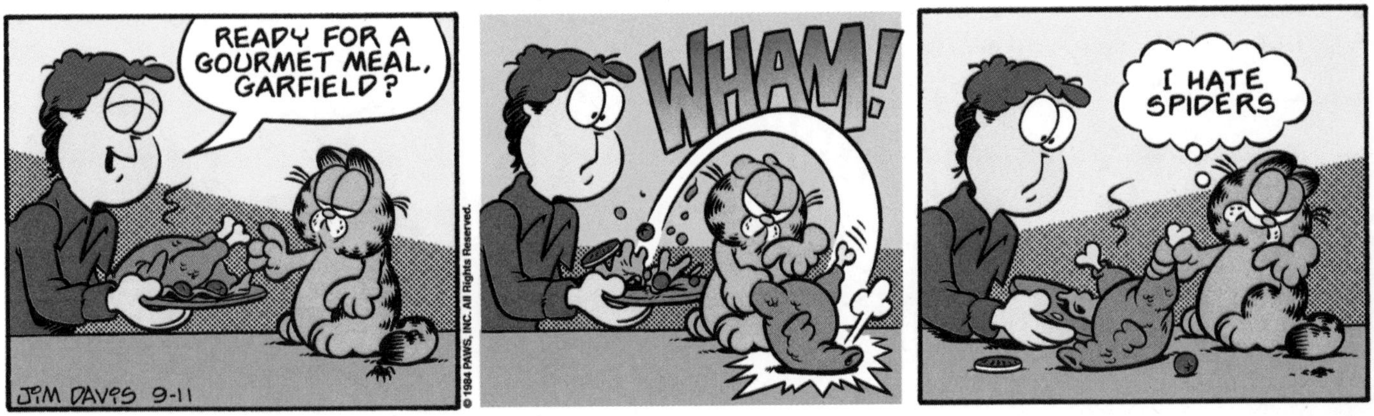
READY FOR A GOURMET MEAL, GARFIELD?
JIM DAVIS 9-11
WHAM!
© 1984 PAWS, INC. All Rights Reserved.
I HATE SPIDERS

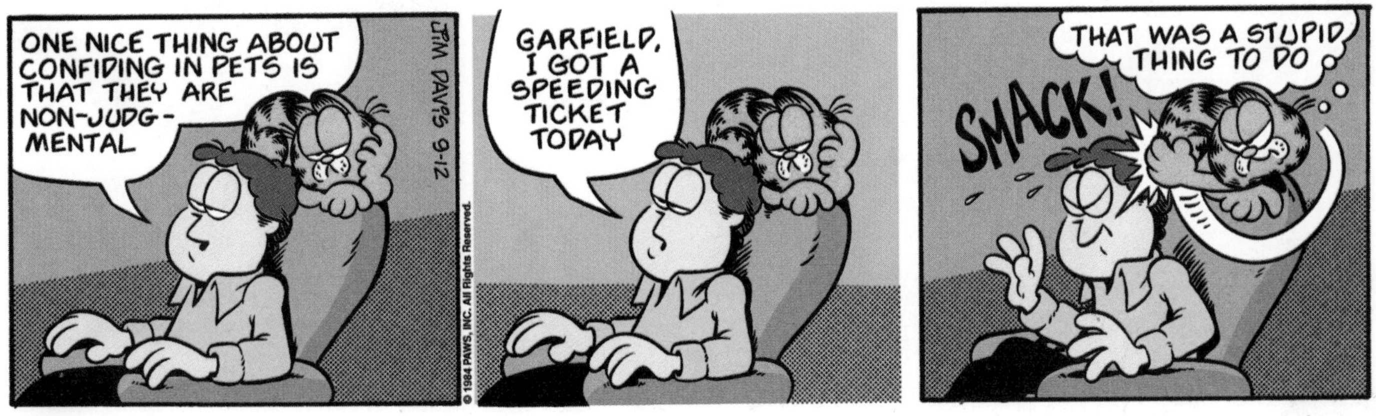
ONE NICE THING ABOUT CONFIDING IN PETS IS THAT THEY ARE NON-JUDG-MENTAL
JIM DAVIS 9-12
GARFIELD, I GOT A SPEEDING TICKET TODAY
© 1984 PAWS, INC. All Rights Reserved.
THAT WAS A STUPID THING TO DO
SMACK!

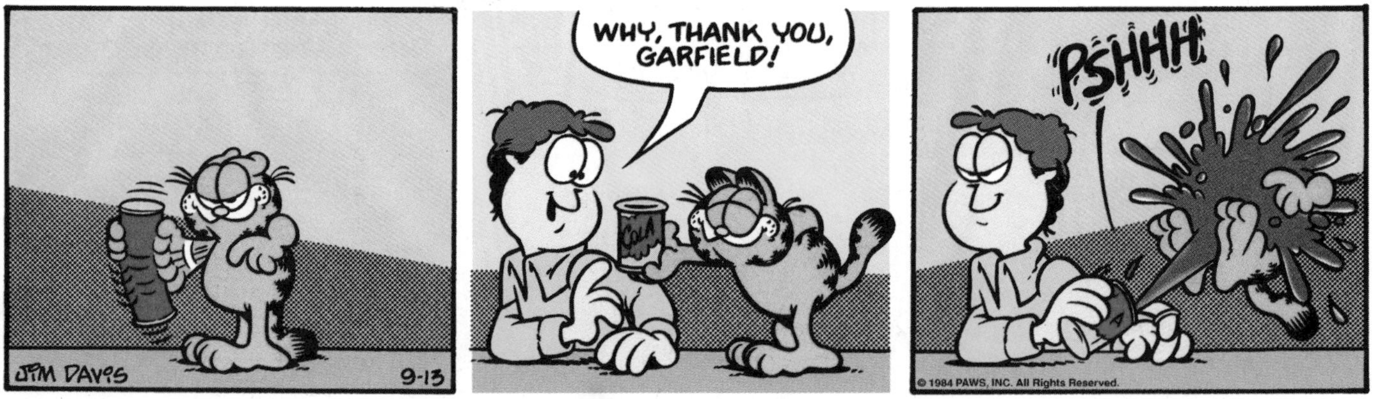
JIM DAVIS
9-13
WHY, THANK YOU, GARFIELD!
COLA
PSHHH
© 1984 PAWS, INC. All Rights Reserved.

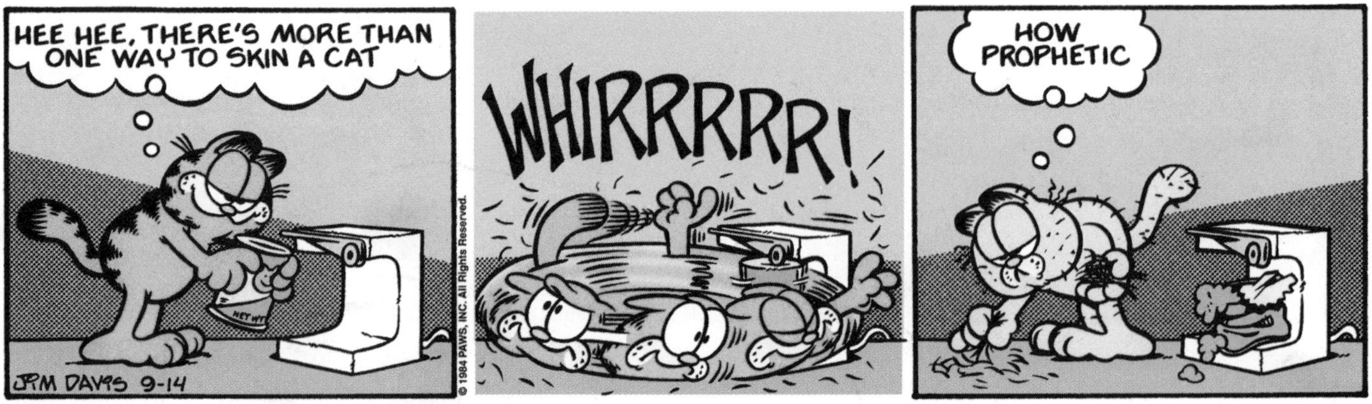
HEE HEE, THERE'S MORE THAN ONE WAY TO SKIN A CAT
JIM DAVIS 9-14
© 1984 PAWS, INC. All Rights Reserved.
WHIRRRRRR!
HOW PROPHETIC

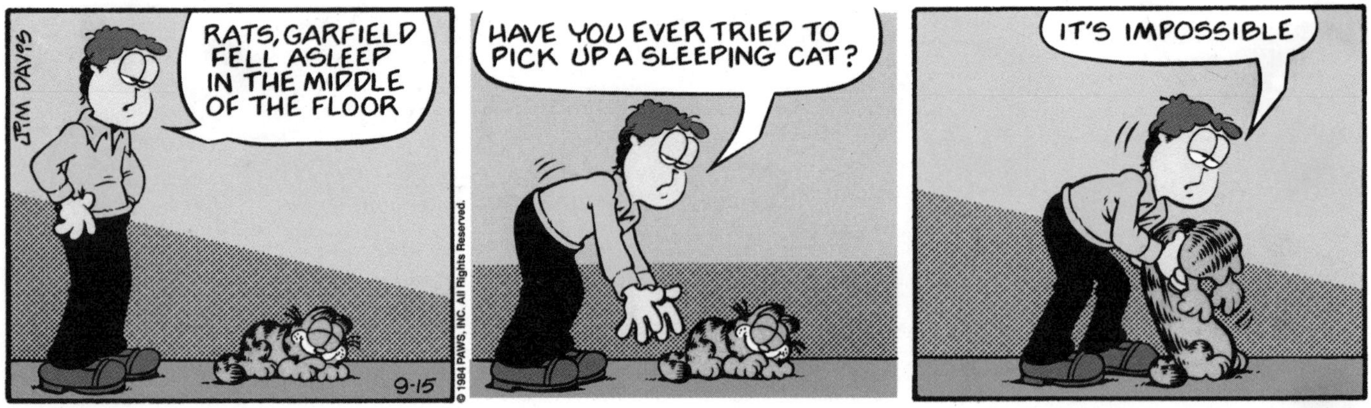
JIM DAVIS
RATS, GARFIELD FELL ASLEEP IN THE MIDDLE OF THE FLOOR
9-15
© 1984 PAWS, INC. All Rights Reserved.
HAVE YOU EVER TRIED TO PICK UP A SLEEPING CAT?
IT'S IMPOSSIBLE

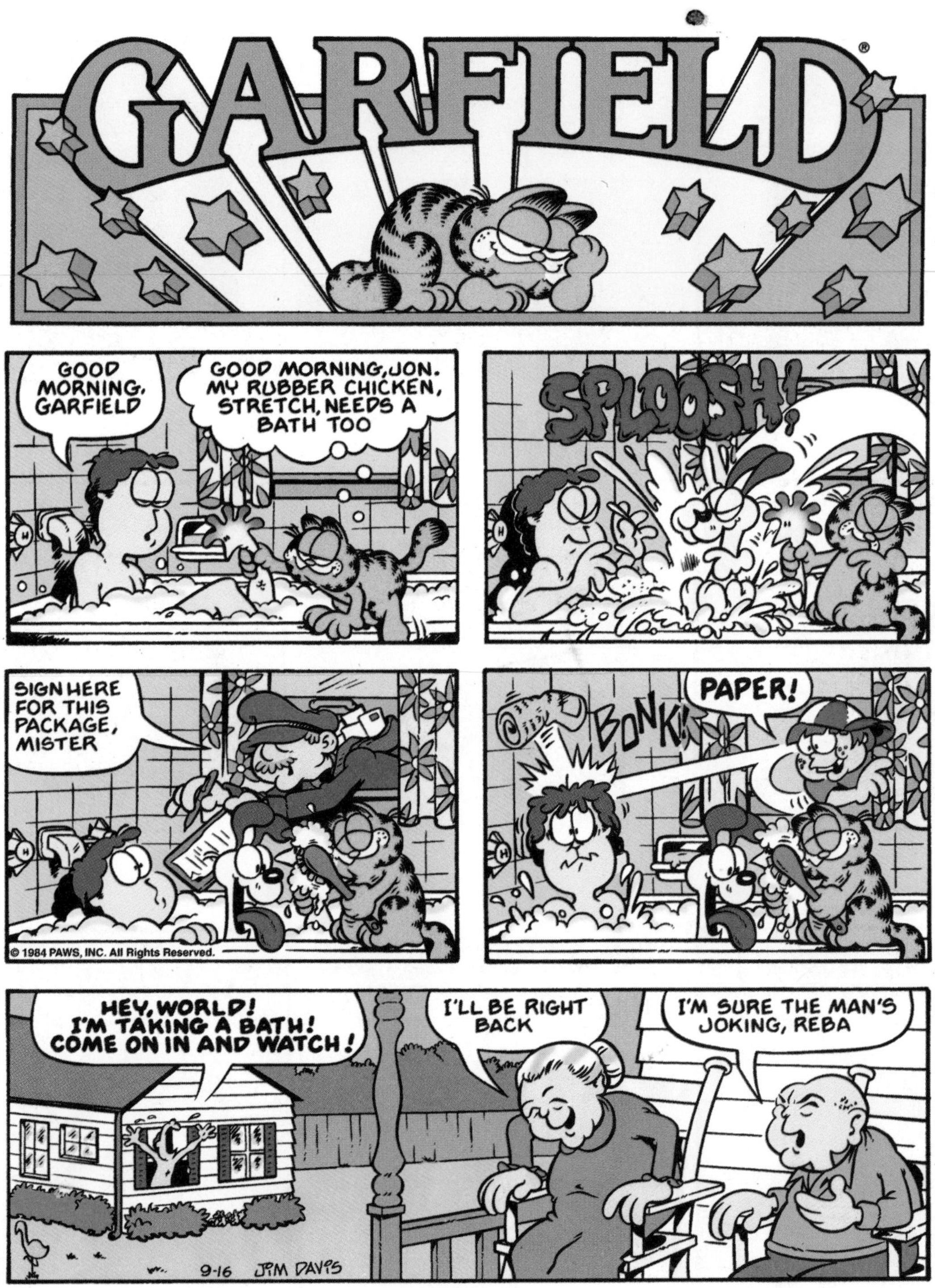
GARFIELD
GOOD MORNING, GARFIELD
GOOD MORNING, JON. MY RUBBER CHICKEN, STRETCH, NEEDS A BATH TOO
SPLOOSH!
SIGN HERE FOR THIS PACKAGE, MISTER
© 1984 PAWS, INC. All Rights Reserved.
BONK!
PAPER!
HEY, WORLD! I'M TAKING A BATH! COME ON IN AND WATCH!
I'LL BE RIGHT BACK
I'M SURE THE MAN'S JOKING, REBA
9-16 JIM DAVIS

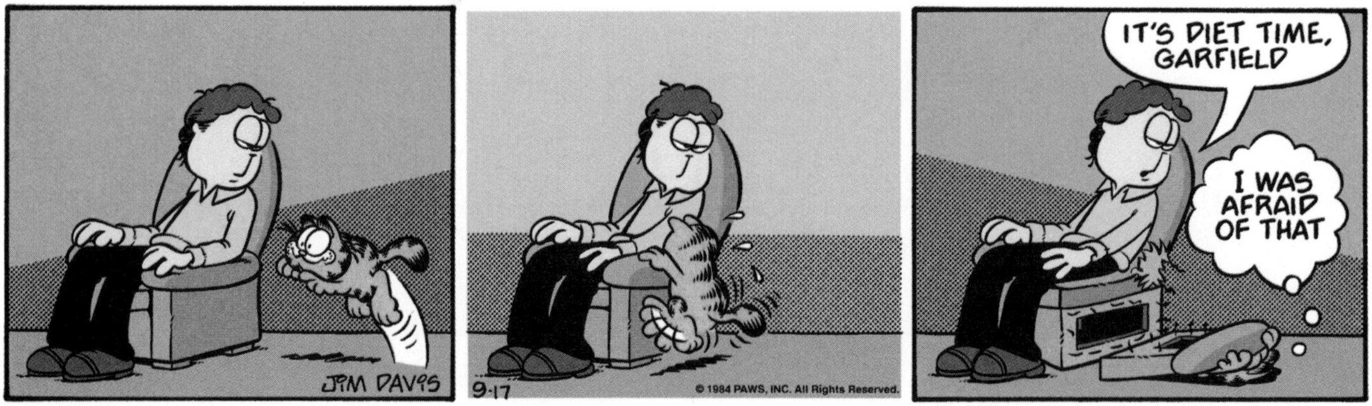
JIM DAVIS
9-17
© 1984 PAWS, INC. All Rights Reserved.
IT'S DIET TIME, GARFIELD
I WAS AFRAID OF THAT

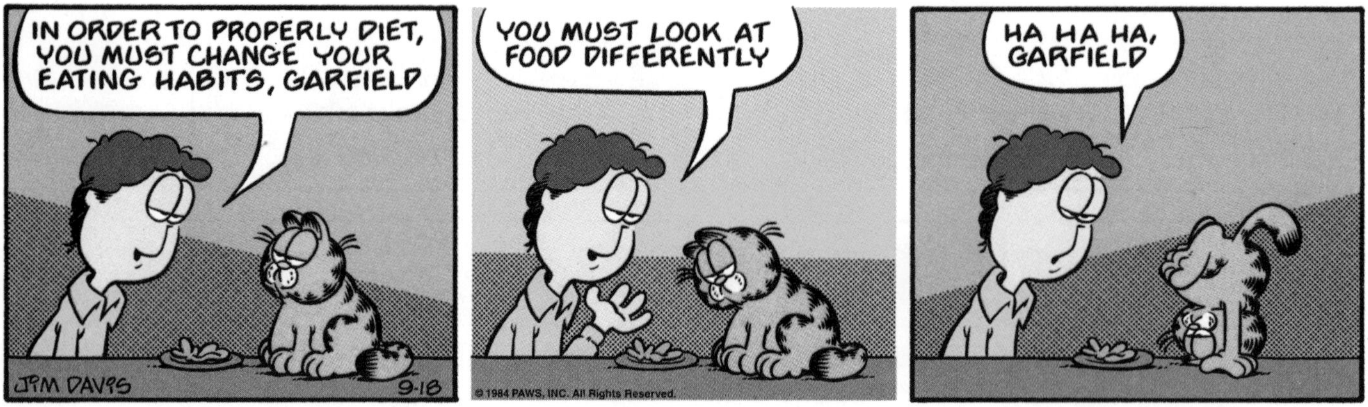
IN ORDER TO PROPERLY DIET, YOU MUST CHANGE YOUR EATING HABITS, GARFIELD
JIM DAVIS
9-18
YOU MUST LOOK AT FOOD DIFFERENTLY
© 1984 PAWS, INC. All Rights Reserved.
HA HA HA, GARFIELD

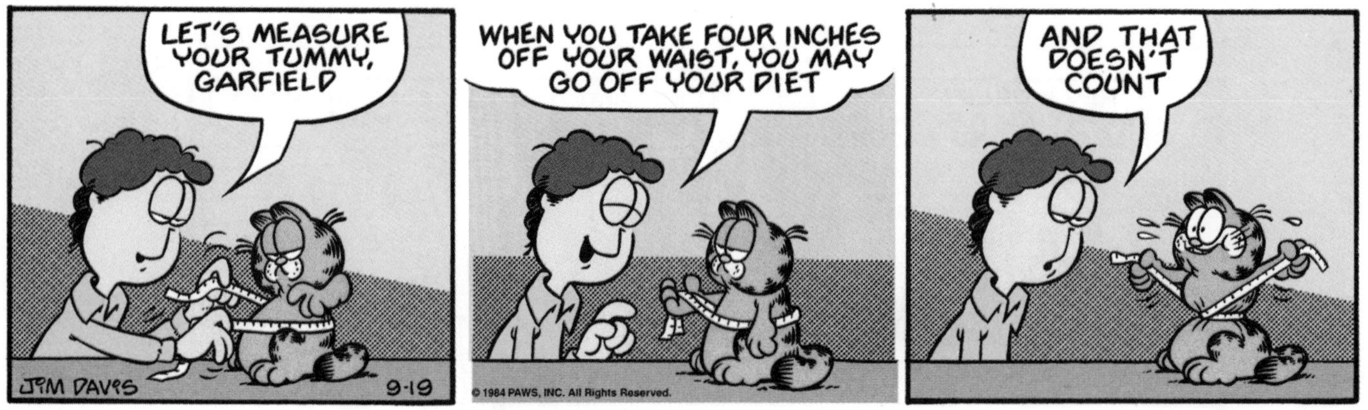
LET'S MEASURE YOUR TUMMY, GARFIELD
JIM DAVIS
9-19
WHEN YOU TAKE FOUR INCHES OFF YOUR WAIST, YOU MAY GO OFF YOUR DIET
© 1984 PAWS, INC. All Rights Reserved.
AND THAT DOESN'T COUNT

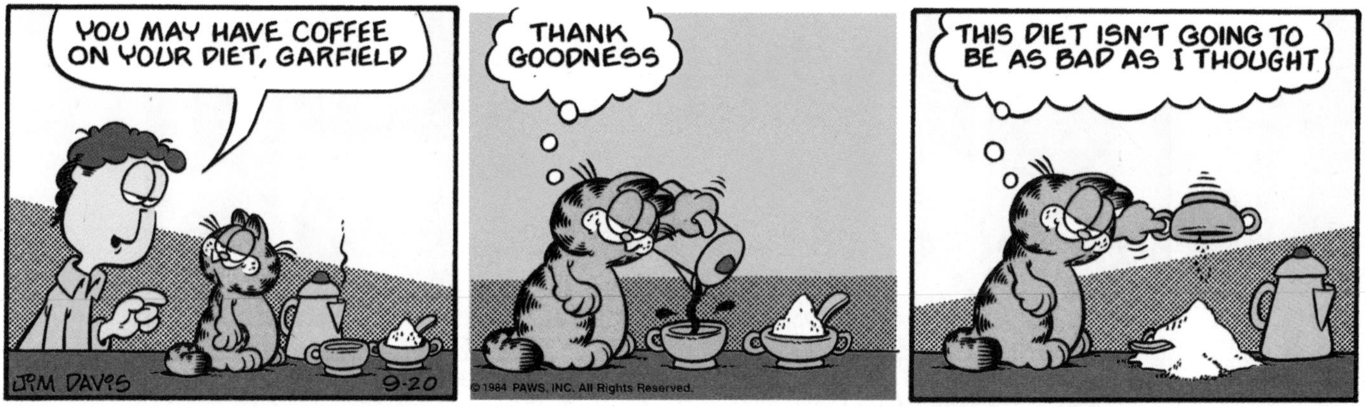
YOU MAY HAVE COFFEE ON YOUR DIET, GARFIELD
JIM DAVIS
9-20
THANK GOODNESS
© 1984 PAWS, INC. All Rights Reserved.
THIS DIET ISN'T GOING TO BE AS BAD AS I THOUGHT

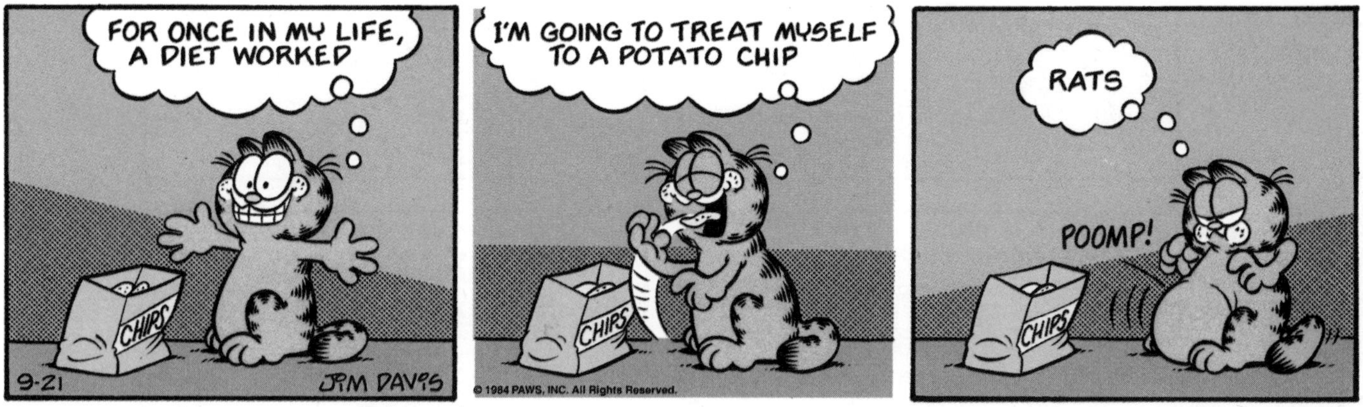
FOR ONCE IN MY LIFE, A DIET WORKED
CHIPS
9-21
JIM DAVIS
I'M GOING TO TREAT MYSELF TO A POTATO CHIP
CHIPS
© 1984 PAWS, INC. All Rights Reserved.
RATS
POOMP!
CHIPS

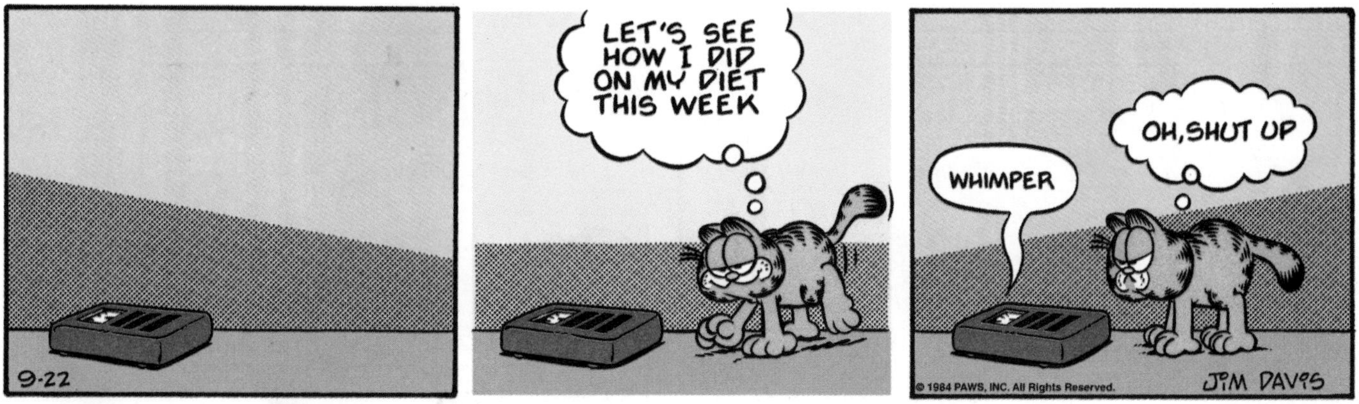
9-22
LET'S SEE HOW I DID ON MY DIET THIS WEEK
OH, SHUT UP
WHIMPER
© 1984 PAWS, INC. All Rights Reserved.
JIM DAVIS

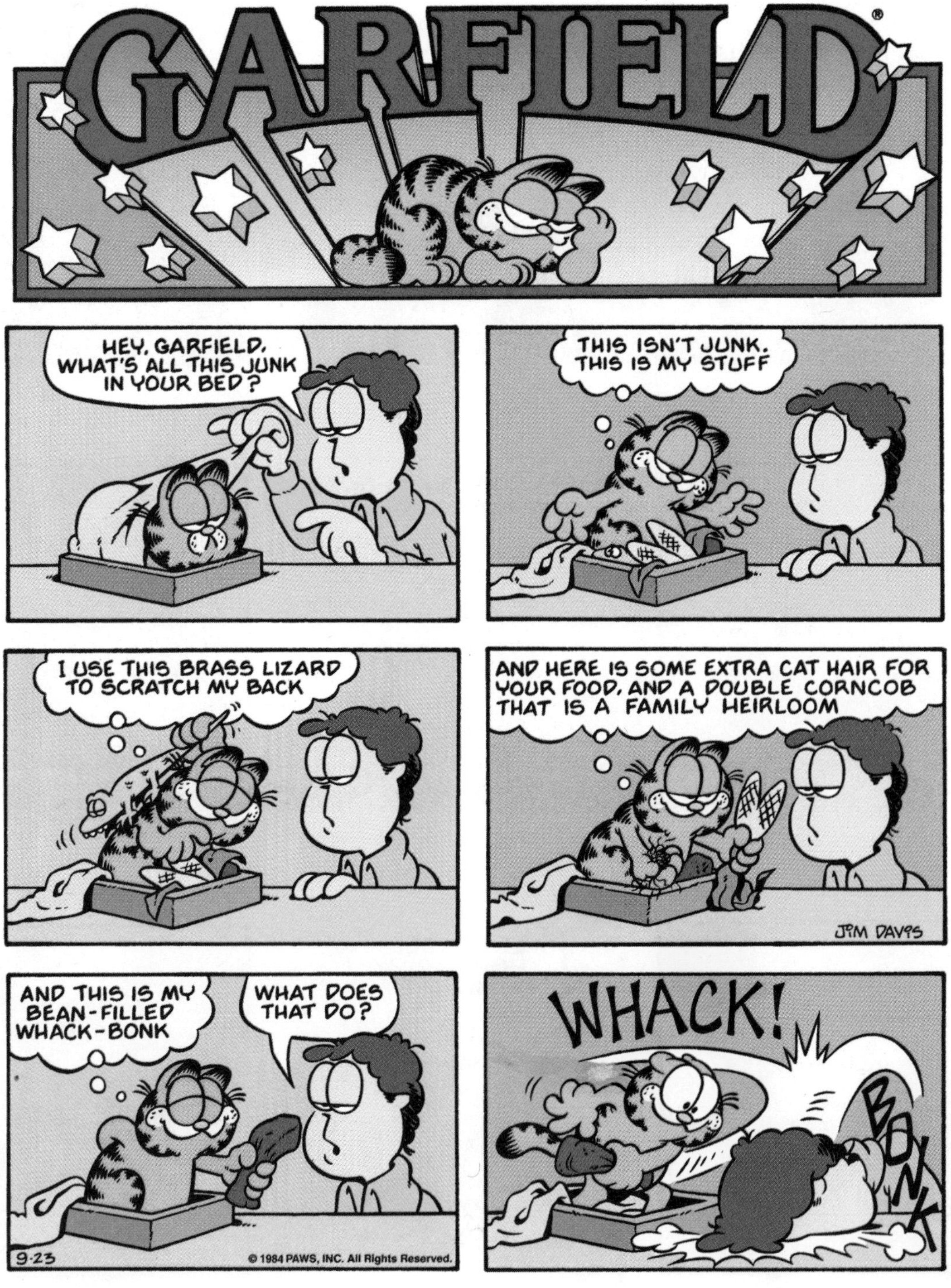
GARFIELD®
HEY, GARFIELD, WHAT'S ALL THIS JUNK IN YOUR BED?
THIS ISN'T JUNK. THIS IS MY STUFF
I USE THIS BRASS LIZARD TO SCRATCH MY BACK
AND HERE IS SOME EXTRA CAT HAIR FOR YOUR FOOD, AND A DOUBLE CORNCOB THAT IS A FAMILY HEIRLOOM
JIM DAVIS
AND THIS IS MY BEAN-FILLED WHACK-BONK
WHAT DOES THAT DO?
9·23
WHACK!
BONK

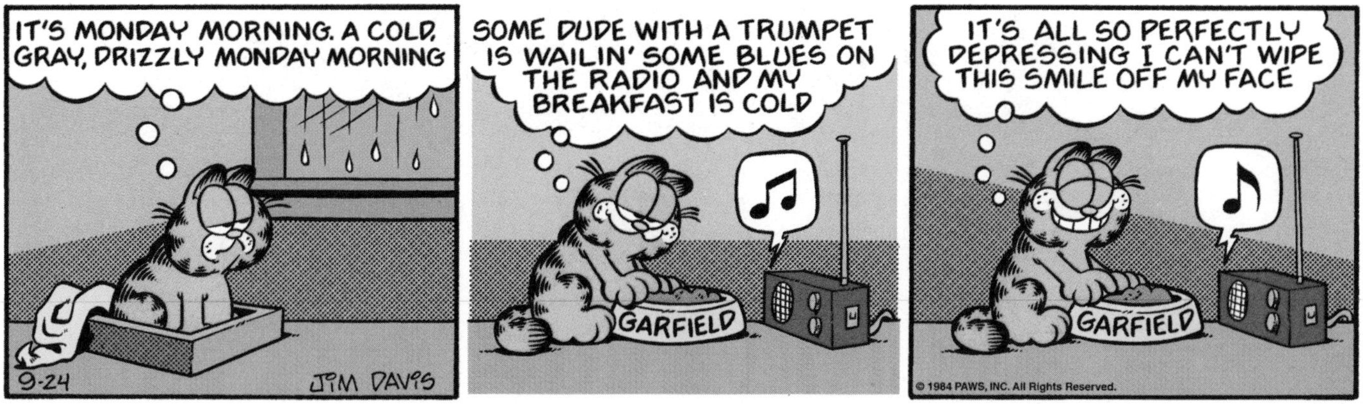
IT'S MONDAY MORNING. A COLD, GRAY, DRIZZLY MONDAY MORNING
9-24
JIM DAVIS
SOME DUDE WITH A TRUMPET IS WAILIN' SOME BLUES ON THE RADIO AND MY BREAKFAST IS COLD
GARFIELD
IT'S ALL SO PERFECTLY DEPRESSING I CAN'T WIPE THIS SMILE OFF MY FACE
GARFIELD
© 1984 PAWS, INC. All Rights Reserved.

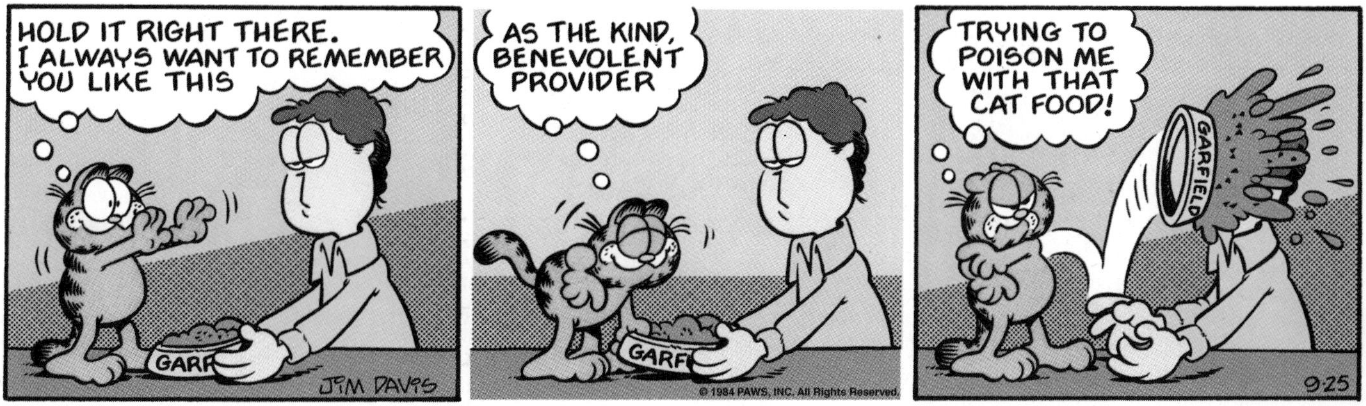
HOLD IT RIGHT THERE. I ALWAYS WANT TO REMEMBER YOU LIKE THIS
GARF
JIM DAVIS
AS THE KIND, BENEVOLENT PROVIDER
GARF
© 1984 PAWS, INC. All Rights Reserved.
TRYING TO POISON ME WITH THAT CAT FOOD!
GARFIELD
9-25

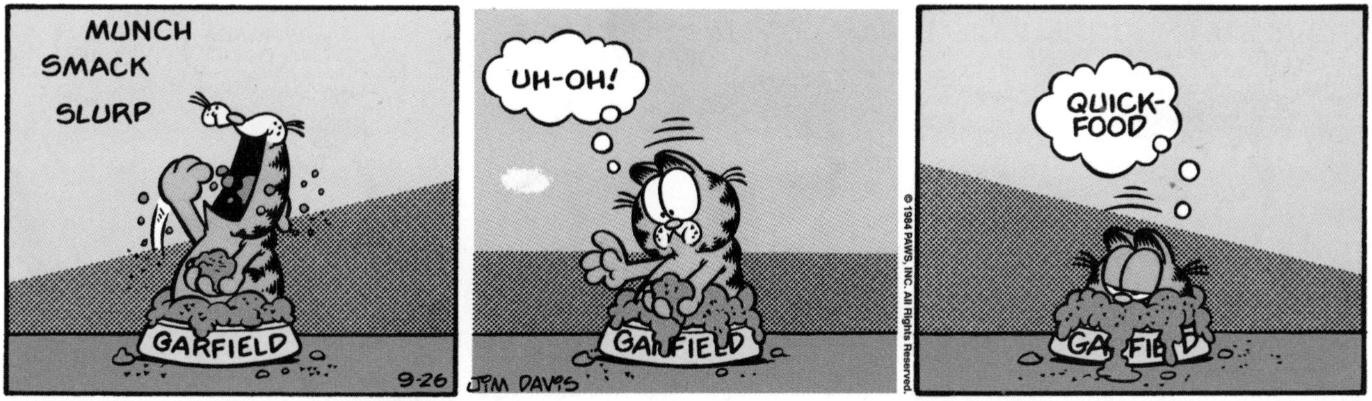
MUNCH
SMACK
SLURP
GARFIELD
9-26
JIM DAVIS
UH-OH!
© 1984 PAWS, INC. All Rights Reserved.
QUICK-FOOD

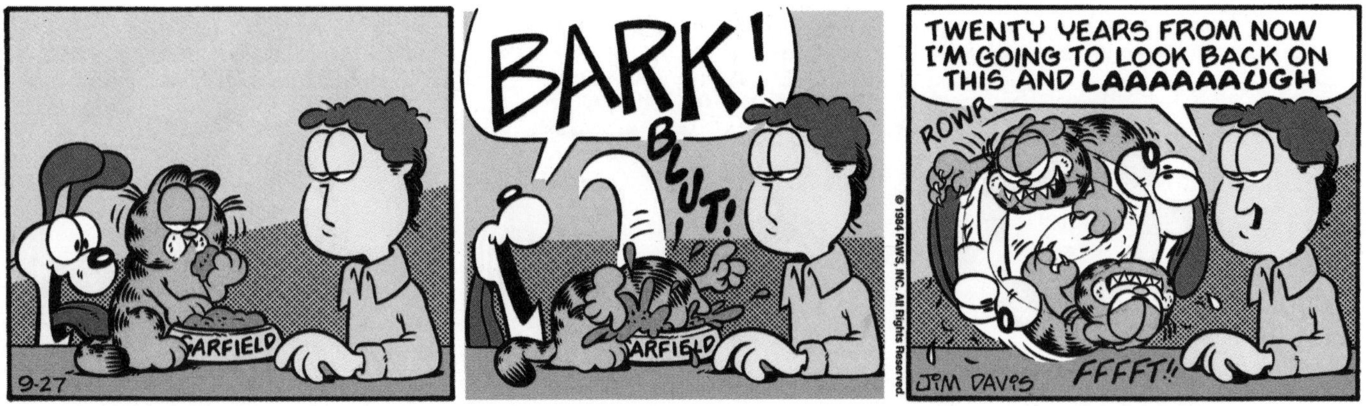
9-27
BARK!
BLUT!
© 1984 PAWS, INC. All Rights Reserved.
TWENTY YEARS FROM NOW I'M GOING TO LOOK BACK ON THIS AND LAAAAAAUGH
ROWR
FFFFT!!
JIM DAVIS

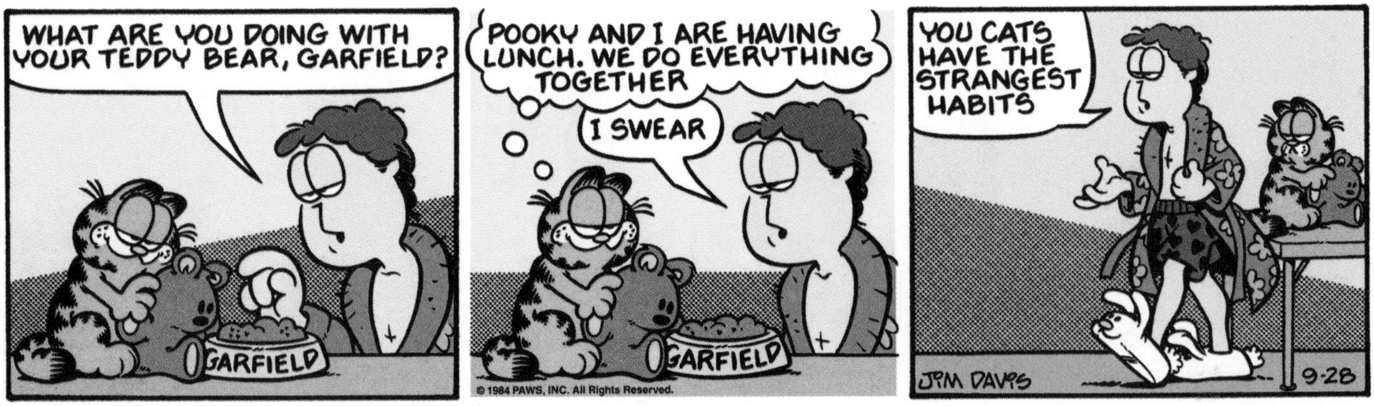
WHAT ARE YOU DOING WITH YOUR TEDDY BEAR, GARFIELD?
POOKY AND I ARE HAVING LUNCH. WE DO EVERYTHING TOGETHER
I SWEAR
© 1984 PAWS, INC. All Rights Reserved.
YOU CATS HAVE THE STRANGEST HABITS
JIM DAVIS
9-28

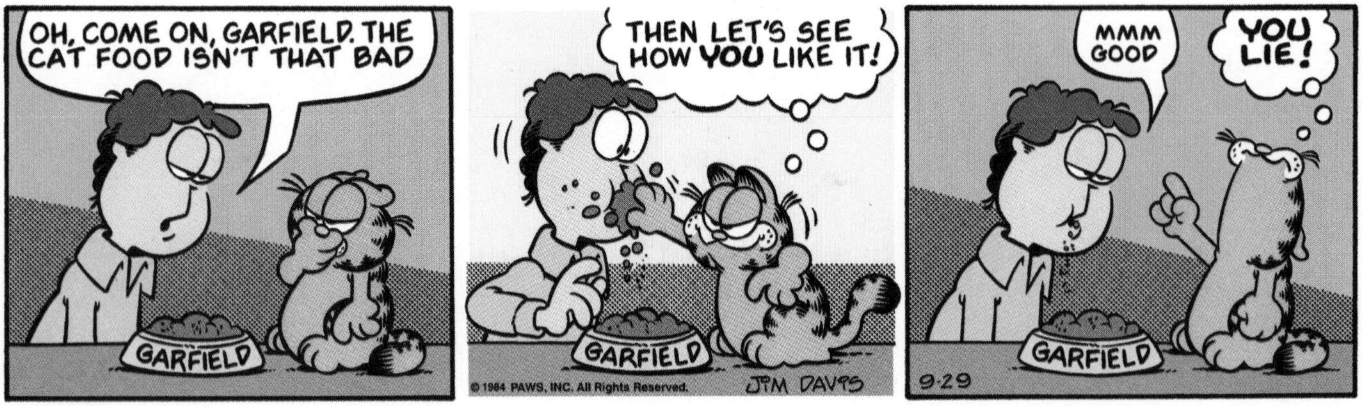
OH, COME ON, GARFIELD. THE CAT FOOD ISN'T THAT BAD
THEN LET'S SEE HOW YOU LIKE IT!
© 1984 PAWS, INC. All Rights Reserved.
JIM DAVIS
MMM GOOD
YOU LIE!
9-29

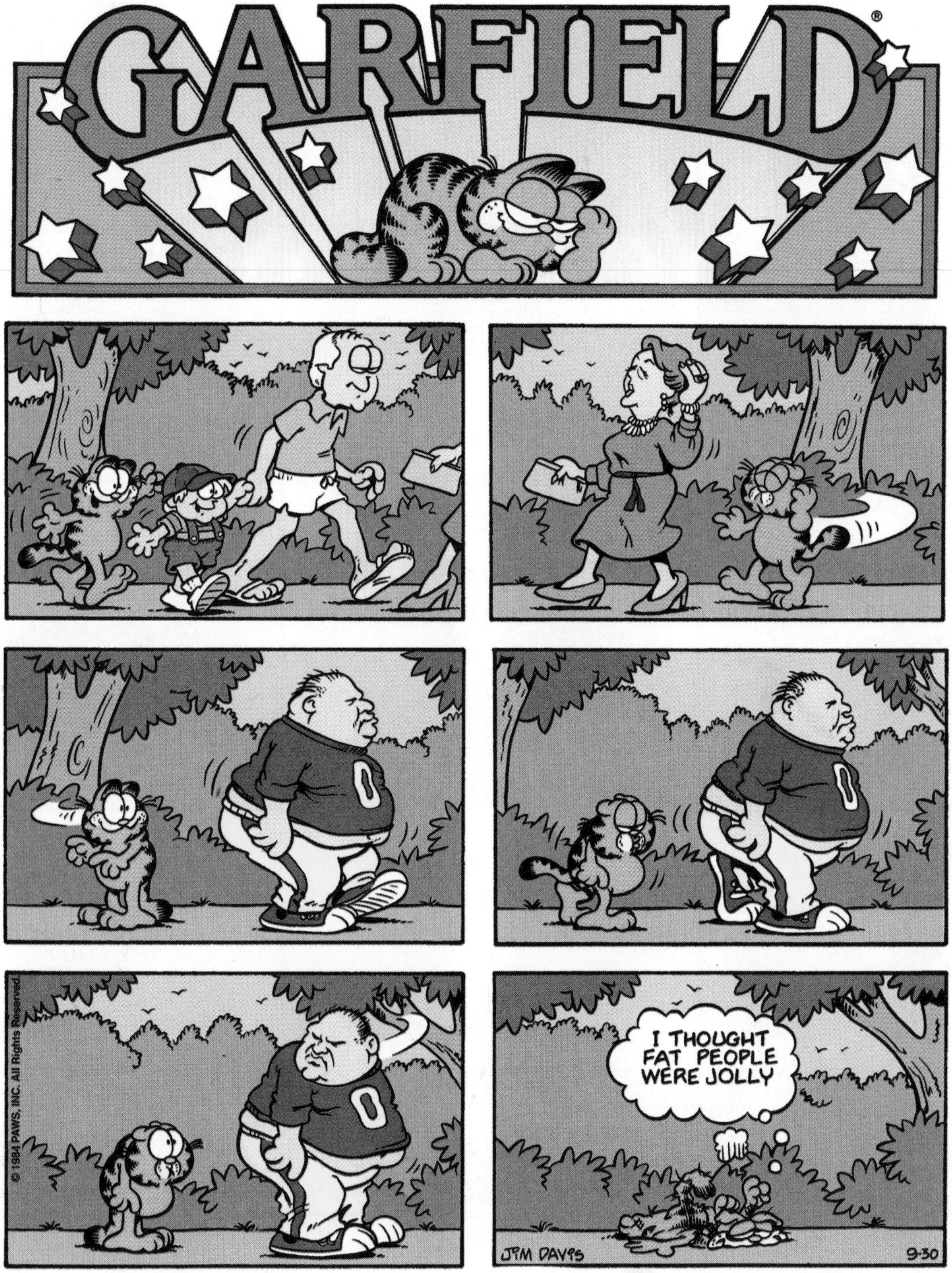
GARFIELD
I THOUGHT FAT PEOPLE WERE JOLLY
© 1984 PAWS, INC. All Rights Reserved
JIM DAVIS
9-30

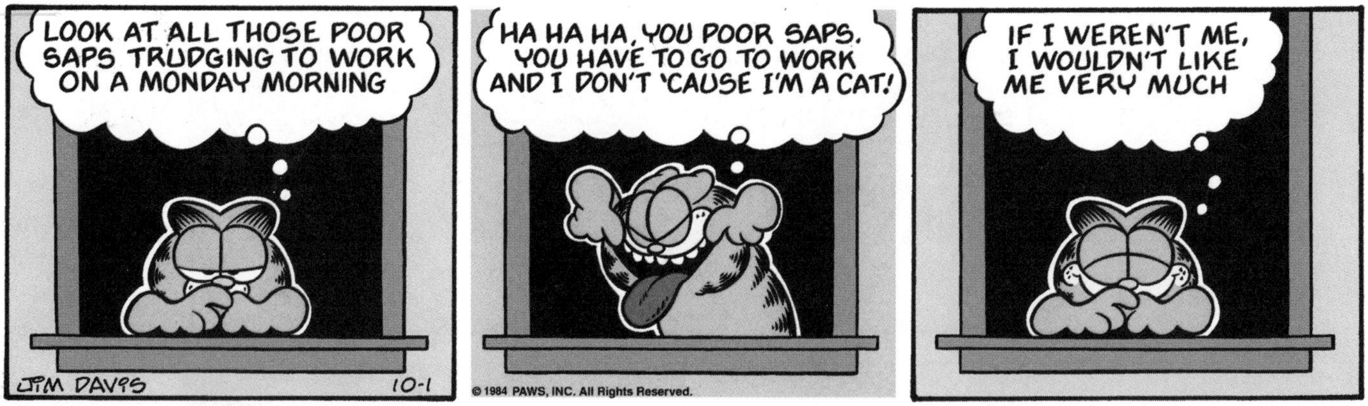
LOOK AT ALL THOSE POOR SAPS TRUDGING TO WORK ON A MONDAY MORNING
JIM DAVIS 10-1
HA HA HA, YOU POOR SAPS. YOU HAVE TO GO TO WORK AND I DON'T 'CAUSE I'M A CAT!
© 1984 PAWS, INC. All Rights Reserved.
IF I WEREN'T ME, I WOULDN'T LIKE ME VERY MUCH

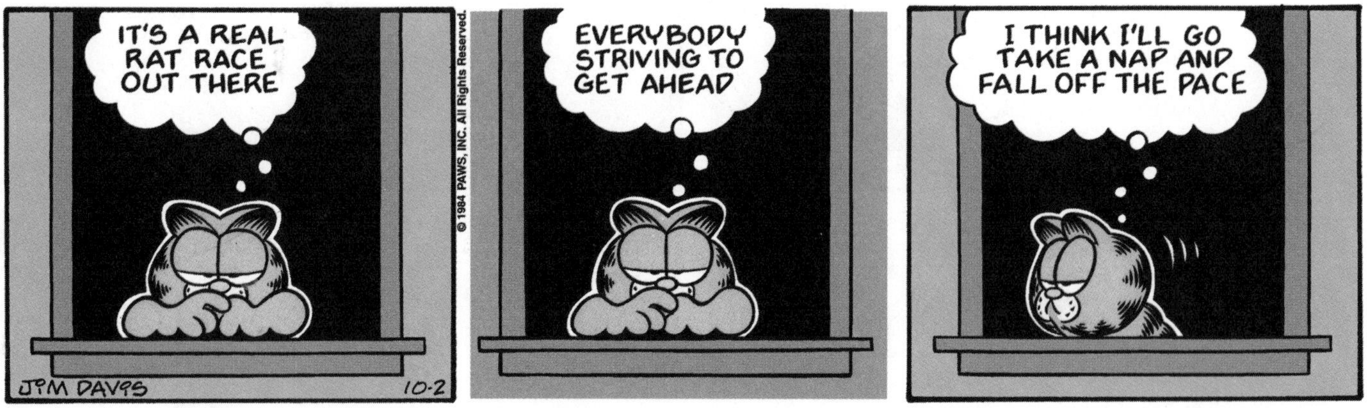
IT'S A REAL RAT RACE OUT THERE
JIM DAVIS 10-2
© 1984 PAWS, INC. All Rights Reserved.
EVERYBODY STRIVING TO GET AHEAD
I THINK I'LL GO TAKE A NAP AND FALL OFF THE PACE

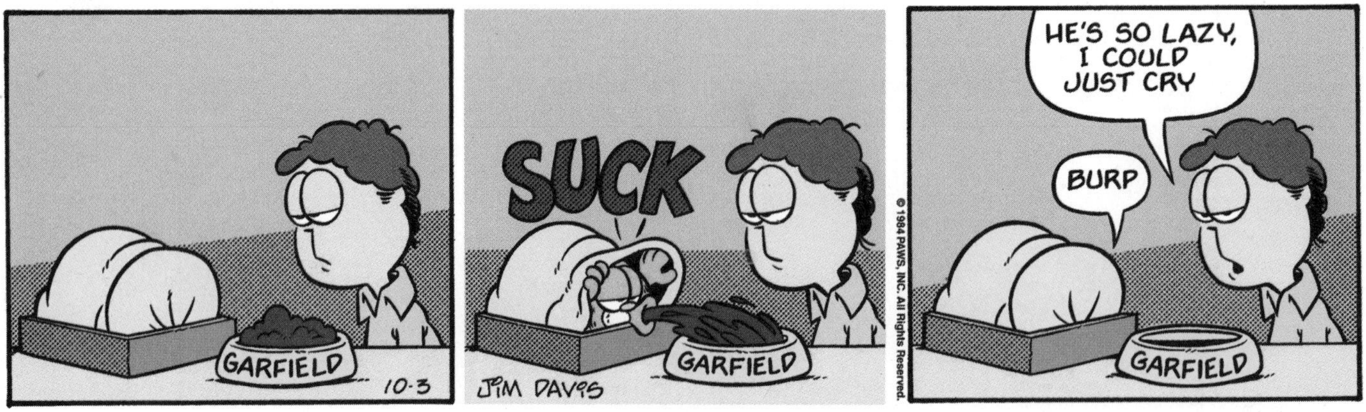
GARFIELD
10-3
SUCK
GARFIELD
JIM DAVIS
© 1984 PAWS, INC. All Rights Reserved.
HE'S SO LAZY, I COULD JUST CRY
BURP
GARFIELD

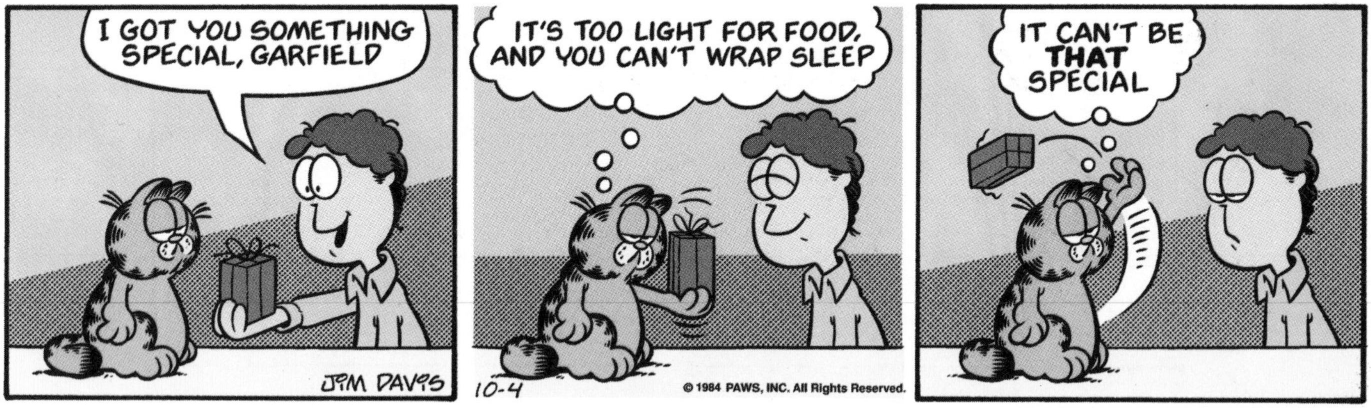
I GOT YOU SOMETHING SPECIAL, GARFIELD
JIM DAVIS
IT'S TOO LIGHT FOR FOOD, AND YOU CAN'T WRAP SLEEP
10-4
© 1984 PAWS, INC. All Rights Reserved.
IT CAN'T BE **THAT** SPECIAL

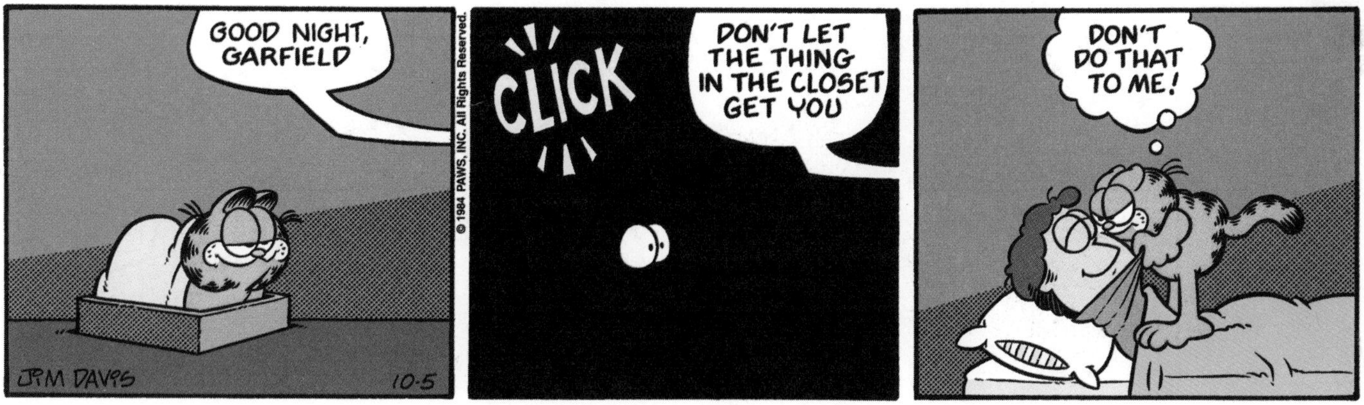
GOOD NIGHT, GARFIELD
JIM DAVIS
10-5
© 1984 PAWS, INC. All Rights Reserved.
CLICK
DON'T LET THE THING IN THE CLOSET GET YOU
DON'T DO THAT TO ME!

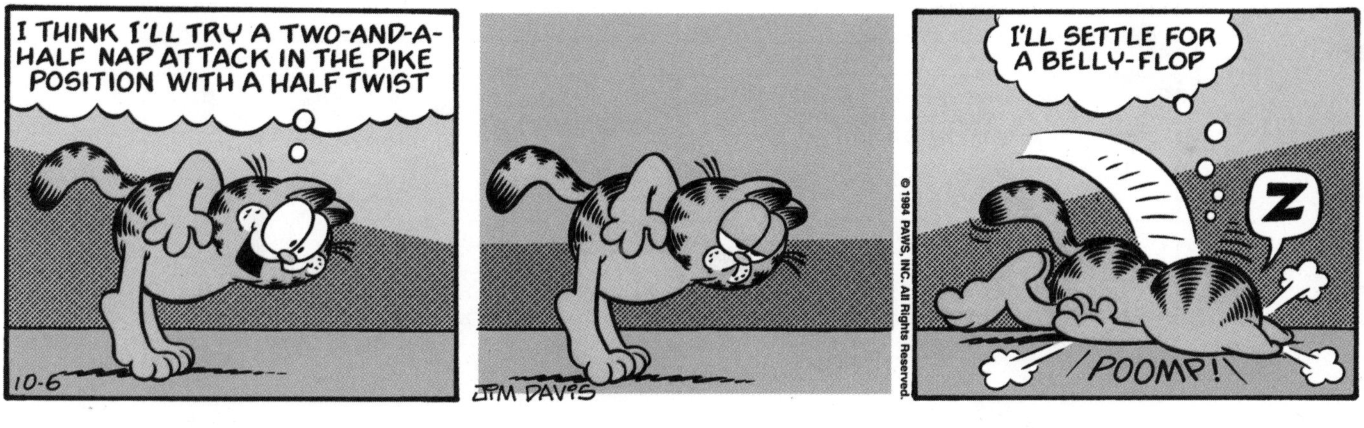
I THINK I'LL TRY A TWO-AND-A-HALF NAP ATTACK IN THE PIKE POSITION WITH A HALF TWIST
10-6
JIM DAVIS
© 1984 PAWS, INC. All Rights Reserved.
I'LL SETTLE FOR A BELLY-FLOP
Z
POOMP!

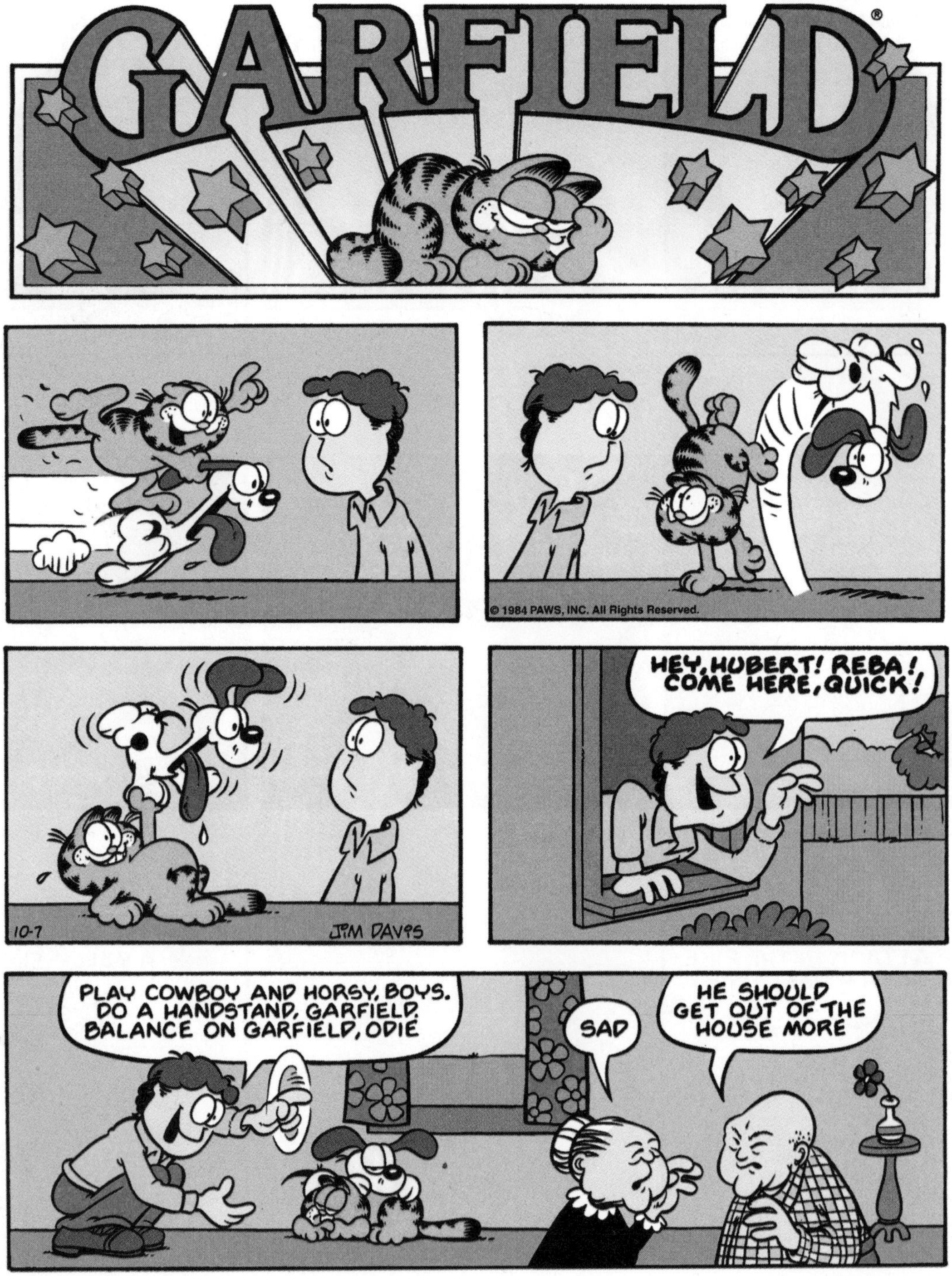
GARFIELD®
© 1984 PAWS, INC. All Rights Reserved.
10-7
JIM DAVIS
HEY, HUBERT! REBA! COME HERE, QUICK!
PLAY COWBOY AND HORSY, BOYS. DO A HANDSTAND, GARFIELD. BALANCE ON GARFIELD, ODIE
SAD
HE SHOULD GET OUT OF THE HOUSE MORE

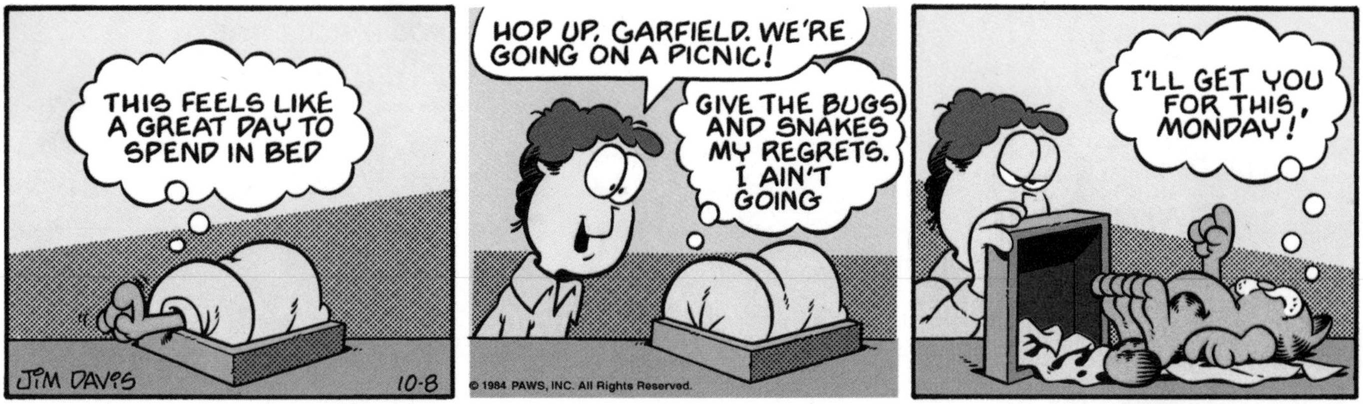
THIS FEELS LIKE A GREAT DAY TO SPEND IN BED
JIM DAVIS
10-8
HOP UP, GARFIELD. WE'RE GOING ON A PICNIC!
GIVE THE BUGS AND SNAKES MY REGRETS. I AIN'T GOING
© 1984 PAWS, INC. All Rights Reserved.
I'LL GET YOU FOR THIS, MONDAY!

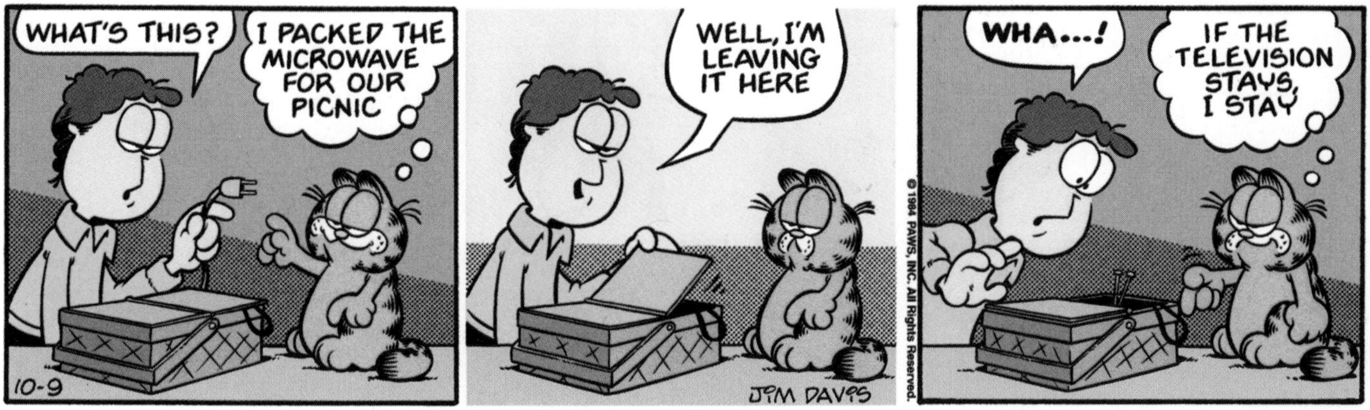
WHAT'S THIS?
I PACKED THE MICROWAVE FOR OUR PICNIC
10-9
WELL, I'M LEAVING IT HERE
JIM DAVIS
© 1984 PAWS, INC. All Rights Reserved.
WHA...!
IF THE TELEVISION STAYS, I STAY

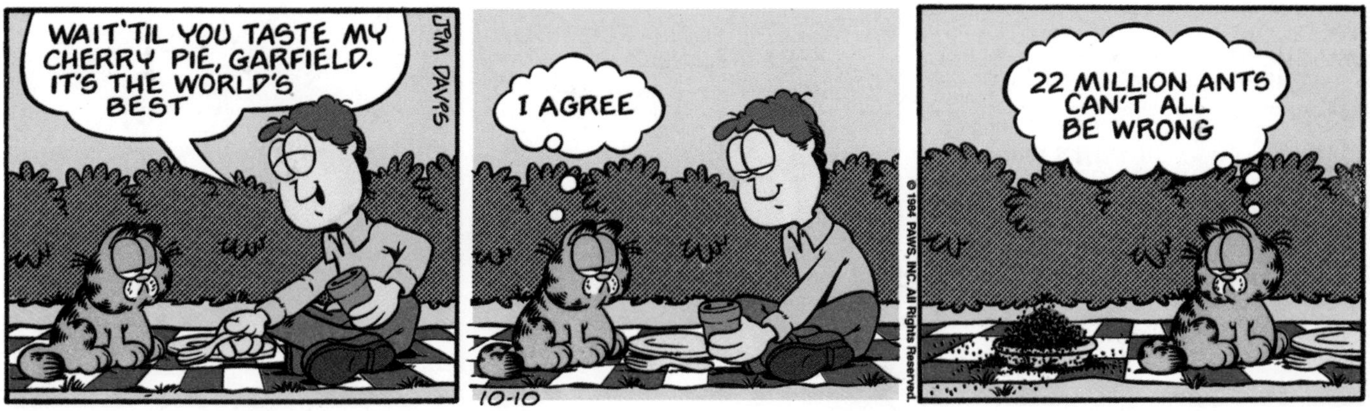
WAIT 'TIL YOU TASTE MY CHERRY PIE, GARFIELD. IT'S THE WORLD'S BEST
JIM DAVIS
I AGREE
10-10
© 1984 PAWS, INC. All Rights Reserved.
22 MILLION ANTS CAN'T ALL BE WRONG

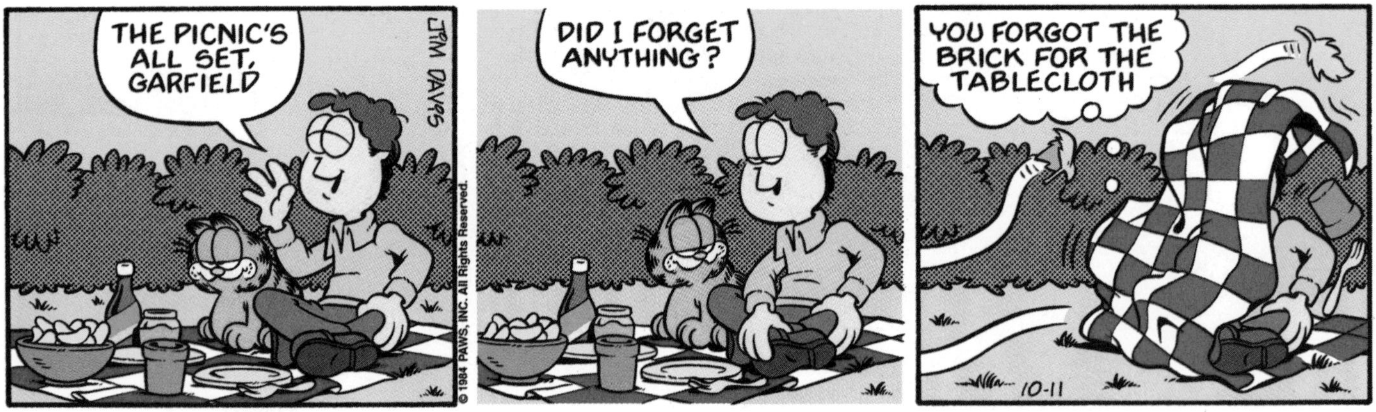
THE PICNIC'S ALL SET, GARFIELD
JIM DAVIS
© 1984 PAWS, INC. All Rights Reserved.
DID I FORGET ANYTHING?
YOU FORGOT THE BRICK FOR THE TABLECLOTH
10-11

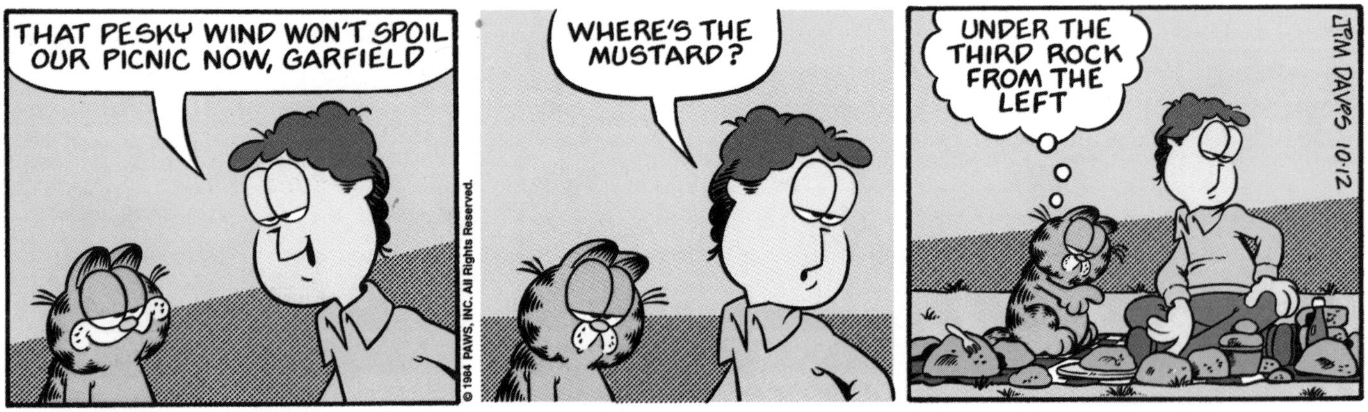
THAT PESKY WIND WON'T SPOIL OUR PICNIC NOW, GARFIELD
© 1984 PAWS, INC. All Rights Reserved.
WHERE'S THE MUSTARD?
UNDER THE THIRD ROCK FROM THE LEFT
JIM DAVIS 10-12

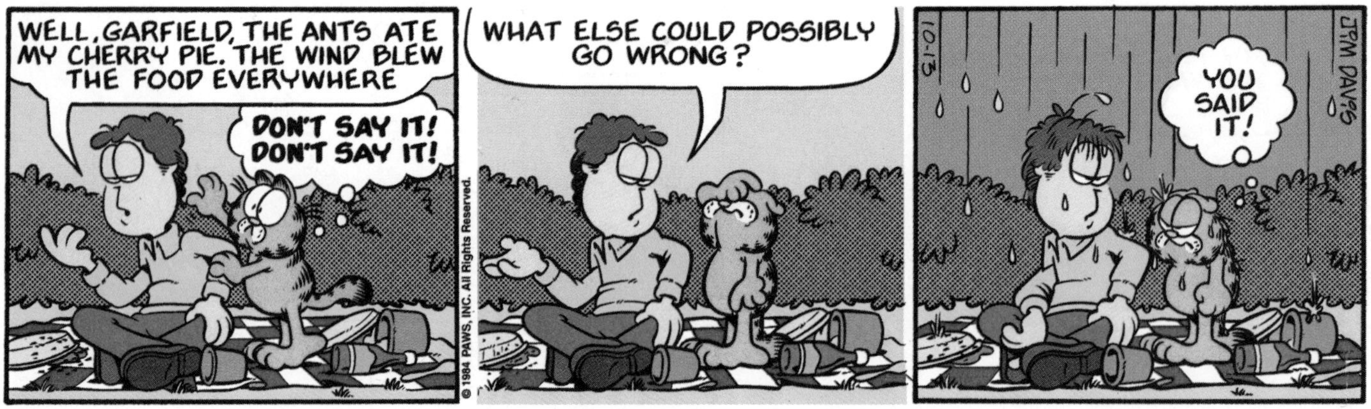
WELL, GARFIELD, THE ANTS ATE MY CHERRY PIE. THE WIND BLEW THE FOOD EVERYWHERE
DON'T SAY IT! DON'T SAY IT!
© 1984 PAWS, INC. All Rights Reserved.
WHAT ELSE COULD POSSIBLY GO WRONG?
10-13
JIM DAVIS
YOU SAID IT!

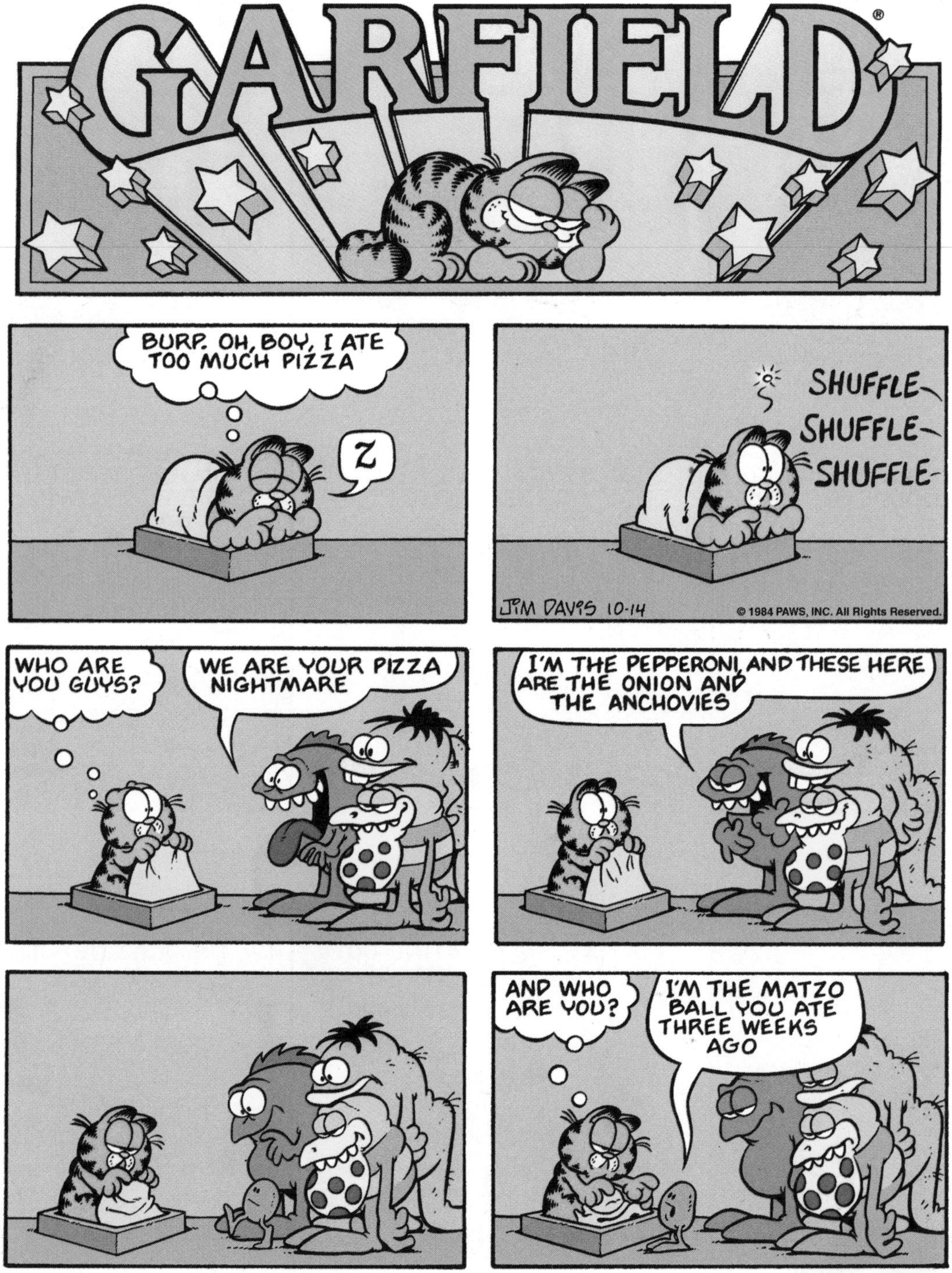
GARFIELD®
BURP. OH, BOY, I ATE TOO MUCH PIZZA
Z
SHUFFLE SHUFFLE SHUFFLE
JIM DAVIS 10-14
© 1984 PAWS, INC. All Rights Reserved.
WHO ARE YOU GUYS?
WE ARE YOUR PIZZA NIGHTMARE
I'M THE PEPPERONI, AND THESE HERE ARE THE ONION AND THE ANCHOVIES
AND WHO ARE YOU?
I'M THE MATZO BALL YOU ATE THREE WEEKS AGO

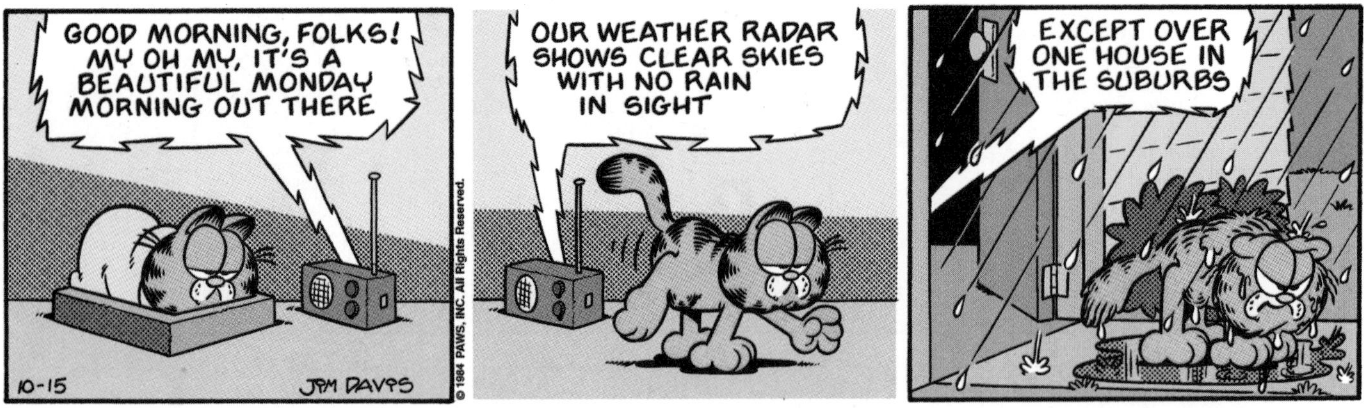
GOOD MORNING, FOLKS! MY OH MY, IT'S A BEAUTIFUL MONDAY MORNING OUT THERE
10-15
JIM DAVIS
© 1984 PAWS, INC. All Rights Reserved.
OUR WEATHER RADAR SHOWS CLEAR SKIES WITH NO RAIN IN SIGHT
EXCEPT OVER ONE HOUSE IN THE SUBURBS

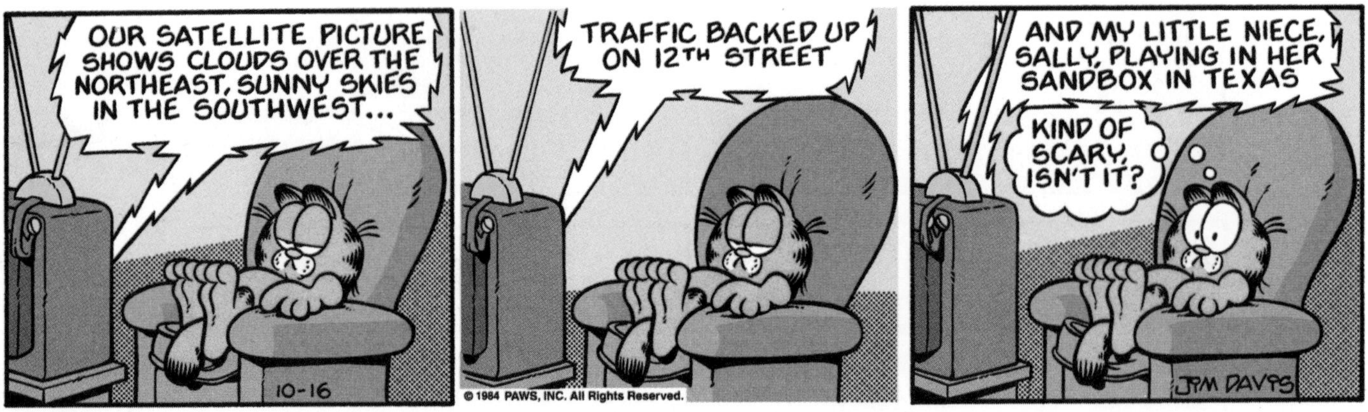
OUR SATELLITE PICTURE SHOWS CLOUDS OVER THE NORTHEAST, SUNNY SKIES IN THE SOUTHWEST...
10-16
TRAFFIC BACKED UP ON 12TH STREET
© 1984 PAWS, INC. All Rights Reserved.
AND MY LITTLE NIECE, SALLY, PLAYING IN HER SANDBOX IN TEXAS
KIND OF SCARY, ISN'T IT?
JIM DAVIS

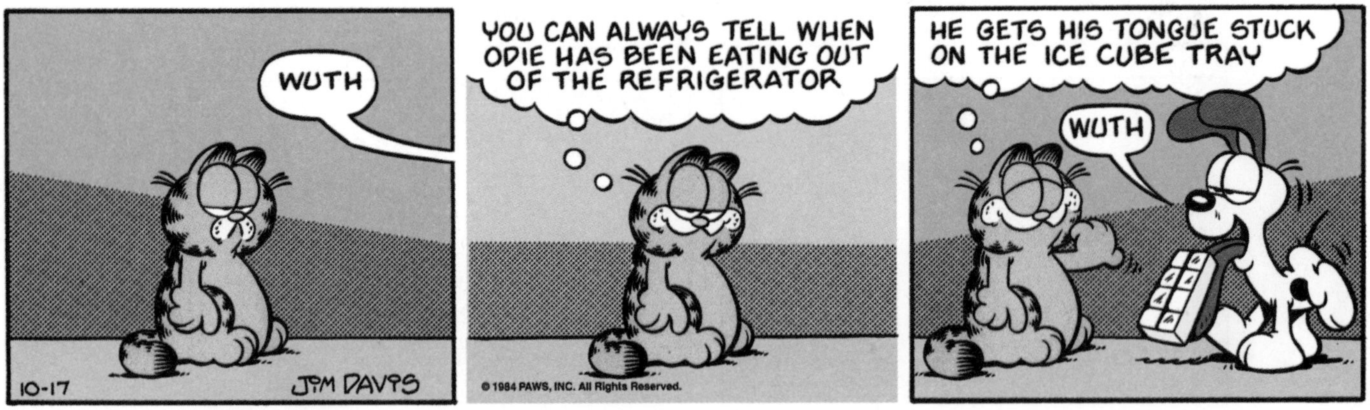
WUTH
10-17
JIM DAVIS
YOU CAN ALWAYS TELL WHEN ODIE HAS BEEN EATING OUT OF THE REFRIGERATOR
© 1984 PAWS, INC. All Rights Reserved.
HE GETS HIS TONGUE STUCK ON THE ICE CUBE TRAY
WUTH

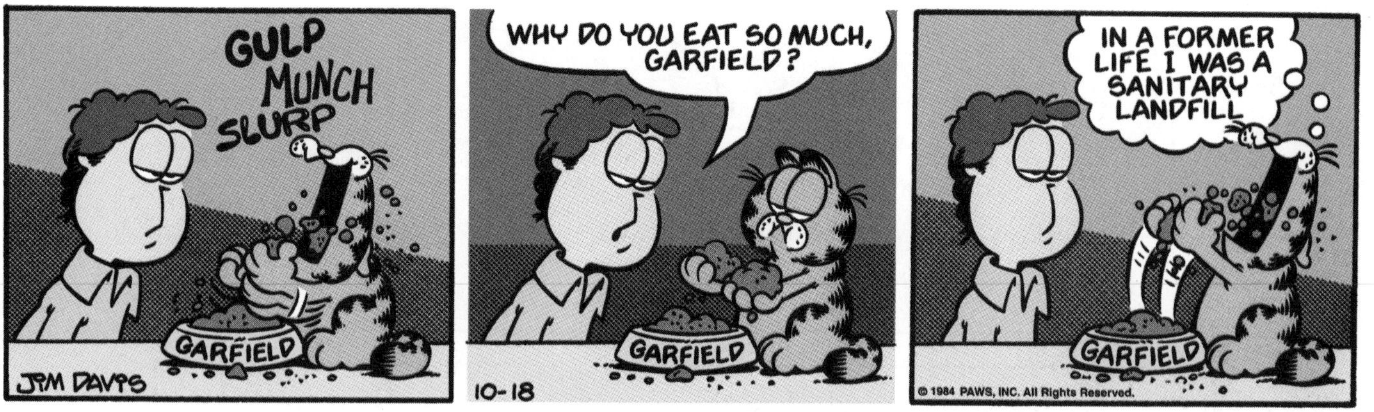
GULP
MUNCH
SLURP
GARFIELD
JIM DAVIS
WHY DO YOU EAT SO MUCH, GARFIELD?
GARFIELD
10-18
IN A FORMER LIFE I WAS A SANITARY LANDFILL
GARFIELD
© 1984 PAWS, INC. All Rights Reserved.

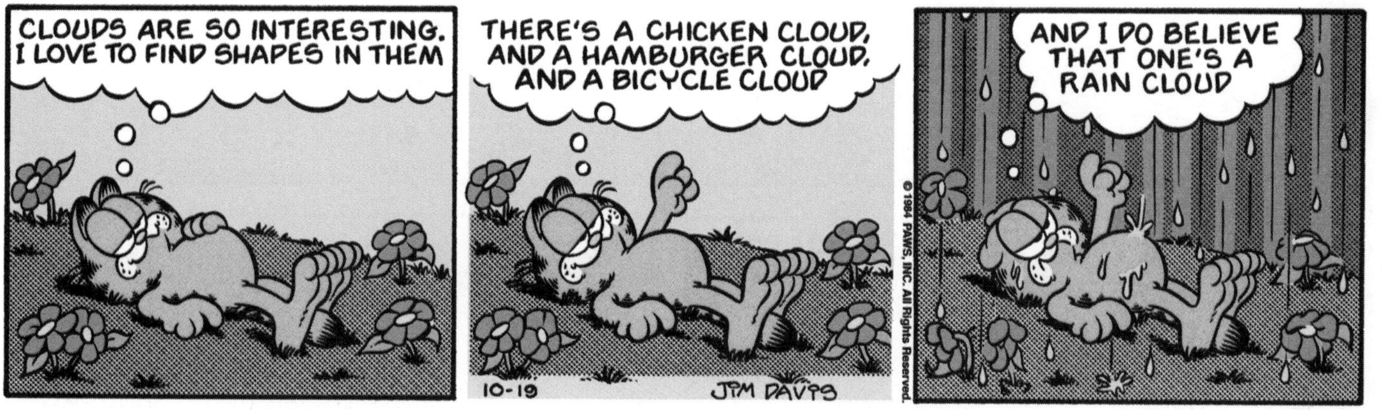
CLOUDS ARE SO INTERESTING. I LOVE TO FIND SHAPES IN THEM
THERE'S A CHICKEN CLOUD, AND A HAMBURGER CLOUD, AND A BICYCLE CLOUD
10-19
JIM DAVIS
© 1984 PAWS, INC. All Rights Reserved.
AND I DO BELIEVE THAT ONE'S A RAIN CLOUD

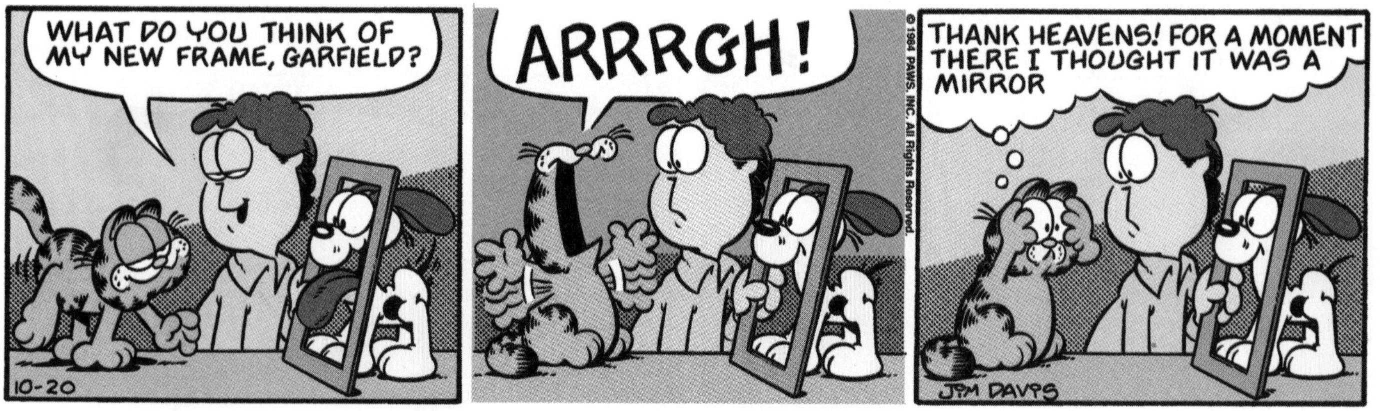
WHAT DO YOU THINK OF MY NEW FRAME, GARFIELD?
10-20
ARRRGH!
© 1984 PAWS, INC. All Rights Reserved.
THANK HEAVENS! FOR A MOMENT THERE I THOUGHT IT WAS A MIRROR
JIM DAVIS

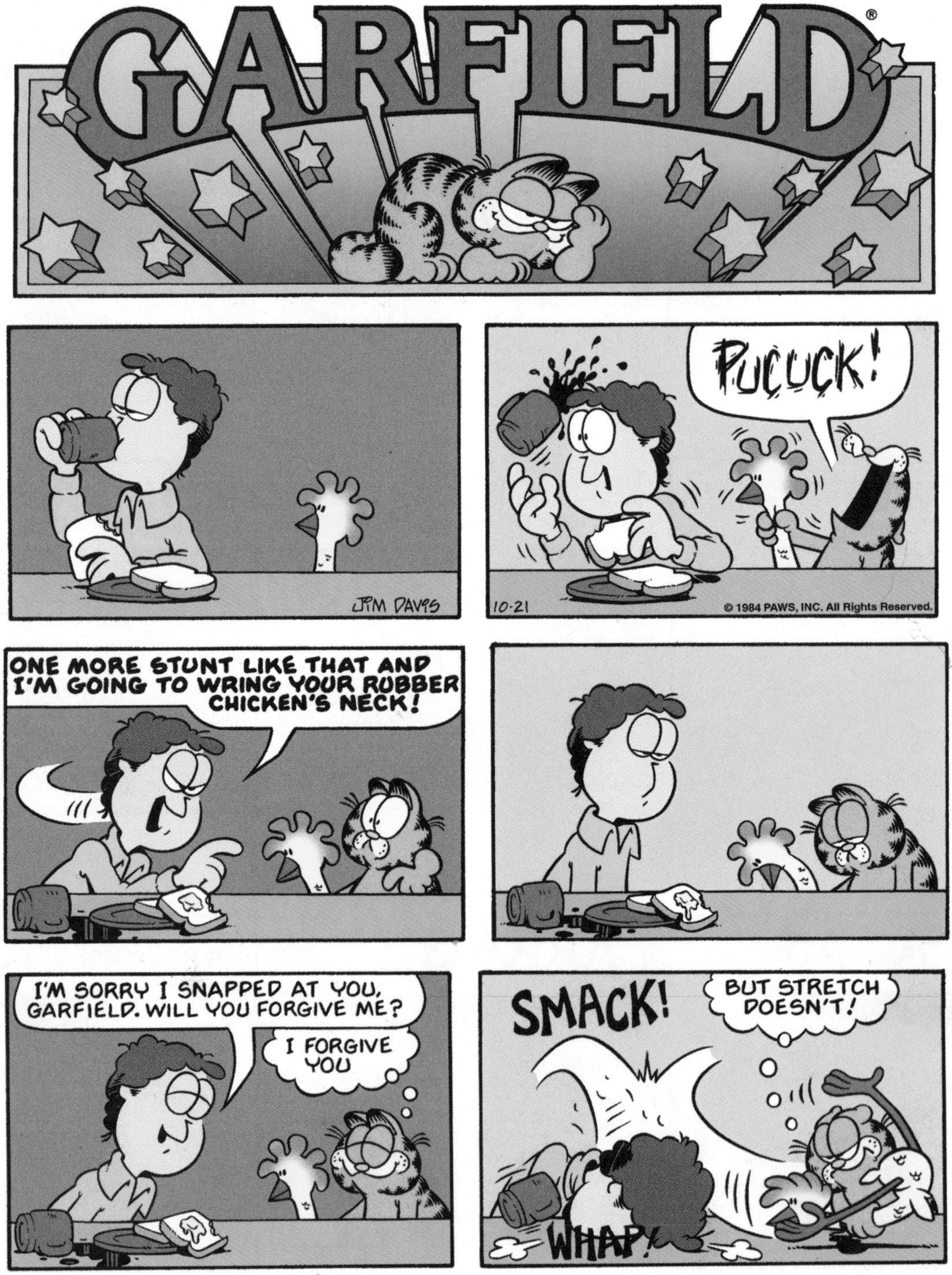
GARFIELD®
JIM DAVIS
PUCUCK!
10-21
© 1984 PAWS, INC. All Rights Reserved.
ONE MORE STUNT LIKE THAT AND I'M GOING TO WRING YOUR RUBBER CHICKEN'S NECK!
I'M SORRY I SNAPPED AT YOU, GARFIELD. WILL YOU FORGIVE ME?
I FORGIVE YOU
SMACK!
BUT STRETCH DOESN'T!
WHAP!

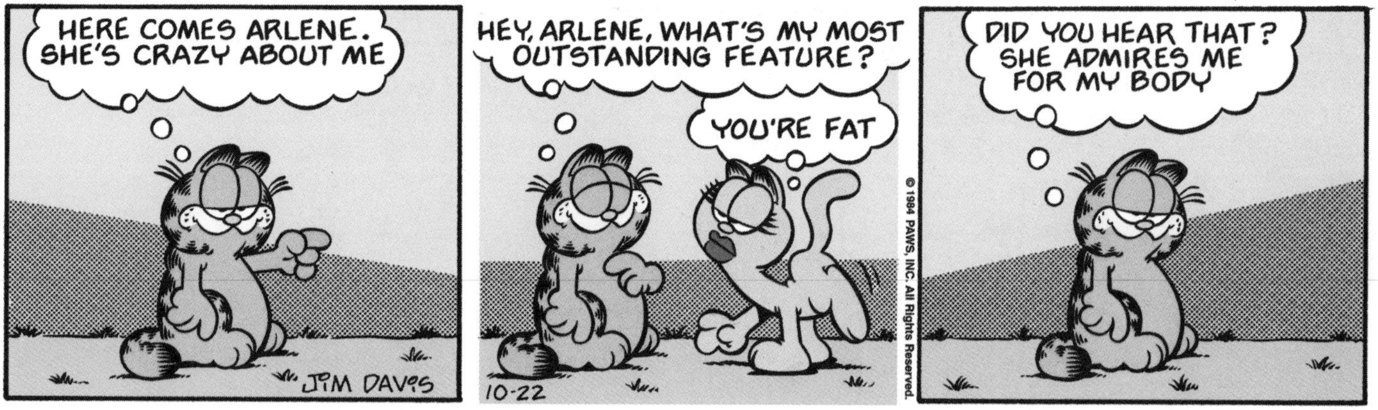
HERE COMES ARLENE. SHE'S CRAZY ABOUT ME
JIM DAVIS
HEY, ARLENE, WHAT'S MY MOST OUTSTANDING FEATURE?
YOU'RE FAT
10-22
© 1984 PAWS, INC. All Rights Reserved.
DID YOU HEAR THAT? SHE ADMIRES ME FOR MY BODY

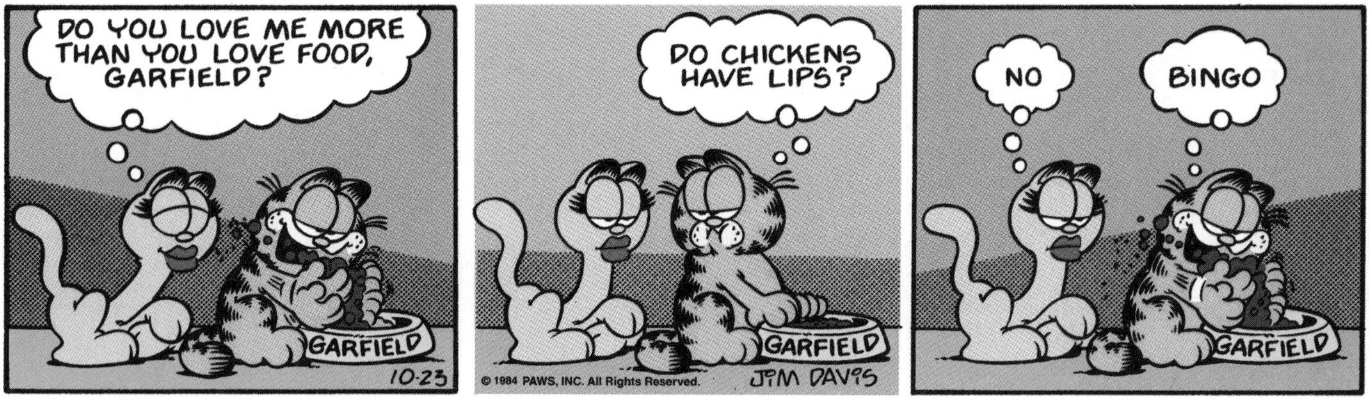
DO YOU LOVE ME MORE THAN YOU LOVE FOOD, GARFIELD?
GARFIELD
10-23
DO CHICKENS HAVE LIPS?
GARFIELD
© 1984 PAWS, INC. All Rights Reserved.
JIM DAVIS
NO
BINGO
GARFIELD

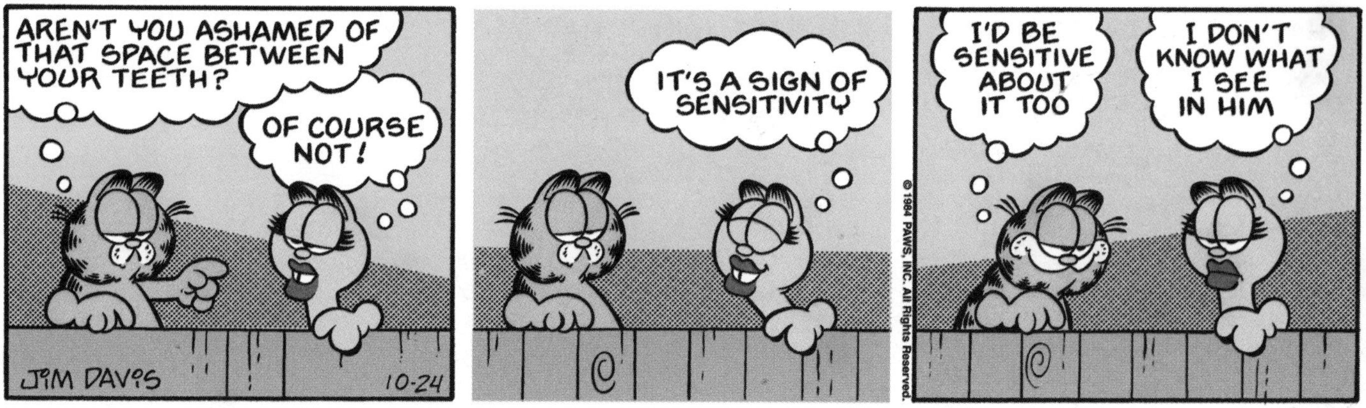
AREN'T YOU ASHAMED OF THAT SPACE BETWEEN YOUR TEETH?
OF COURSE NOT!
JIM DAVIS
10-24
IT'S A SIGN OF SENSITIVITY
© 1984 PAWS, INC. All Rights Reserved.
I'D BE SENSITIVE ABOUT IT TOO
I DON'T KNOW WHAT I SEE IN HIM

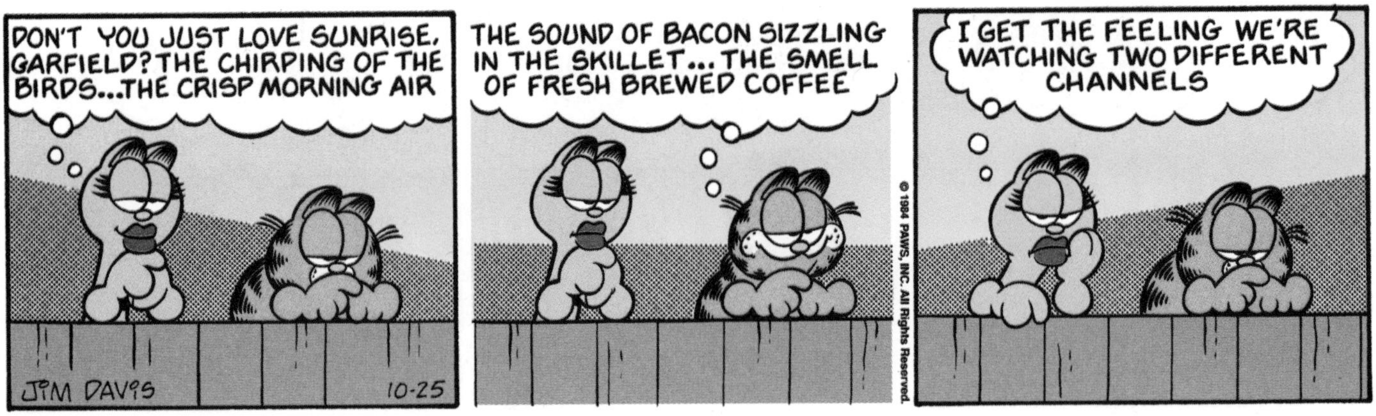
DON'T YOU JUST LOVE SUNRISE, GARFIELD? THE CHIRPING OF THE BIRDS...THE CRISP MORNING AIR
JIM DAVIS
10-25
THE SOUND OF BACON SIZZLING IN THE SKILLET... THE SMELL OF FRESH BREWED COFFEE
© 1984 PAWS, INC. All Rights Reserved.
I GET THE FEELING WE'RE WATCHING TWO DIFFERENT CHANNELS

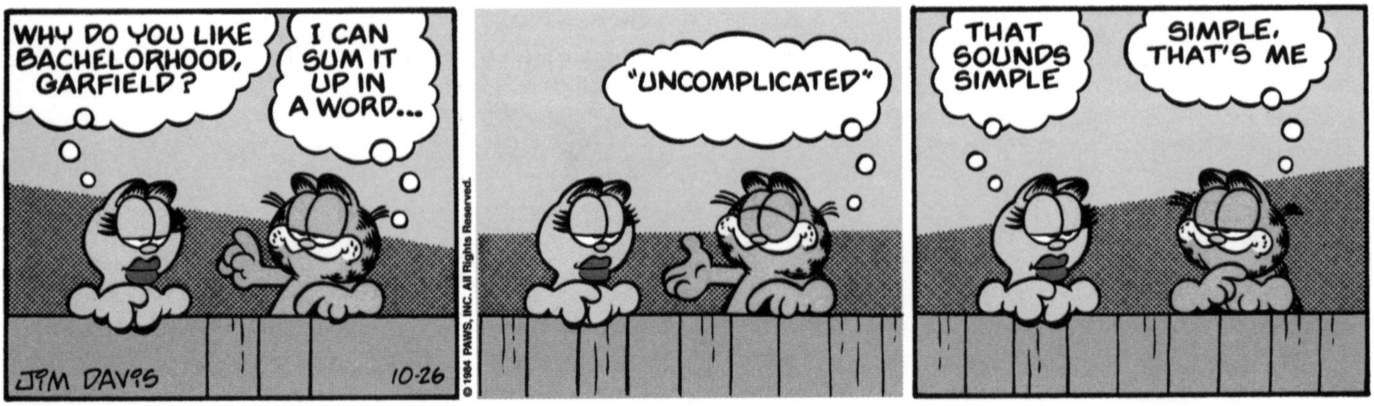
WHY DO YOU LIKE BACHELORHOOD, GARFIELD?
I CAN SUM IT UP IN A WORD...
JIM DAVIS
10-26
© 1984 PAWS, INC. All Rights Reserved.
"UNCOMPLICATED"
THAT SOUNDS SIMPLE
SIMPLE, THAT'S ME

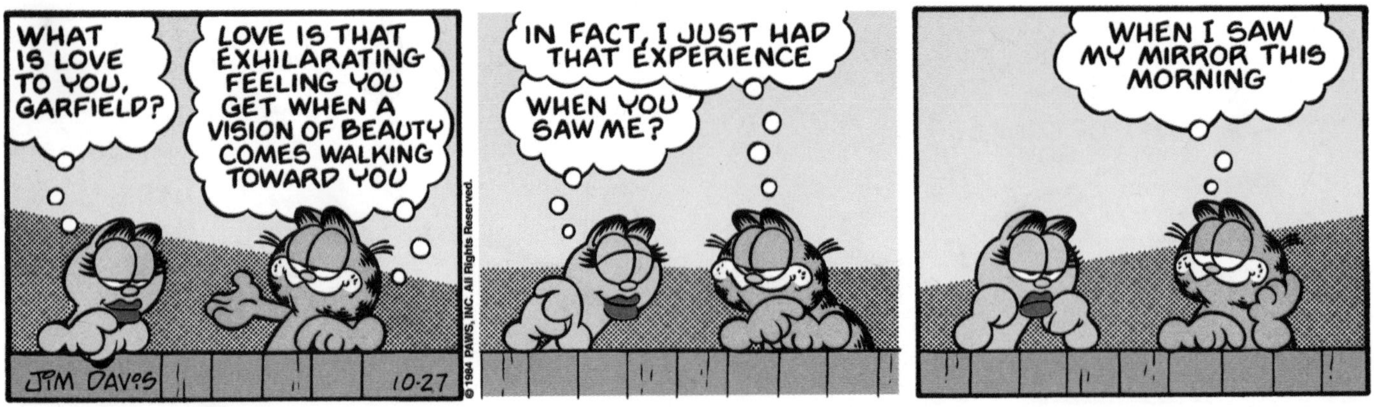
WHAT IS LOVE TO YOU, GARFIELD?
LOVE IS THAT EXHILARATING FEELING YOU GET WHEN A VISION OF BEAUTY COMES WALKING TOWARD YOU
JIM DAVIS
10-27
© 1984 PAWS, INC. All Rights Reserved.
IN FACT, I JUST HAD THAT EXPERIENCE
WHEN YOU SAW ME?
WHEN I SAW MY MIRROR THIS MORNING

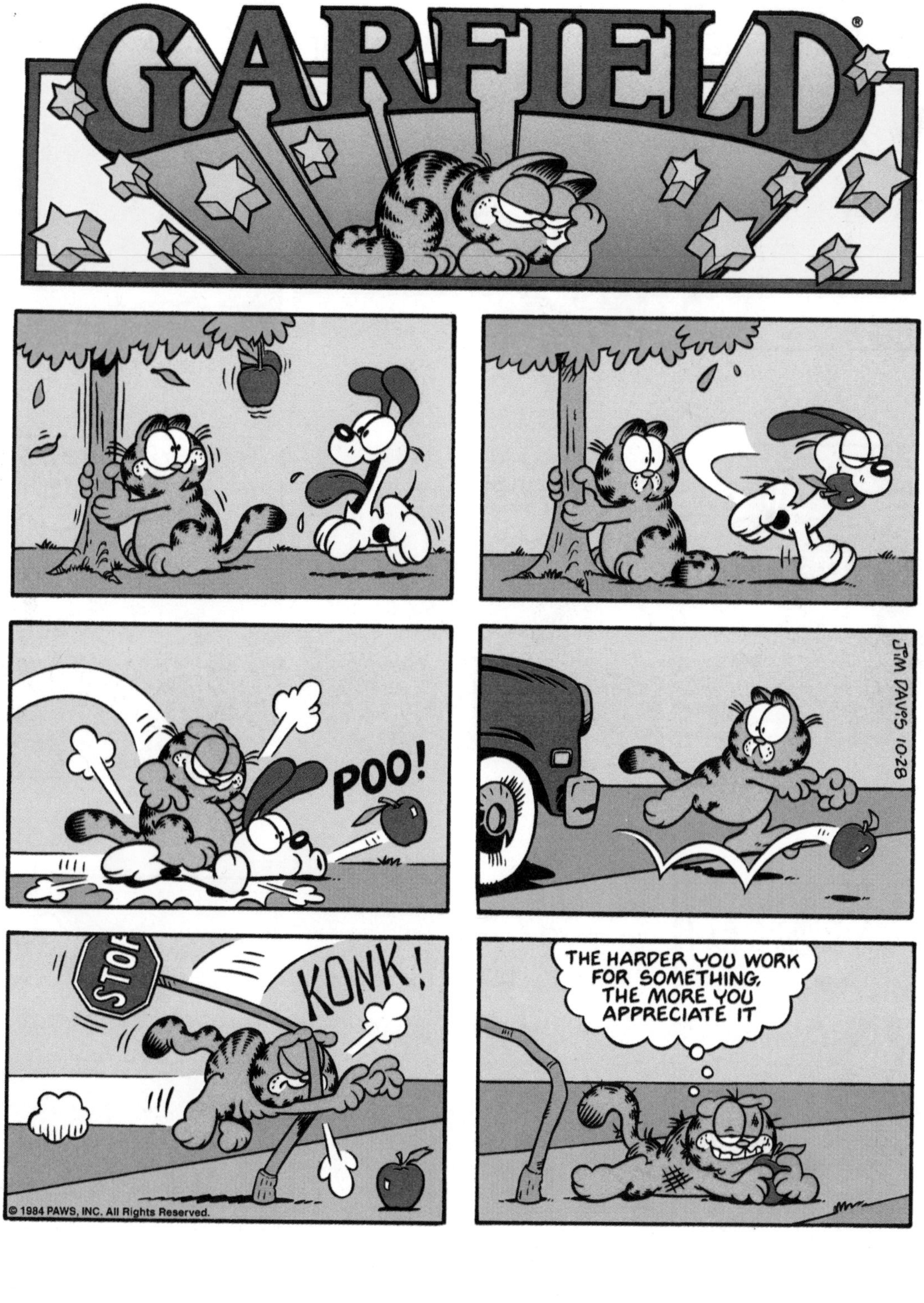
GARFIELD®
JIM DAVIS 10·28
POO!
STOP
KONK!
THE HARDER YOU WORK FOR SOMETHING, THE MORE YOU APPRECIATE IT
© 1984 PAWS, INC. All Rights Reserved.

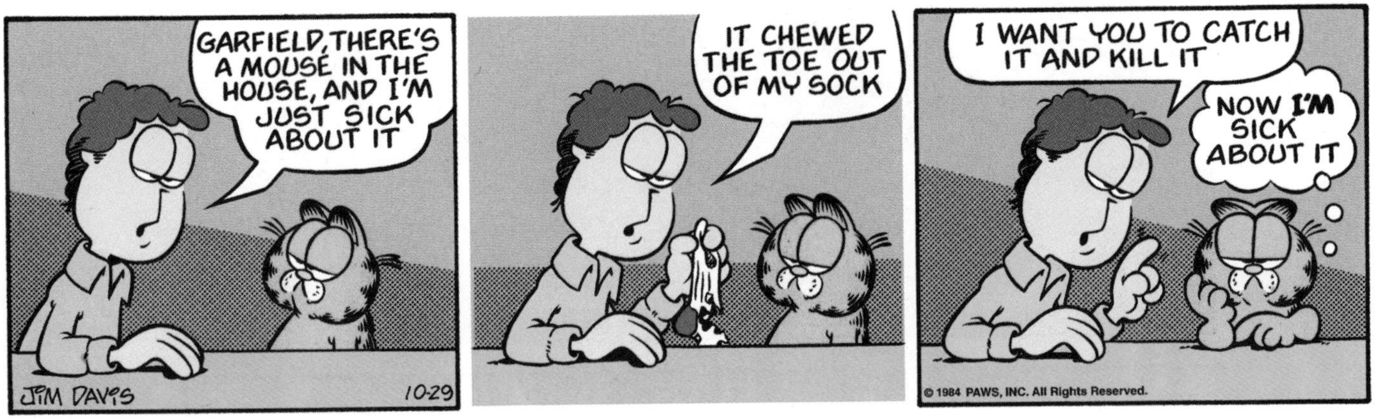
GARFIELD, THERE'S A MOUSE IN THE HOUSE, AND I'M JUST SICK ABOUT IT
JIM DAVIS
10-29
IT CHEWED THE TOE OUT OF MY SOCK
I WANT YOU TO CATCH IT AND KILL IT
NOW **I'M** SICK ABOUT IT
© 1984 PAWS, INC. All Rights Reserved.

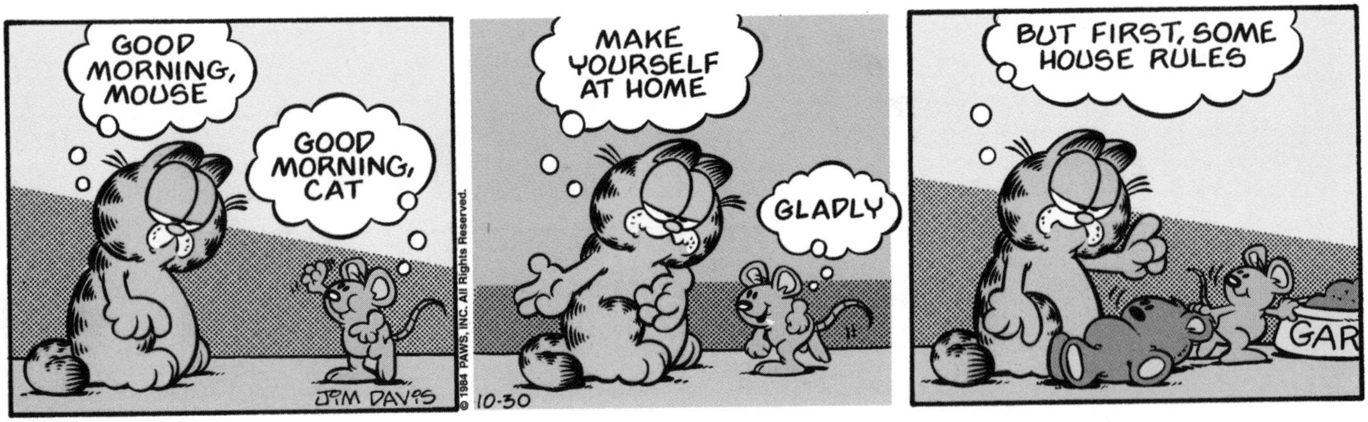
GOOD MORNING, MOUSE
GOOD MORNING, CAT
JIM DAVIS
© 1984 PAWS, INC. All Rights Reserved.
MAKE YOURSELF AT HOME
GLADLY
10-30
BUT FIRST, SOME HOUSE RULES
GAR

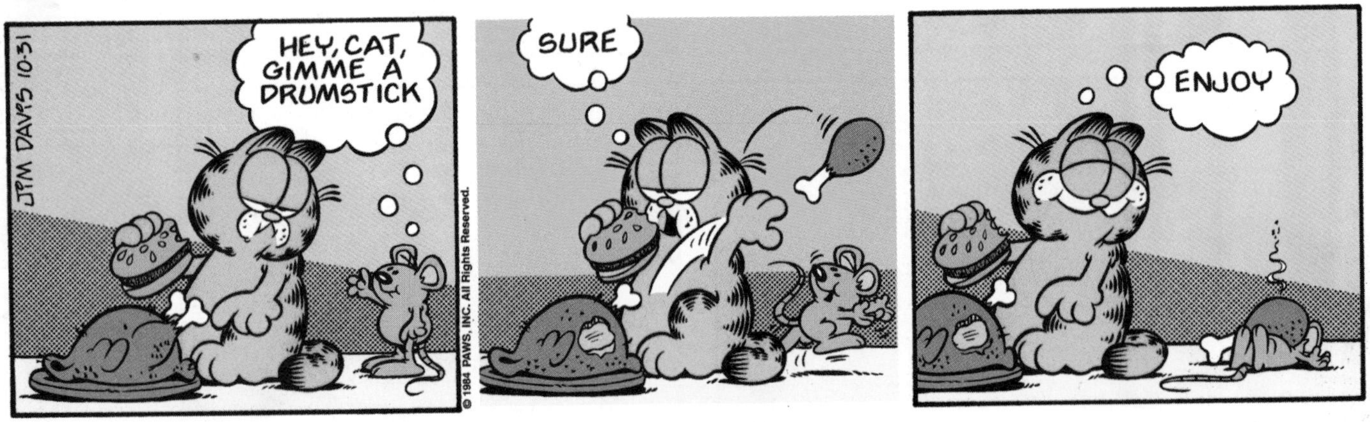
JIM DAVIS 10-31
HEY, CAT, GIMME A DRUMSTICK
© 1984 PAWS, INC. All Rights Reserved.
SURE
ENJOY

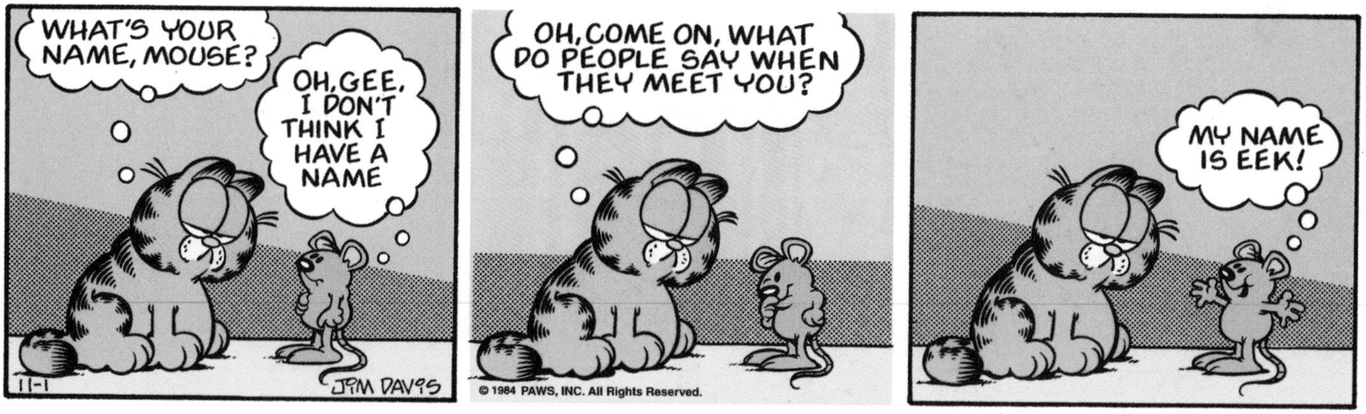
WHAT'S YOUR NAME, MOUSE?
OH, GEE, I DON'T THINK I HAVE A NAME
11-1
JIM DAVIS
OH, COME ON, WHAT DO PEOPLE SAY WHEN THEY MEET YOU?
© 1984 PAWS, INC. All Rights Reserved.
MY NAME IS EEK!

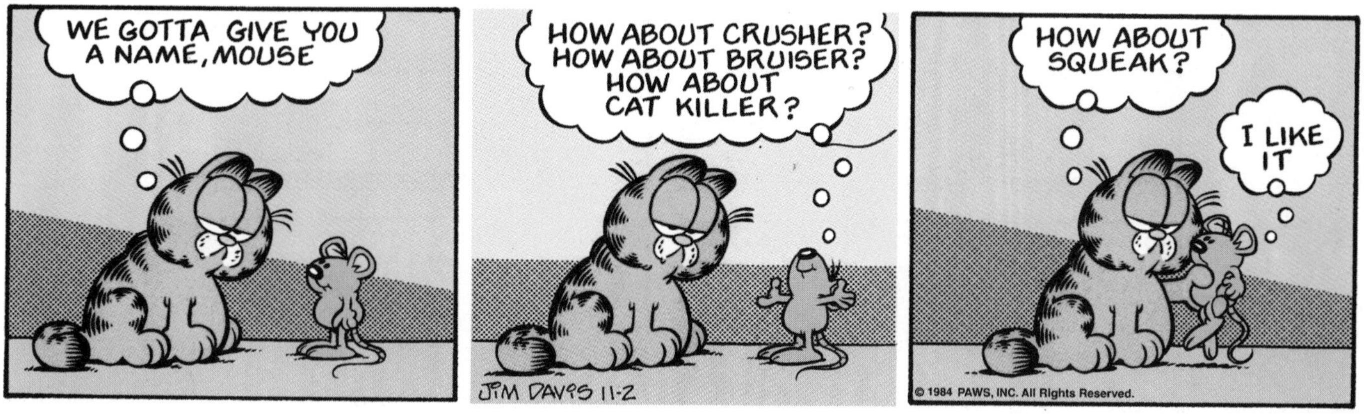
WE GOTTA GIVE YOU A NAME, MOUSE
HOW ABOUT CRUSHER? HOW ABOUT BRUISER? HOW ABOUT CAT KILLER?
JIM DAVIS 11-2
HOW ABOUT SQUEAK?
I LIKE IT
© 1984 PAWS, INC. All Rights Reserved.

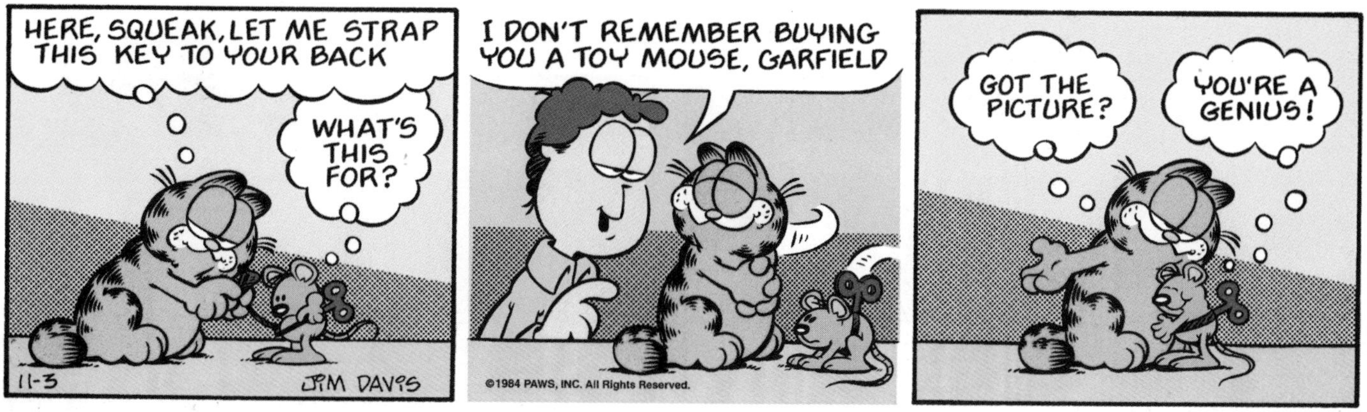
HERE, SQUEAK, LET ME STRAP THIS KEY TO YOUR BACK
WHAT'S THIS FOR?
11-3
JIM DAVIS
I DON'T REMEMBER BUYING YOU A TOY MOUSE, GARFIELD
©1984 PAWS, INC. All Rights Reserved.
GOT THE PICTURE?
YOU'RE A GENIUS!

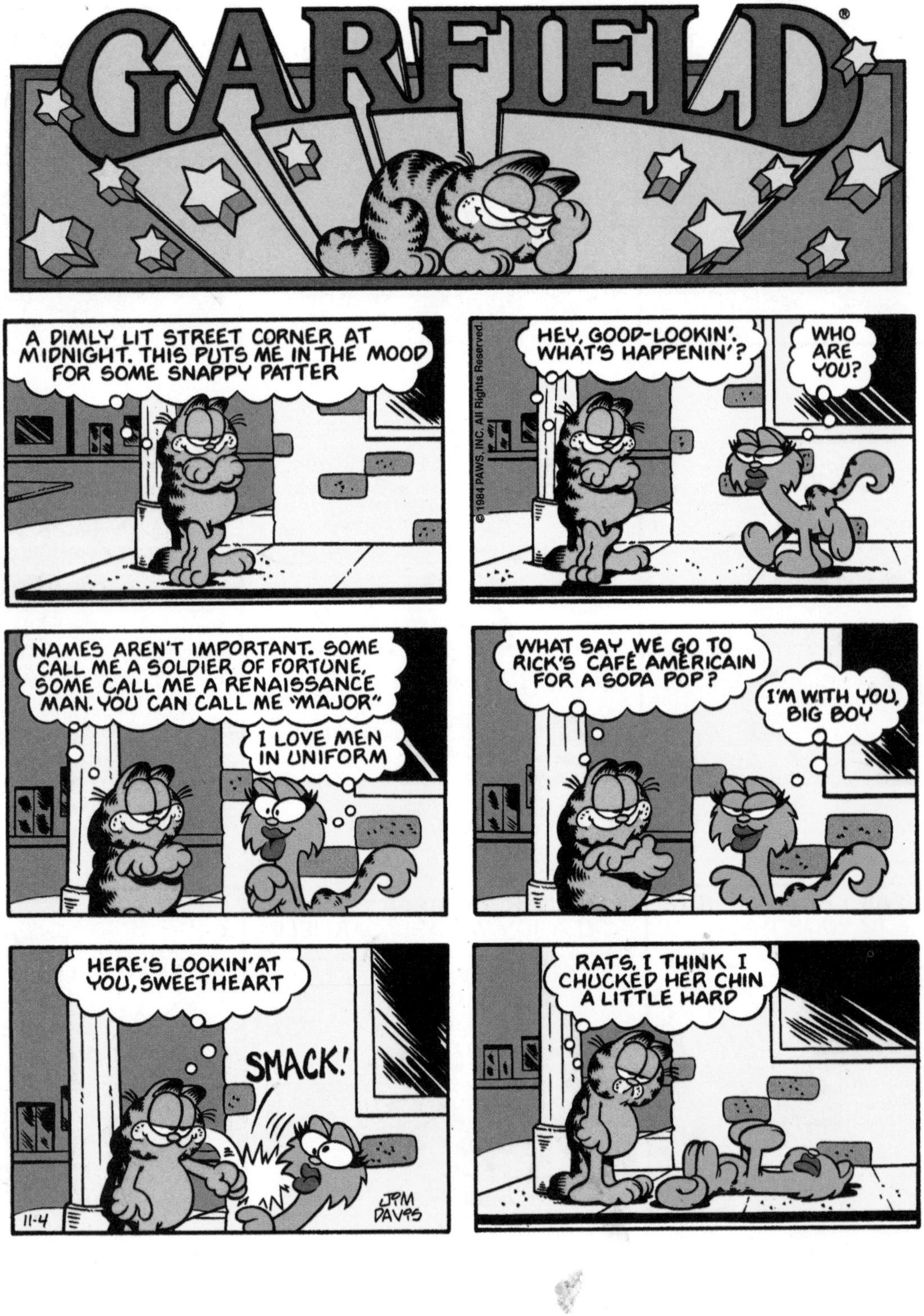
GARFIELD®
A DIMLY LIT STREET CORNER AT MIDNIGHT. THIS PUTS ME IN THE MOOD FOR SOME SNAPPY PATTER
© 1984 PAWS, INC. All Rights Reserved.
HEY, GOOD-LOOKIN'. WHAT'S HAPPENIN'?
WHO ARE YOU?
NAMES AREN'T IMPORTANT. SOME CALL ME A SOLDIER OF FORTUNE, SOME CALL ME A RENAISSANCE MAN. YOU CAN CALL ME "MAJOR"
I LOVE MEN IN UNIFORM
WHAT SAY WE GO TO RICK'S CAFÉ AMÉRICAIN FOR A SODA POP?
I'M WITH YOU, BIG BOY
HERE'S LOOKIN' AT YOU, SWEETHEART
SMACK!
11-4
JPM DAVPS
RATS. I THINK I CHUCKED HER CHIN A LITTLE HARD

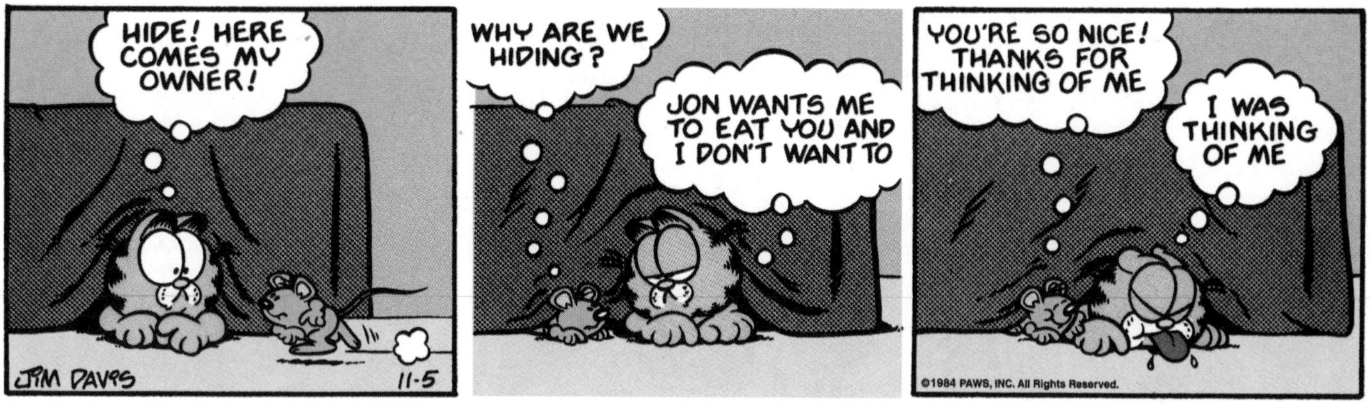
HIDE! HERE COMES MY OWNER!
JIM DAVIS
11-5
WHY ARE WE HIDING?
JON WANTS ME TO EAT YOU AND I DON'T WANT TO
YOU'RE SO NICE! THANKS FOR THINKING OF ME
I WAS THINKING OF ME
©1984 PAWS, INC. All Rights Reserved.

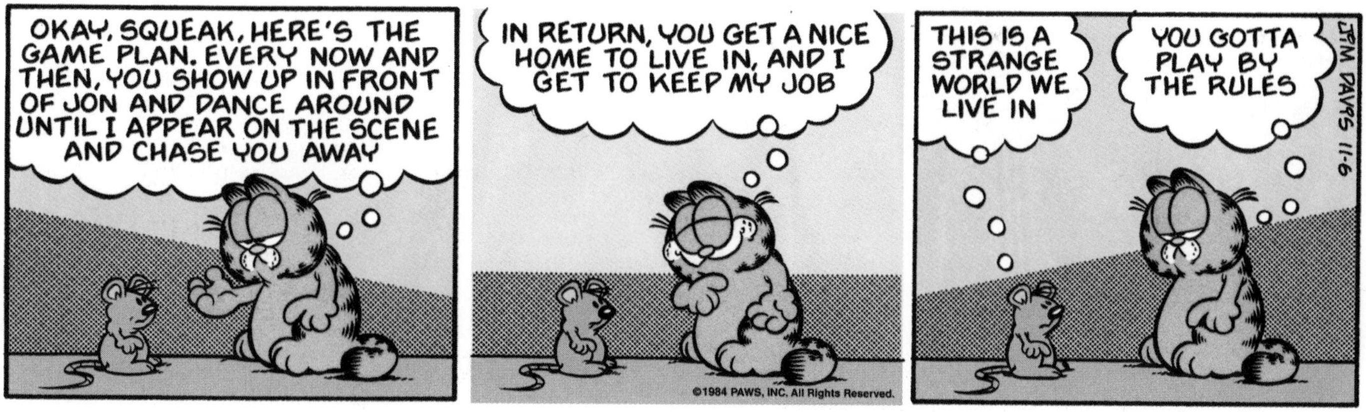
OKAY, SQUEAK, HERE'S THE GAME PLAN. EVERY NOW AND THEN, YOU SHOW UP IN FRONT OF JON AND DANCE AROUND UNTIL I APPEAR ON THE SCENE AND CHASE YOU AWAY
IN RETURN, YOU GET A NICE HOME TO LIVE IN, AND I GET TO KEEP MY JOB
©1984 PAWS, INC. All Rights Reserved.
THIS IS A STRANGE WORLD WE LIVE IN
YOU GOTTA PLAY BY THE RULES
JIM DAVIS 11-6

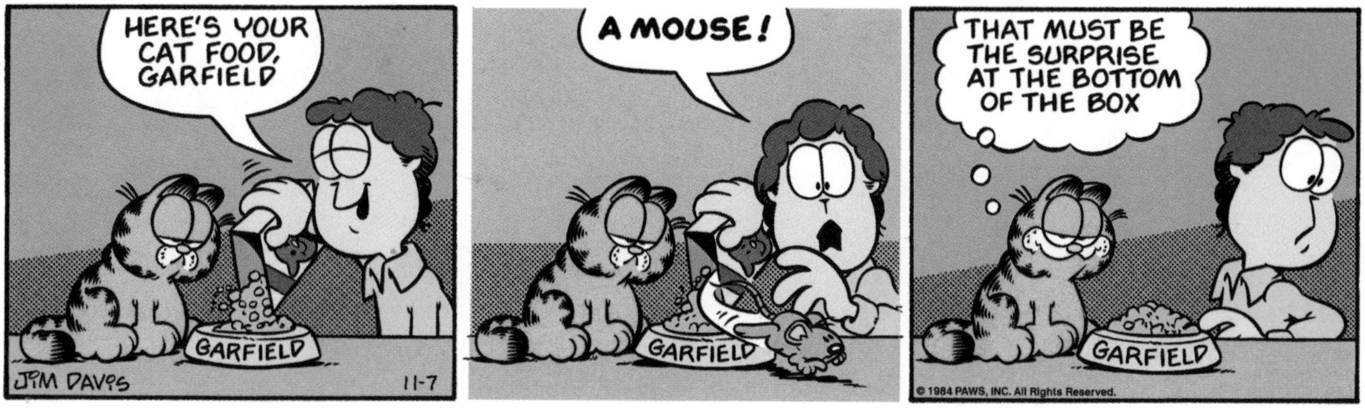
HERE'S YOUR CAT FOOD, GARFIELD
GARFIELD
JIM DAVIS
11-7
A MOUSE!
GARFIELD
THAT MUST BE THE SURPRISE AT THE BOTTOM OF THE BOX
GARFIELD
© 1984 PAWS, INC. All Rights Reserved.

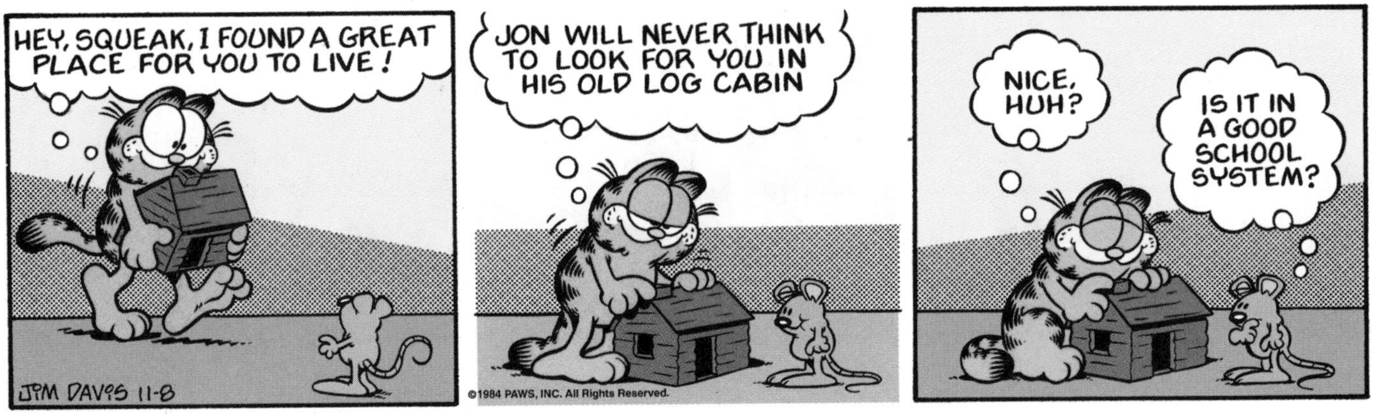
HEY, SQUEAK, I FOUND A GREAT PLACE FOR YOU TO LIVE!
JIM DAVIS 11-8
JON WILL NEVER THINK TO LOOK FOR YOU IN HIS OLD LOG CABIN
©1984 PAWS, INC. All Rights Reserved.
NICE, HUH?
IS IT IN A GOOD SCHOOL SYSTEM?

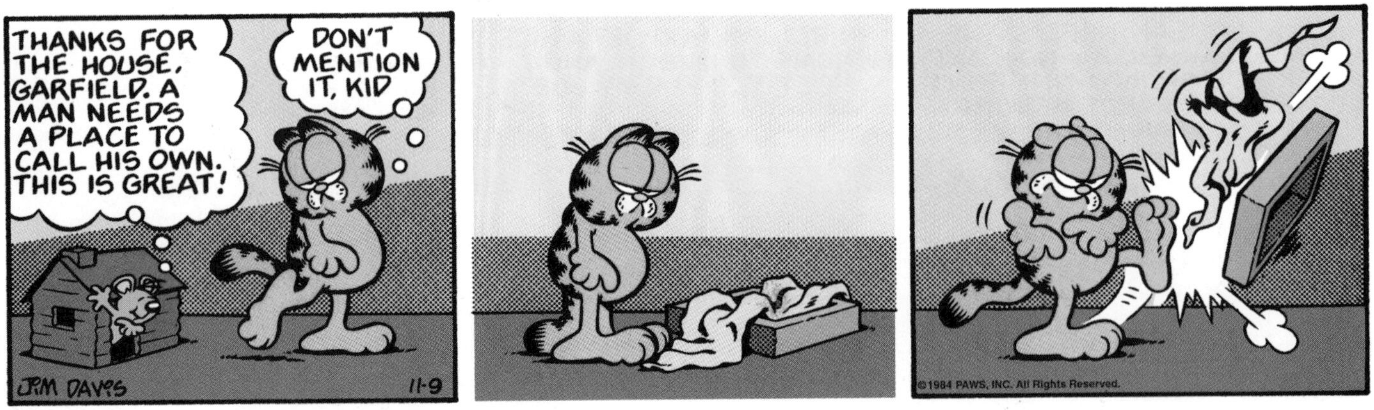
THANKS FOR THE HOUSE, GARFIELD. A MAN NEEDS A PLACE TO CALL HIS OWN. THIS IS GREAT!
DON'T MENTION IT, KID
JIM DAVIS 11-9
©1984 PAWS, INC. All Rights Reserved.

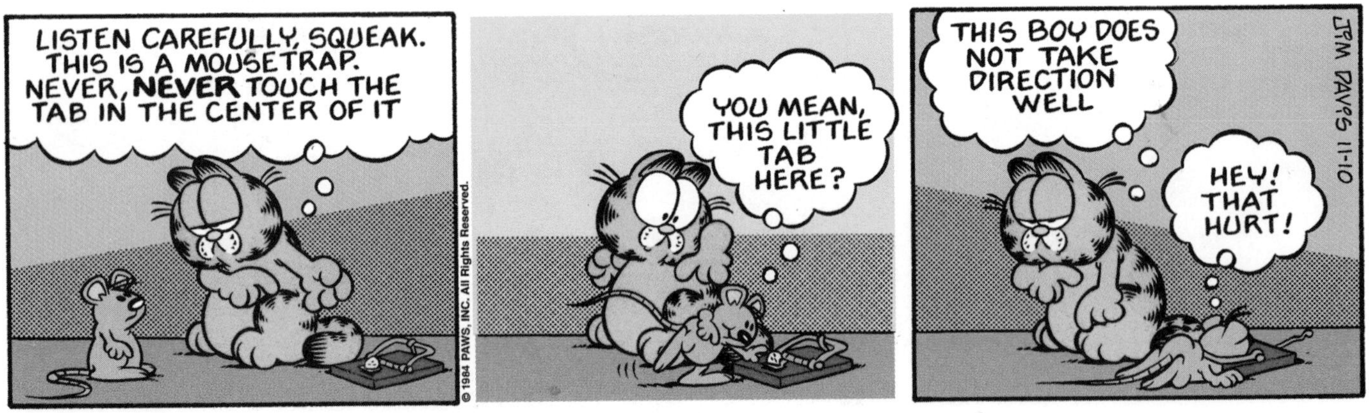
LISTEN CAREFULLY, SQUEAK. THIS IS A MOUSETRAP. NEVER, **NEVER** TOUCH THE TAB IN THE CENTER OF IT
© 1984 PAWS, INC. All Rights Reserved.
YOU MEAN, THIS LITTLE TAB HERE?
THIS BOY DOES NOT TAKE DIRECTION WELL
HEY! THAT HURT!
JIM DAVIS 11-10

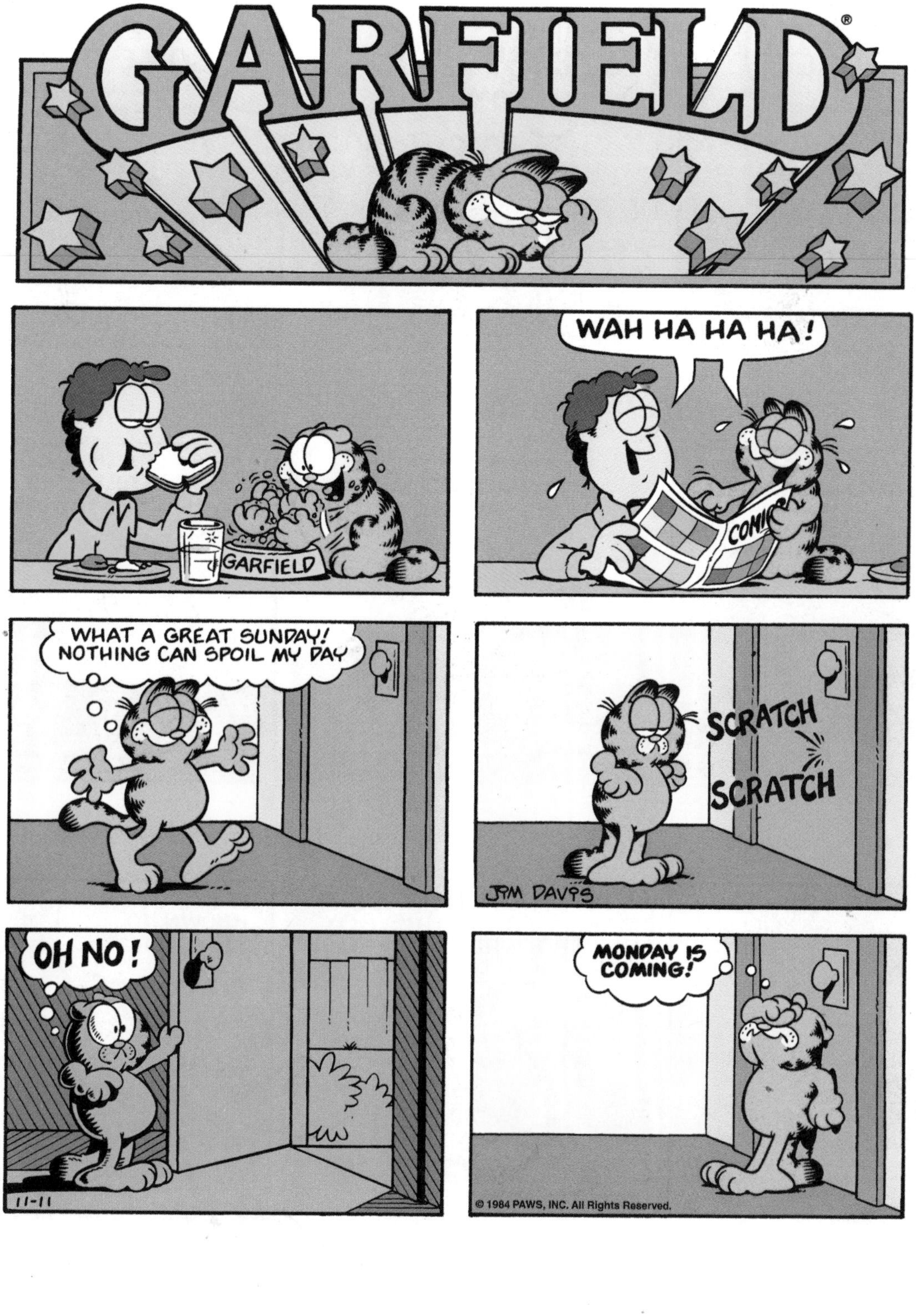
GARFIELD
GARFIELD
WAH HA HA HA!
COMICS
WHAT A GREAT SUNDAY! NOTHING CAN SPOIL MY DAY
SCRATCH
SCRATCH
JPM DAVPS
OH NO!
MONDAY IS COMING!
11-11
© 1984 PAWS, INC. All Rights Reserved.

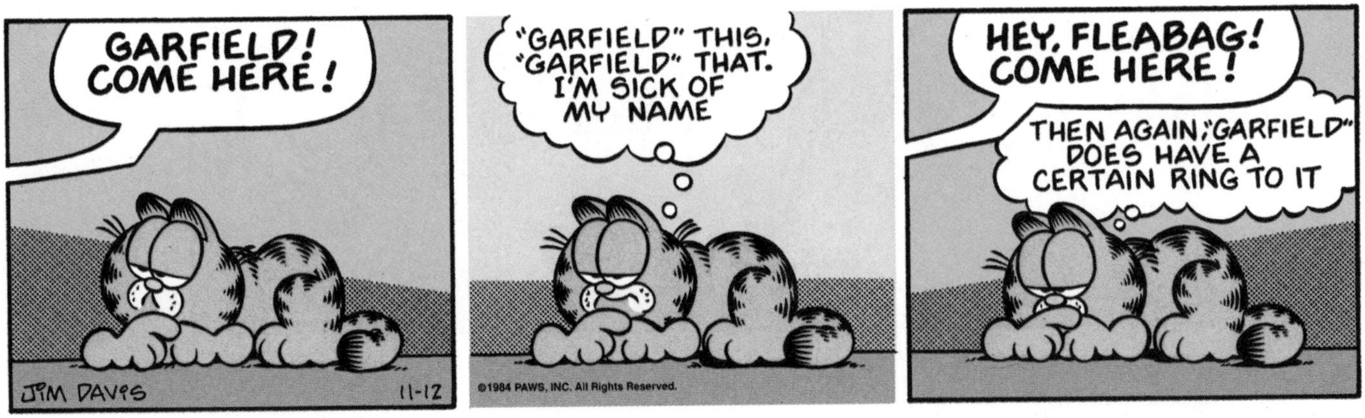
GARFIELD! COME HERE!
JIM DAVIS
11-12
"GARFIELD" THIS, "GARFIELD" THAT. I'M SICK OF MY NAME
©1984 PAWS, INC. All Rights Reserved.
HEY, FLEABAG! COME HERE!
THEN AGAIN, "GARFIELD" DOES HAVE A CERTAIN RING TO IT

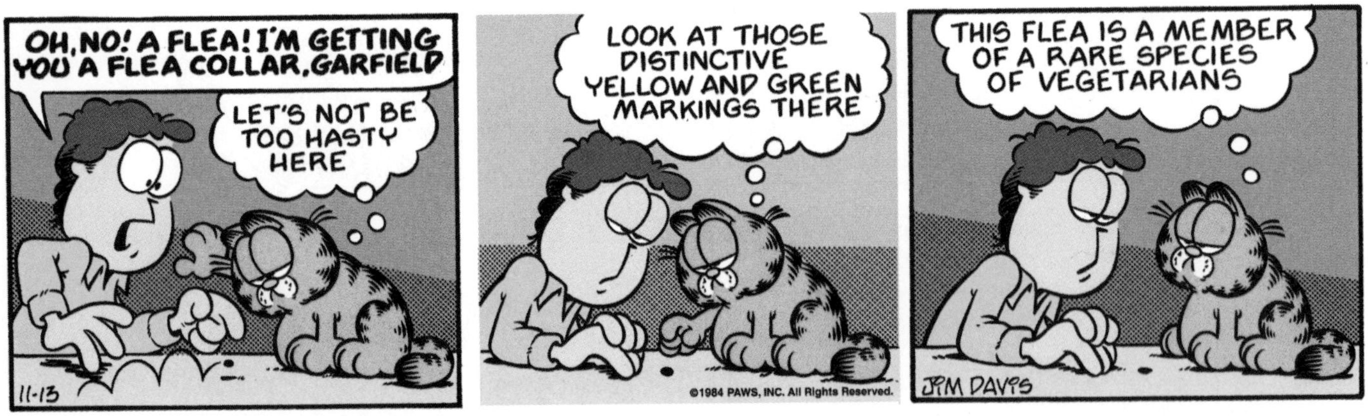
OH, NO! A FLEA! I'M GETTING YOU A FLEA COLLAR, GARFIELD
LET'S NOT BE TOO HASTY HERE
11-13
LOOK AT THOSE DISTINCTIVE YELLOW AND GREEN MARKINGS THERE
©1984 PAWS, INC. All Rights Reserved.
THIS FLEA IS A MEMBER OF A RARE SPECIES OF VEGETARIANS
JIM DAVIS

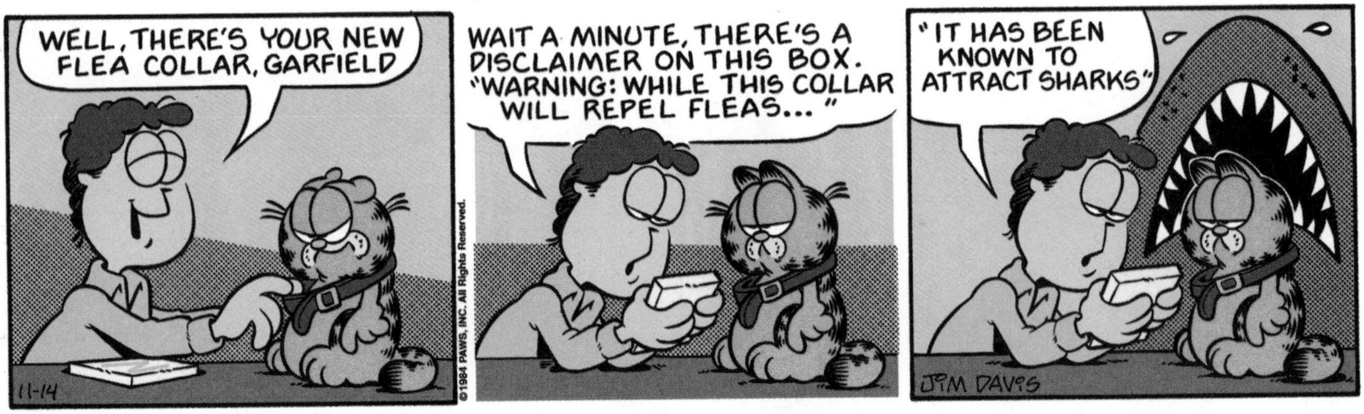
WELL, THERE'S YOUR NEW FLEA COLLAR, GARFIELD
11-14
©1984 PAWS, INC. All Rights Reserved.
WAIT A MINUTE, THERE'S A DISCLAIMER ON THIS BOX. "WARNING: WHILE THIS COLLAR WILL REPEL FLEAS... "
"IT HAS BEEN KNOWN TO ATTRACT SHARKS"
JIM DAVIS

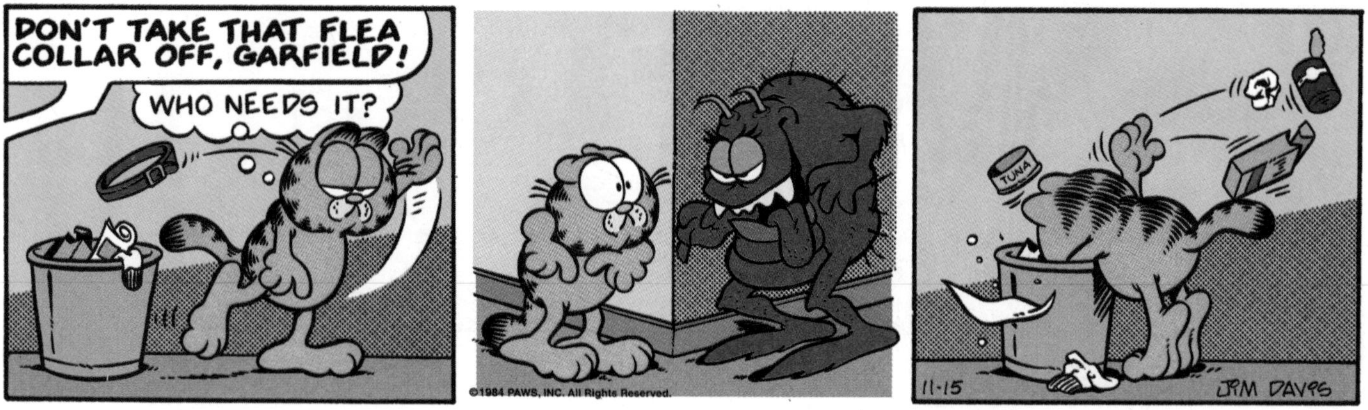
DON'T TAKE THAT FLEA COLLAR OFF, GARFIELD!
WHO NEEDS IT?
©1984 PAWS, INC. All Rights Reserved.
TUNA
11-15
JIM DAVIS

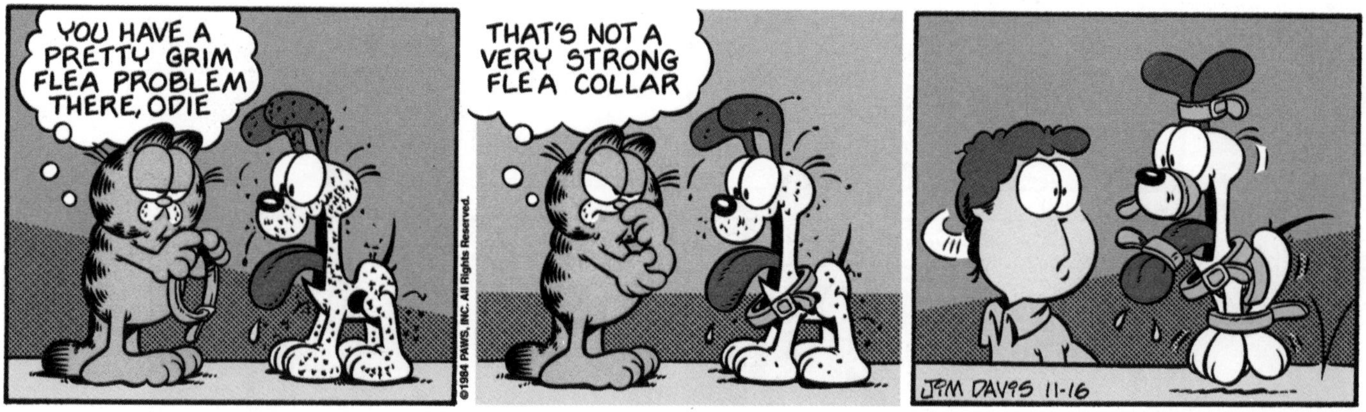
YOU HAVE A PRETTY GRIM FLEA PROBLEM THERE, ODIE
©1984 PAWS, INC. All Rights Reserved.
THAT'S NOT A VERY STRONG FLEA COLLAR
JIM DAVIS 11-16

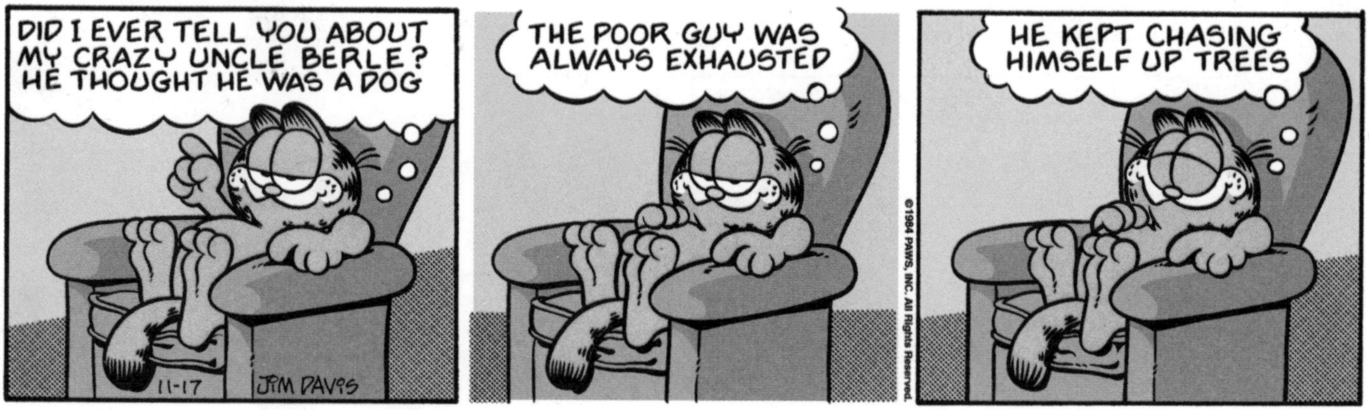
DID I EVER TELL YOU ABOUT MY CRAZY UNCLE BERLE? HE THOUGHT HE WAS A DOG
11-17
JIM DAVIS
THE POOR GUY WAS ALWAYS EXHAUSTED
©1984 PAWS, INC. All Rights Reserved.
HE KEPT CHASING HIMSELF UP TREES

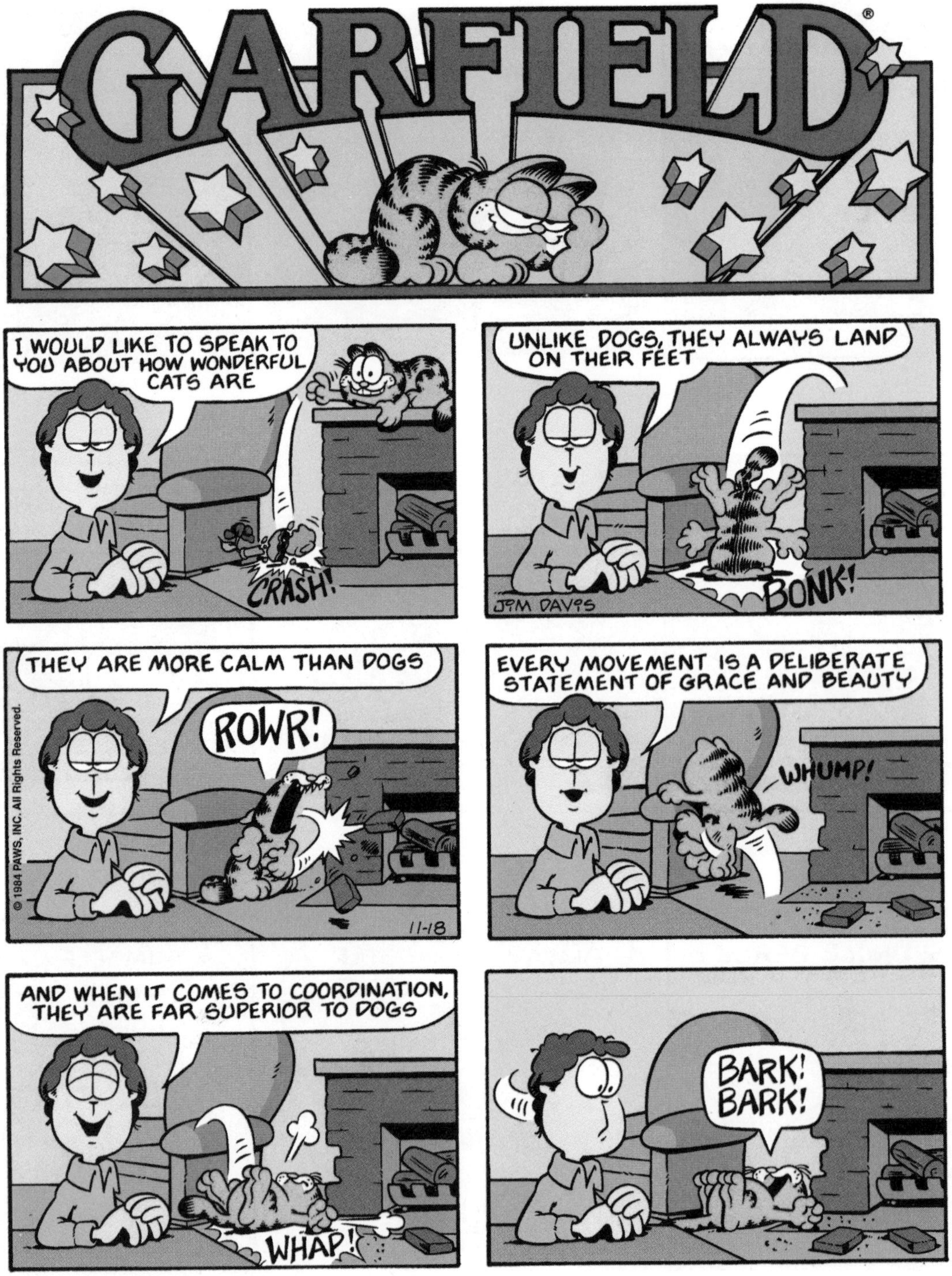
GARFIELD®
I WOULD LIKE TO SPEAK TO YOU ABOUT HOW WONDERFUL CATS ARE
CRASH!
UNLIKE DOGS, THEY ALWAYS LAND ON THEIR FEET
BONK!
JIM DAVIS
THEY ARE MORE CALM THAN DOGS
ROWR!
© 1984 PAWS, INC. All Rights Reserved.
11-18
EVERY MOVEMENT IS A DELIBERATE STATEMENT OF GRACE AND BEAUTY
WHUMP!
AND WHEN IT COMES TO COORDINATION, THEY ARE FAR SUPERIOR TO DOGS
WHAP!
BARK! BARK!

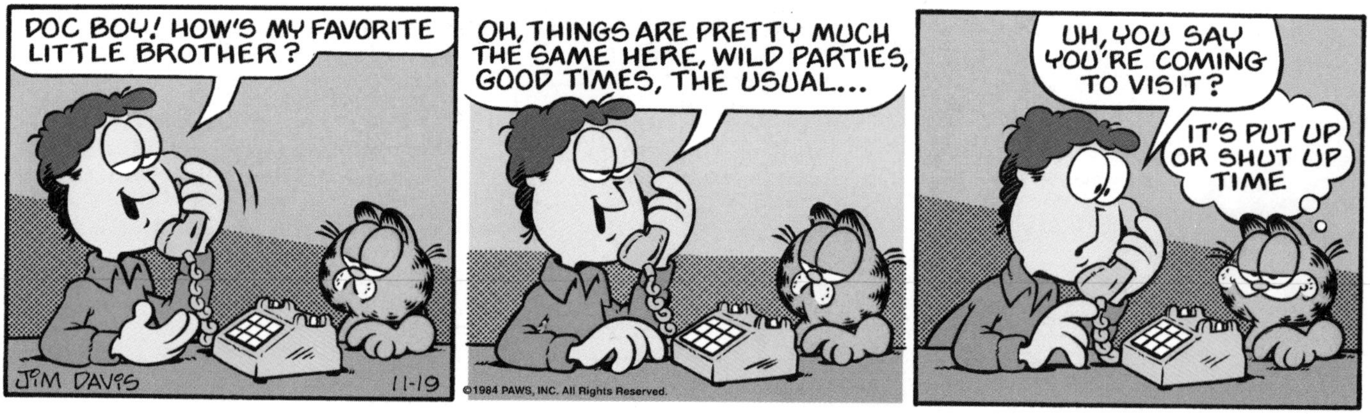
DOC BOY! HOW'S MY FAVORITE LITTLE BROTHER?
OH, THINGS ARE PRETTY MUCH THE SAME HERE, WILD PARTIES, GOOD TIMES, THE USUAL...
UH, YOU SAY YOU'RE COMING TO VISIT?
IT'S PUT UP OR SHUT UP TIME
JIM DAVIS
11-19
©1984 PAWS, INC. All Rights Reserved.

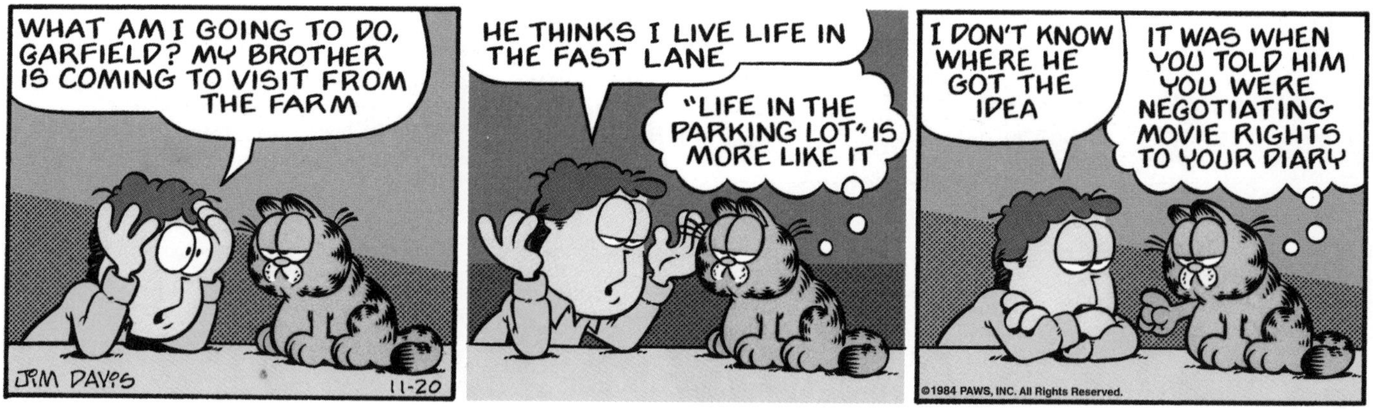
WHAT AM I GOING TO DO, GARFIELD? MY BROTHER IS COMING TO VISIT FROM THE FARM
HE THINKS I LIVE LIFE IN THE FAST LANE
"LIFE IN THE PARKING LOT" IS MORE LIKE IT
I DON'T KNOW WHERE HE GOT THE IDEA
IT WAS WHEN YOU TOLD HIM YOU WERE NEGOTIATING MOVIE RIGHTS TO YOUR DIARY
JIM DAVIS
11-20
©1984 PAWS, INC. All Rights Reserved.

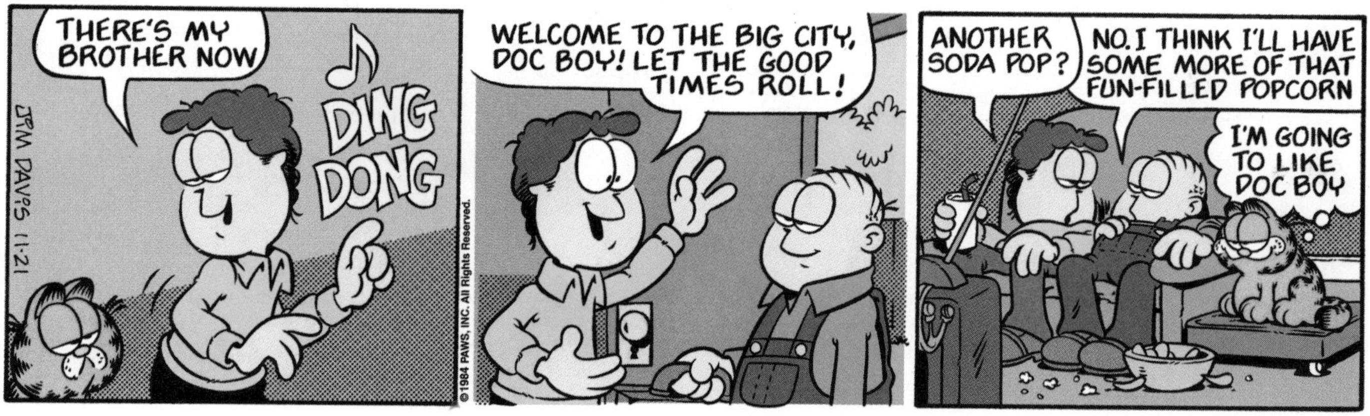
THERE'S MY BROTHER NOW
DING DONG
WELCOME TO THE BIG CITY, DOC BOY! LET THE GOOD TIMES ROLL!
ANOTHER SODA POP?
NO. I THINK I'LL HAVE SOME MORE OF THAT FUN-FILLED POPCORN
I'M GOING TO LIKE DOC BOY
JIM DAVIS 11-21
©1984 PAWS, INC. All Rights Reserved.

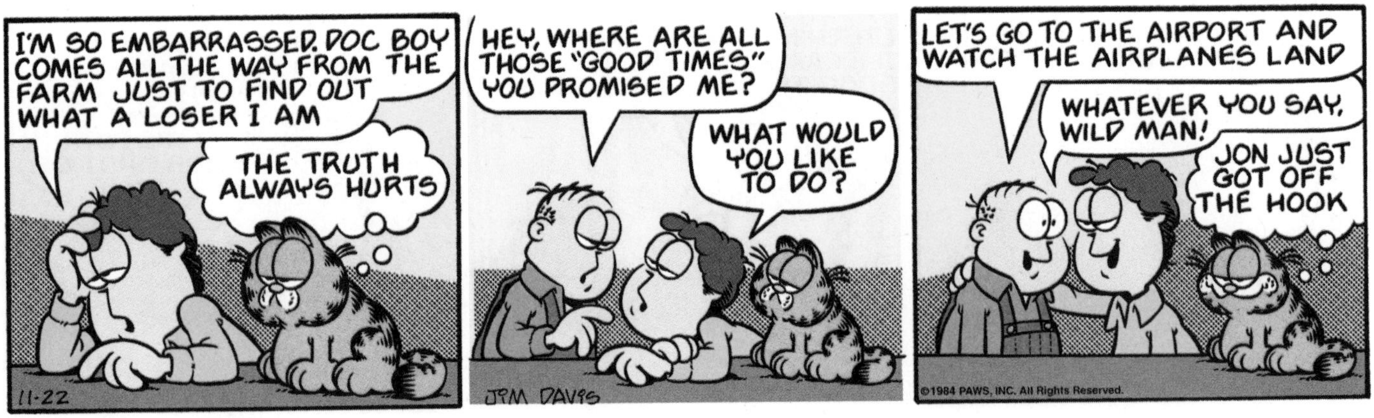
I'M SO EMBARRASSED. DOC BOY COMES ALL THE WAY FROM THE FARM JUST TO FIND OUT WHAT A LOSER I AM
THE TRUTH ALWAYS HURTS
HEY, WHERE ARE ALL THOSE "GOOD TIMES" YOU PROMISED ME?
WHAT WOULD YOU LIKE TO DO?
LET'S GO TO THE AIRPORT AND WATCH THE AIRPLANES LAND
WHATEVER YOU SAY, WILD MAN!
JON JUST GOT OFF THE HOOK
©1984 PAWS, INC. All Rights Reserved.

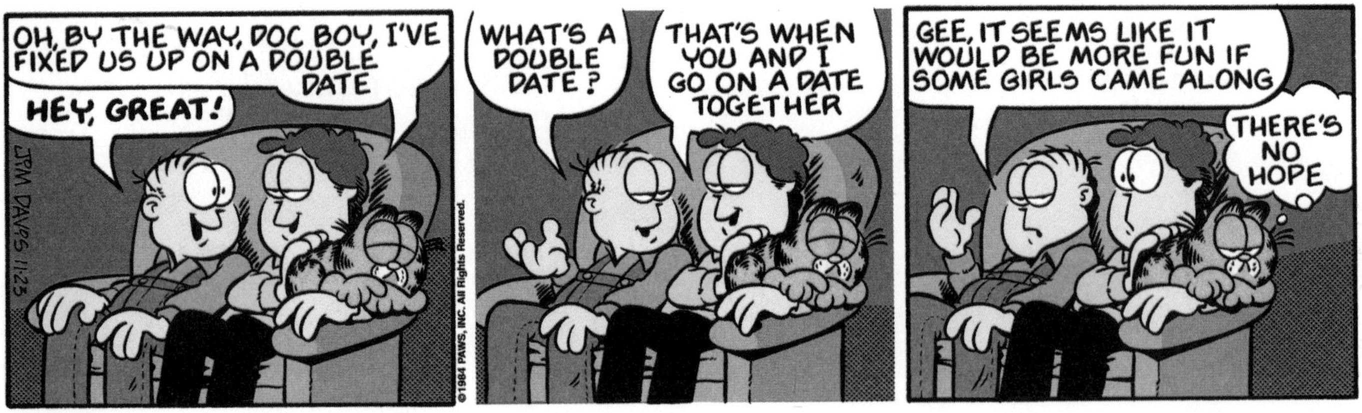
OH, BY THE WAY, DOC BOY, I'VE FIXED US UP ON A DOUBLE DATE
HEY, GREAT!
WHAT'S A DOUBLE DATE?
THAT'S WHEN YOU AND I GO ON A DATE TOGETHER
GEE, IT SEEMS LIKE IT WOULD BE MORE FUN IF SOME GIRLS CAME ALONG
THERE'S NO HOPE
©1984 PAWS, INC. All Rights Reserved.

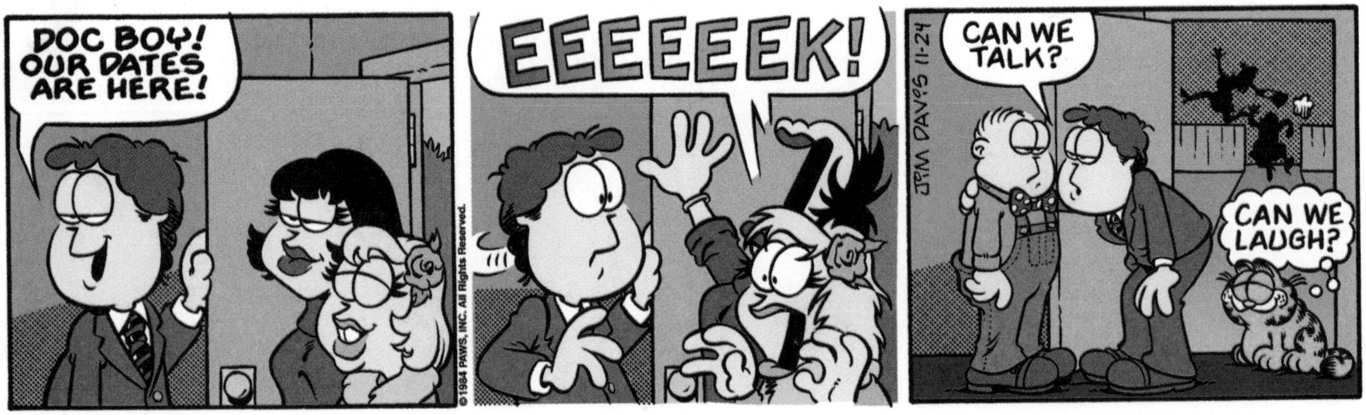
DOC BOY! OUR DATES ARE HERE!
EEEEEEEK!
CAN WE TALK?
CAN WE LAUGH?
©1984 PAWS, INC. All Rights Reserved.

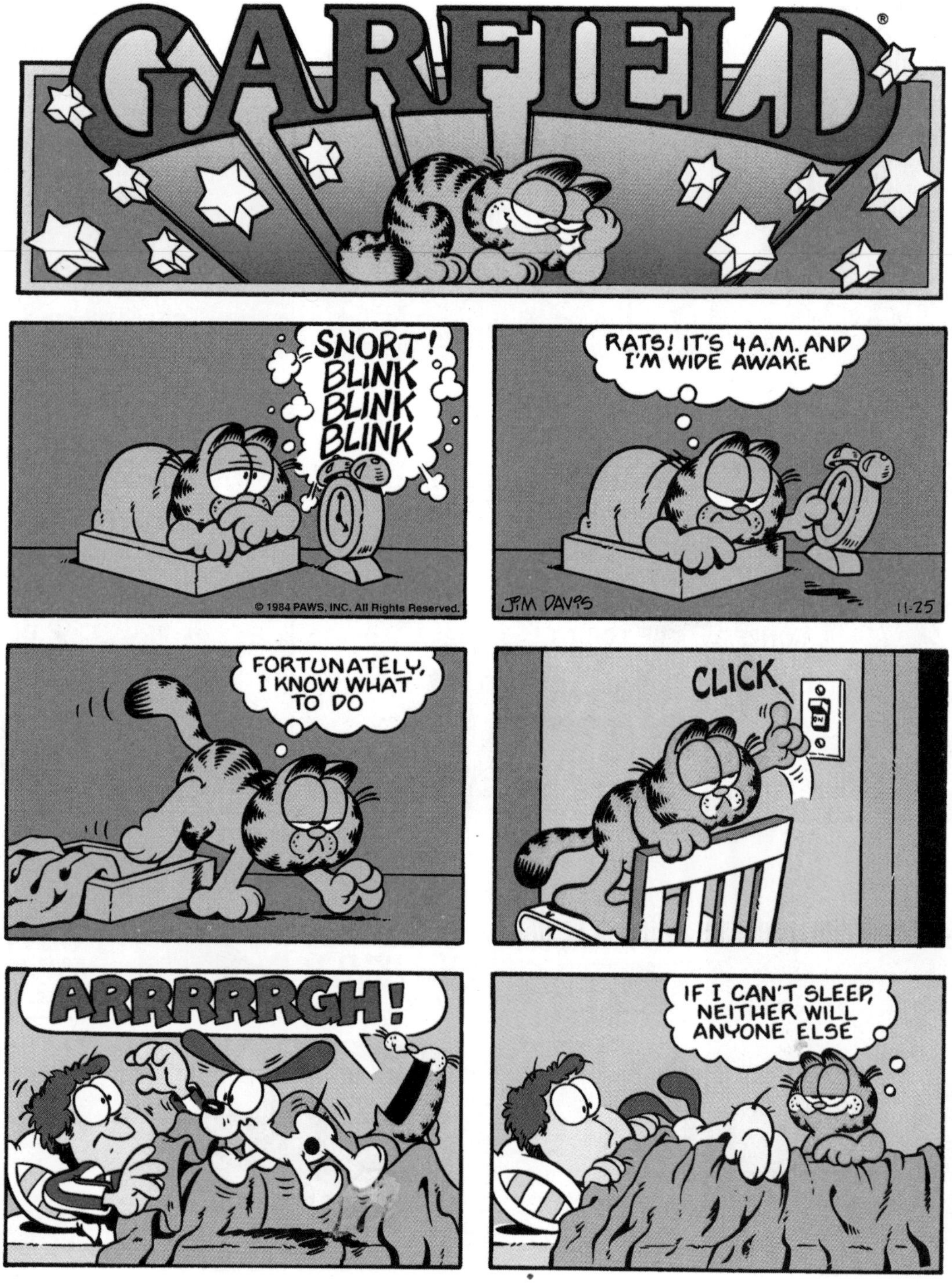
GARFIELD®
SNORT! BLINK BLINK BLINK
© 1984 PAWS, INC. All Rights Reserved.
RATS! IT'S 4 A.M. AND I'M WIDE AWAKE
JIM DAVIS
11-25
FORTUNATELY, I KNOW WHAT TO DO
CLICK
ON
ARRRRRGH!
IF I CAN'T SLEEP, NEITHER WILL ANYONE ELSE

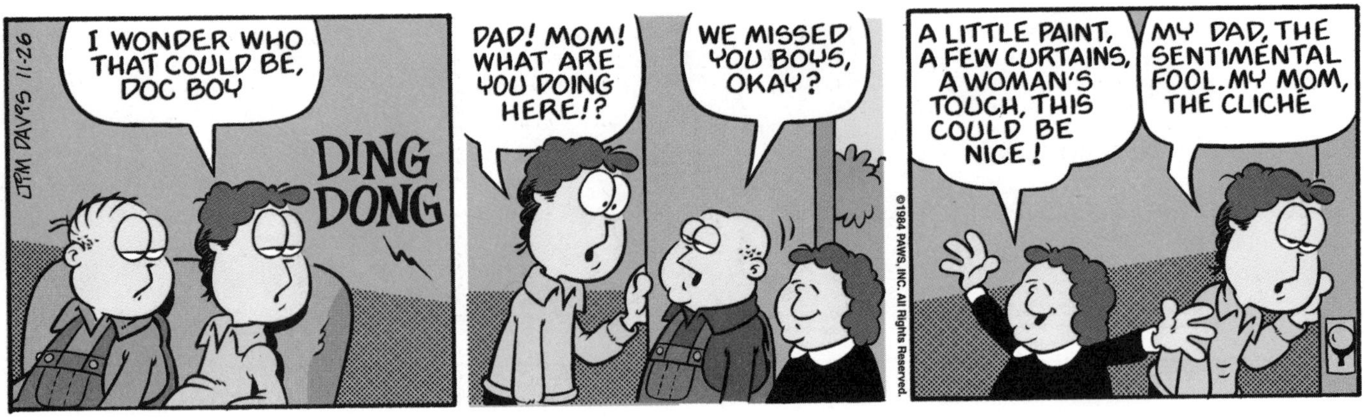
JPM DAVPS 11-26
I WONDER WHO THAT COULD BE, DOC BOY
DING DONG
DAD! MOM! WHAT ARE YOU DOING HERE!?
WE MISSED YOU BOYS, OKAY?
©1984 PAWS, INC. All Rights Reserved.
A LITTLE PAINT, A FEW CURTAINS, A WOMAN'S TOUCH, THIS COULD BE NICE!
MY DAD, THE SENTIMENTAL FOOL. MY MOM, THE CLICHÉ

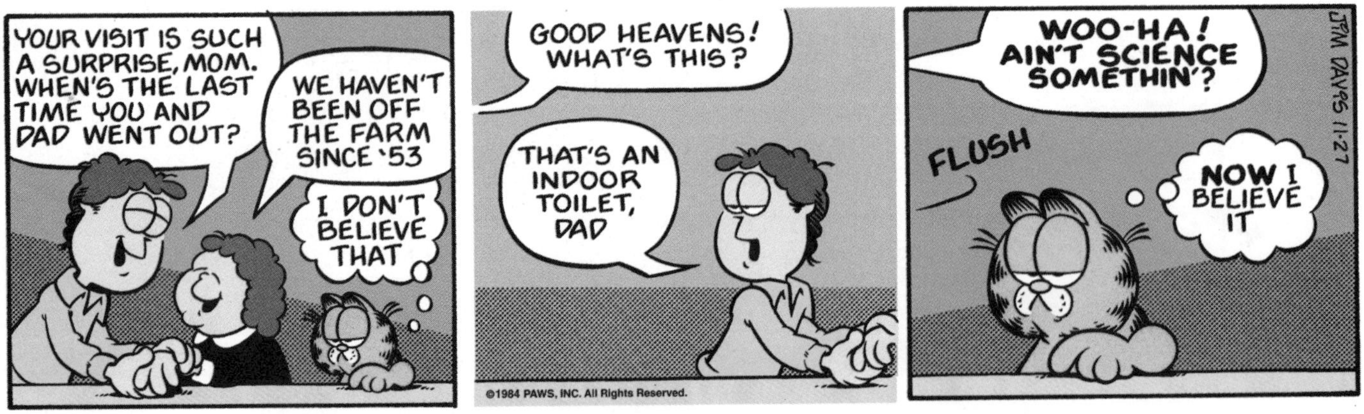
YOUR VISIT IS SUCH A SURPRISE, MOM. WHEN'S THE LAST TIME YOU AND DAD WENT OUT?
WE HAVEN'T BEEN OFF THE FARM SINCE '53
I DON'T BELIEVE THAT
GOOD HEAVENS! WHAT'S THIS?
THAT'S AN INDOOR TOILET, DAD
©1984 PAWS, INC. All Rights Reserved.
JPM DAVPS 11-27
WOO-HA! AIN'T SCIENCE SOMETHIN'?
FLUSH
NOW I BELIEVE IT

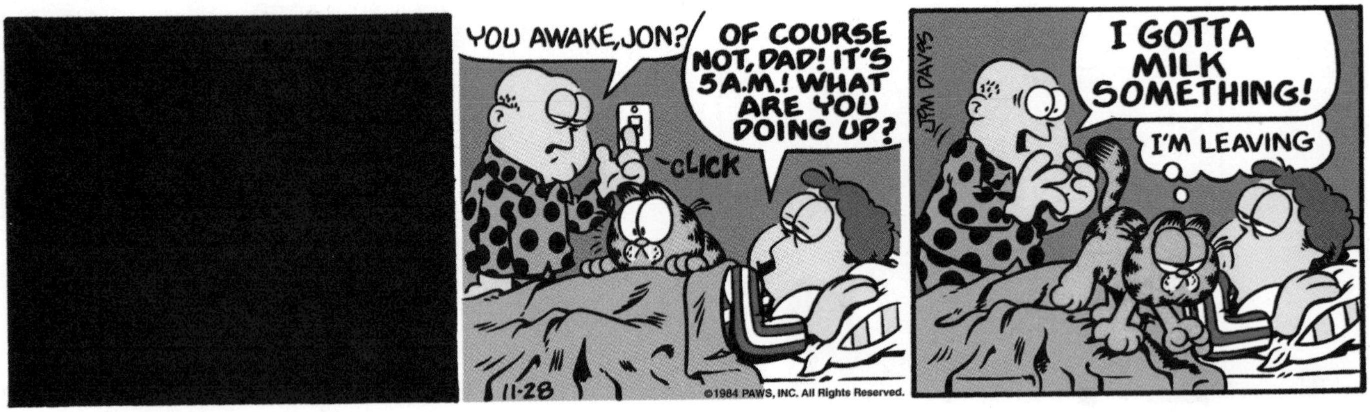
YOU AWAKE, JON?
OF COURSE NOT, DAD! IT'S 5 A.M.! WHAT ARE YOU DOING UP?
CLICK
11-28
©1984 PAWS, INC. All Rights Reserved.
JPM DAVPS
I GOTTA MILK SOMETHING!
I'M LEAVING

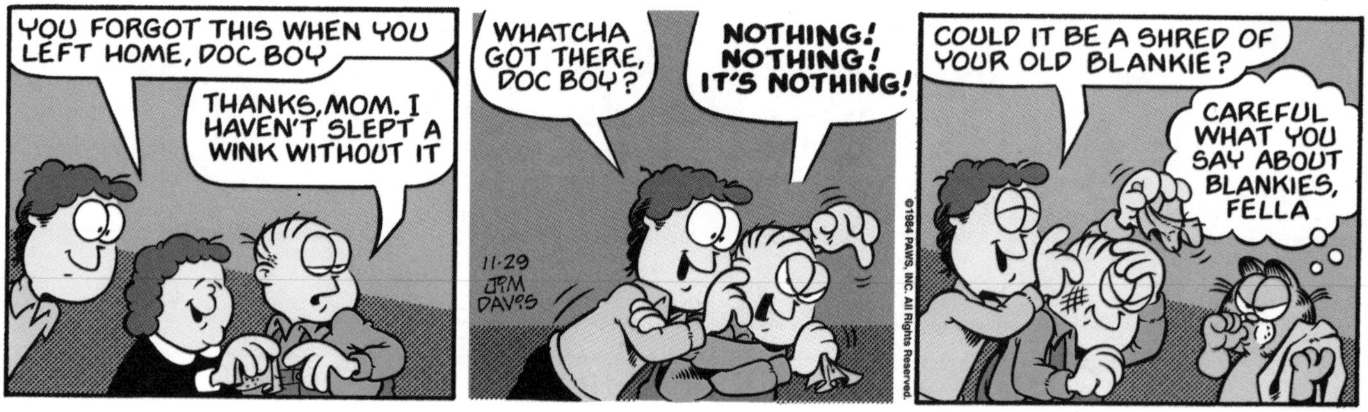
YOU FORGOT THIS WHEN YOU LEFT HOME, DOC BOY
THANKS, MOM. I HAVEN'T SLEPT A WINK WITHOUT IT
WHATCHA GOT THERE, DOC BOY?
NOTHING! NOTHING! IT'S NOTHING!
11-29 JIM DAVIS
©1984 PAWS, INC. All Rights Reserved.
COULD IT BE A SHRED OF YOUR OLD BLANKIE?
CAREFUL WHAT YOU SAY ABOUT BLANKIES, FELLA

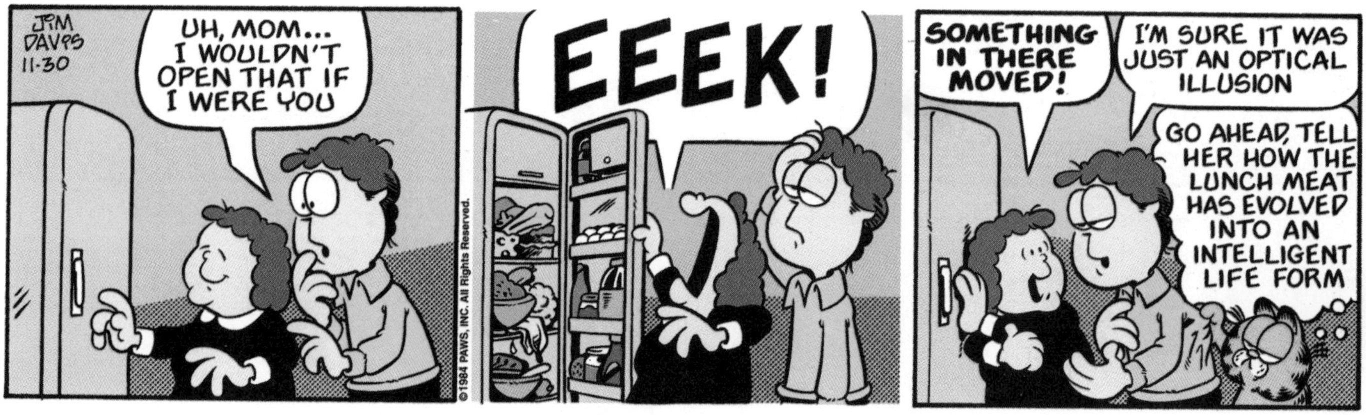
JIM DAVIS 11-30
UH, MOM... I WOULDN'T OPEN THAT IF I WERE YOU
©1984 PAWS, INC. All Rights Reserved.
EEEK!
SOMETHING IN THERE MOVED!
I'M SURE IT WAS JUST AN OPTICAL ILLUSION
GO AHEAD, TELL HER HOW THE LUNCH MEAT HAS EVOLVED INTO AN INTELLIGENT LIFE FORM

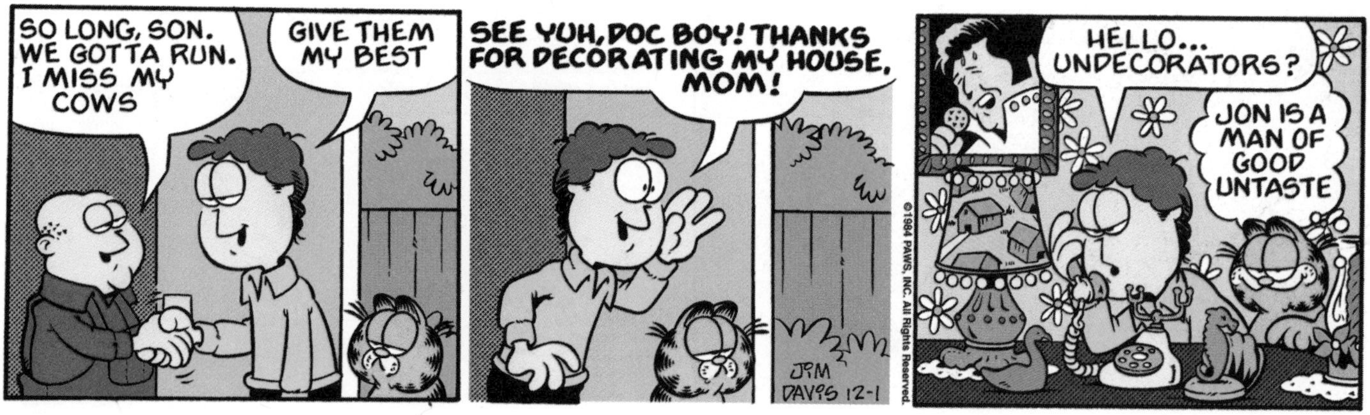
SO LONG, SON. WE GOTTA RUN. I MISS MY COWS
GIVE THEM MY BEST
SEE YUH, DOC BOY! THANKS FOR DECORATING MY HOUSE, MOM!
JIM DAVIS 12-1
©1984 PAWS, INC. All Rights Reserved.
HELLO... UNDECORATORS?
JON IS A MAN OF GOOD UNTASTE

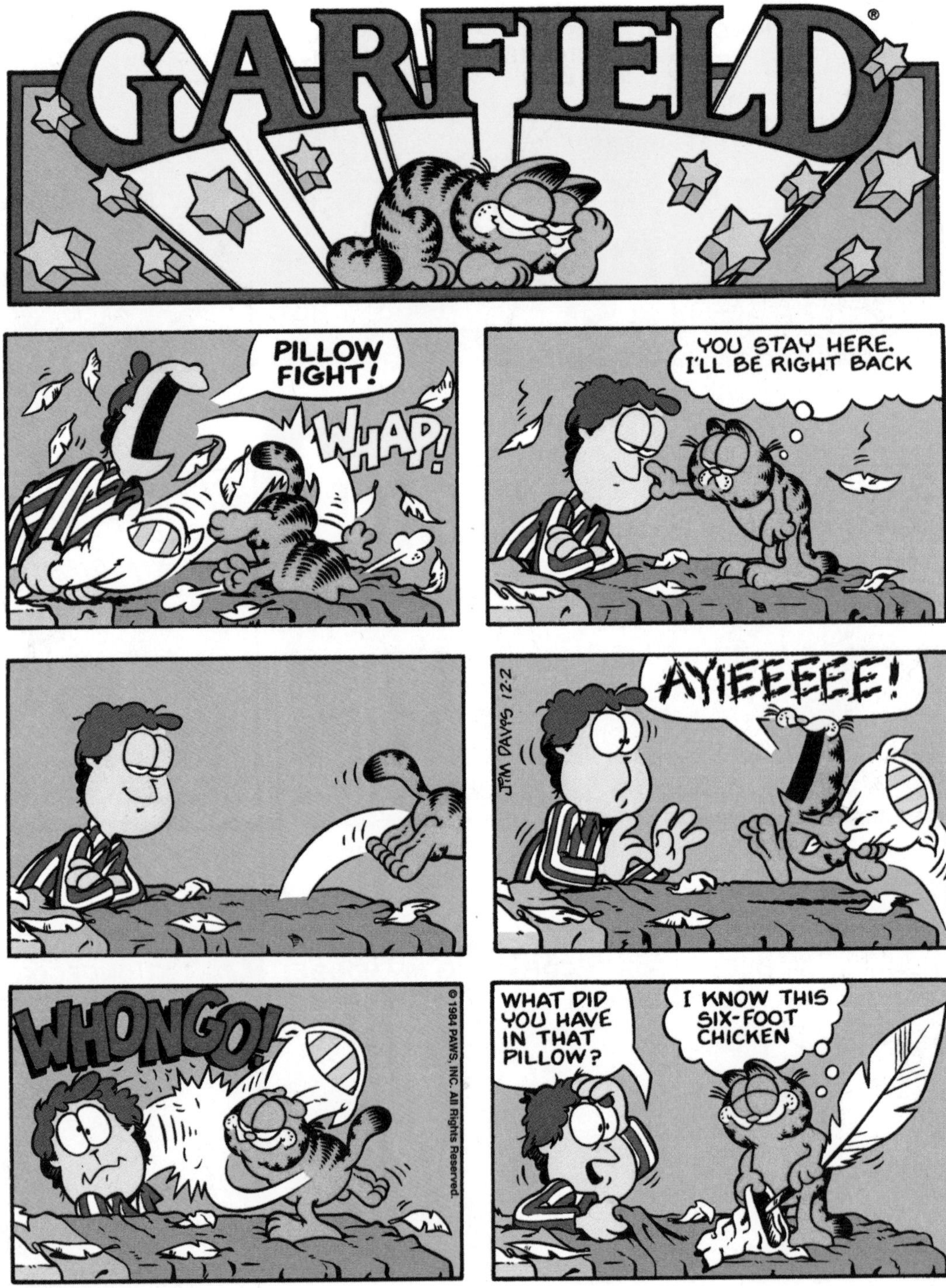
GARFIELD®
PILLOW FIGHT!
WHAP!
YOU STAY HERE. I'LL BE RIGHT BACK
JIM DAVIS 12-2
AYIEEEEEE!
WHONGO!
© 1984 PAWS, INC. All Rights Reserved.
WHAT DID YOU HAVE IN THAT PILLOW?
I KNOW THIS SIX-FOOT CHICKEN

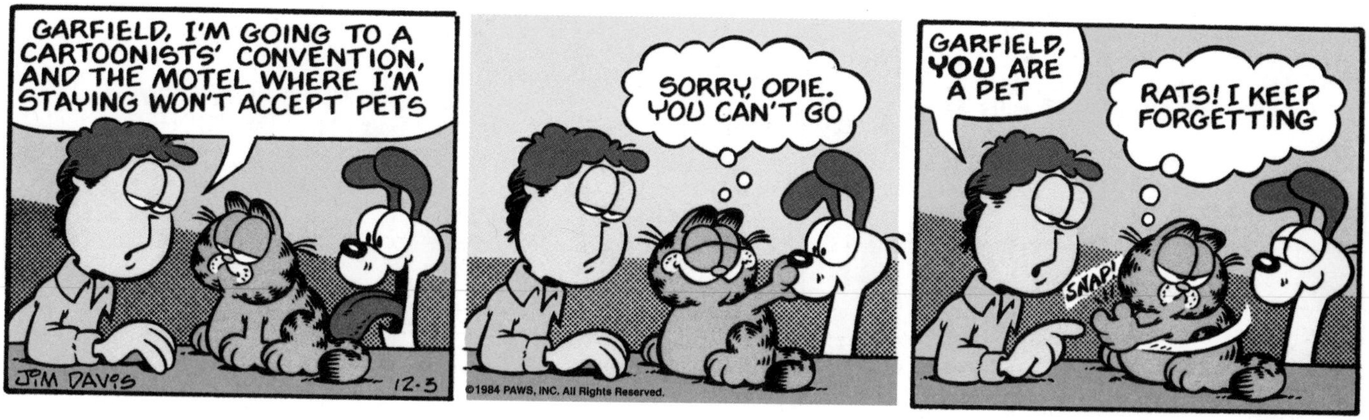
GARFIELD, I'M GOING TO A CARTOONISTS' CONVENTION, AND THE MOTEL WHERE I'M STAYING WON'T ACCEPT PETS
JIM DAVIS 12-3
SORRY, ODIE. YOU CAN'T GO
©1984 PAWS, INC. All Rights Reserved.
GARFIELD, YOU ARE A PET
RATS! I KEEP FORGETTING
SNAP!

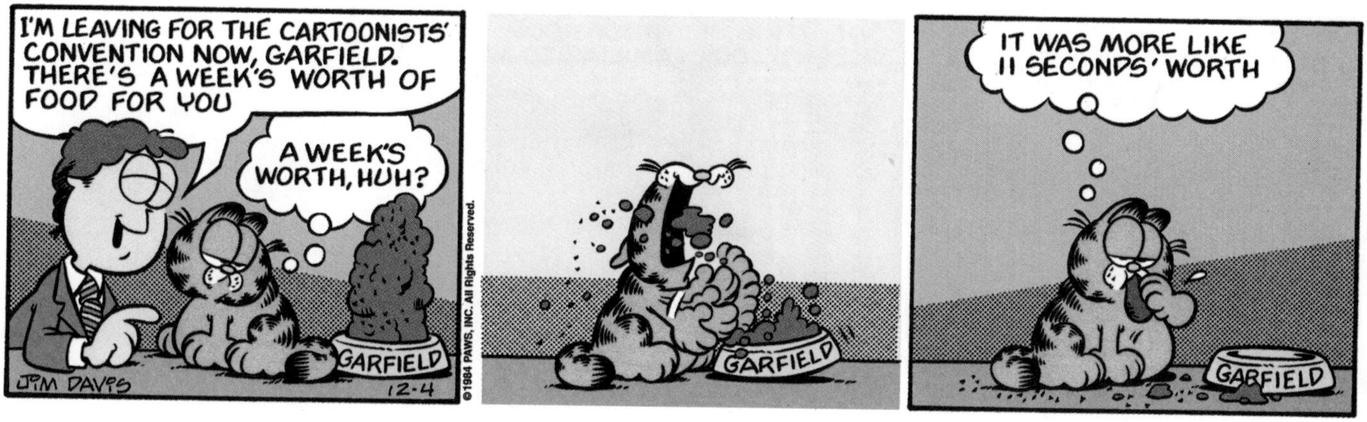
I'M LEAVING FOR THE CARTOONISTS' CONVENTION NOW, GARFIELD. THERE'S A WEEK'S WORTH OF FOOD FOR YOU
A WEEK'S WORTH, HUH?
GARFIELD
JIM DAVIS 12-4
©1984 PAWS, INC. All Rights Reserved.
GARFIELD
IT WAS MORE LIKE 11 SECONDS' WORTH
GARFIELD

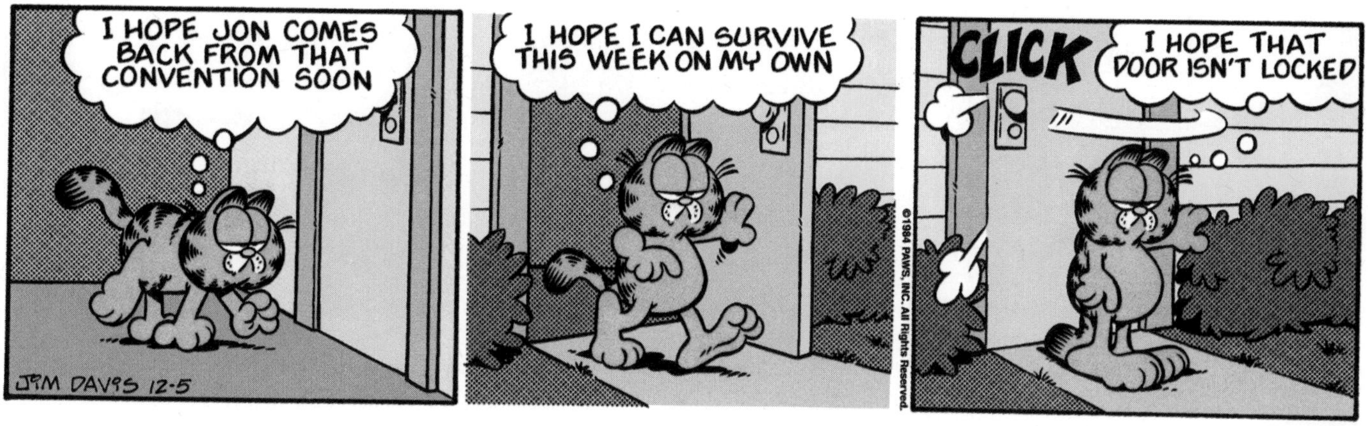
I HOPE JON COMES BACK FROM THAT CONVENTION SOON
JIM DAVIS 12-5
I HOPE I CAN SURVIVE THIS WEEK ON MY OWN
©1984 PAWS, INC. All Rights Reserved.
CLICK
I HOPE THAT DOOR ISN'T LOCKED

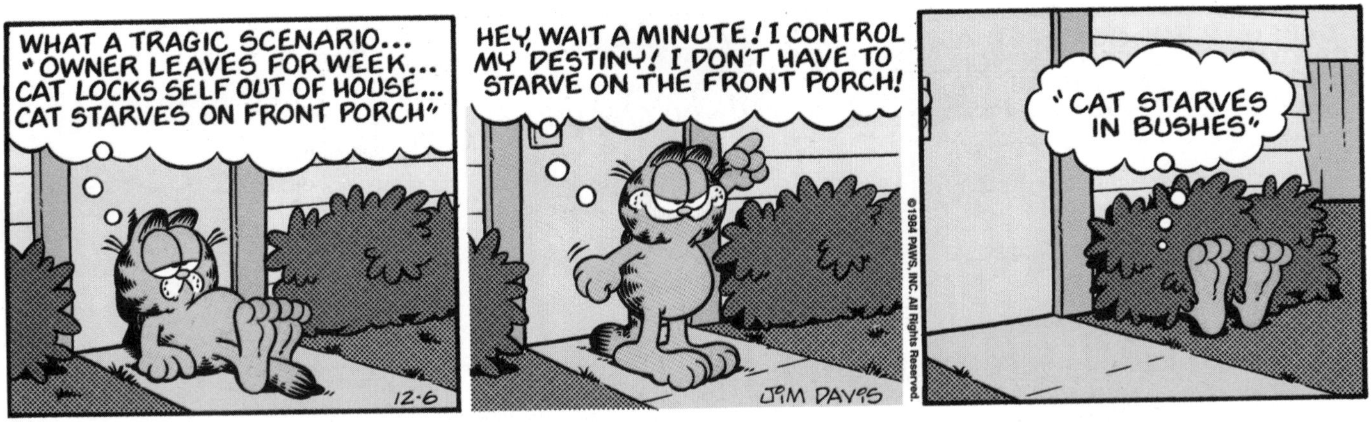
WHAT A TRAGIC SCENARIO... "OWNER LEAVES FOR WEEK... CAT LOCKS SELF OUT OF HOUSE... CAT STARVES ON FRONT PORCH"
12-6
HEY, WAIT A MINUTE! I CONTROL MY DESTINY! I DON'T HAVE TO STARVE ON THE FRONT PORCH!
JIM DAVIS
©1984 PAWS, INC. All Rights Reserved.
"CAT STARVES IN BUSHES"

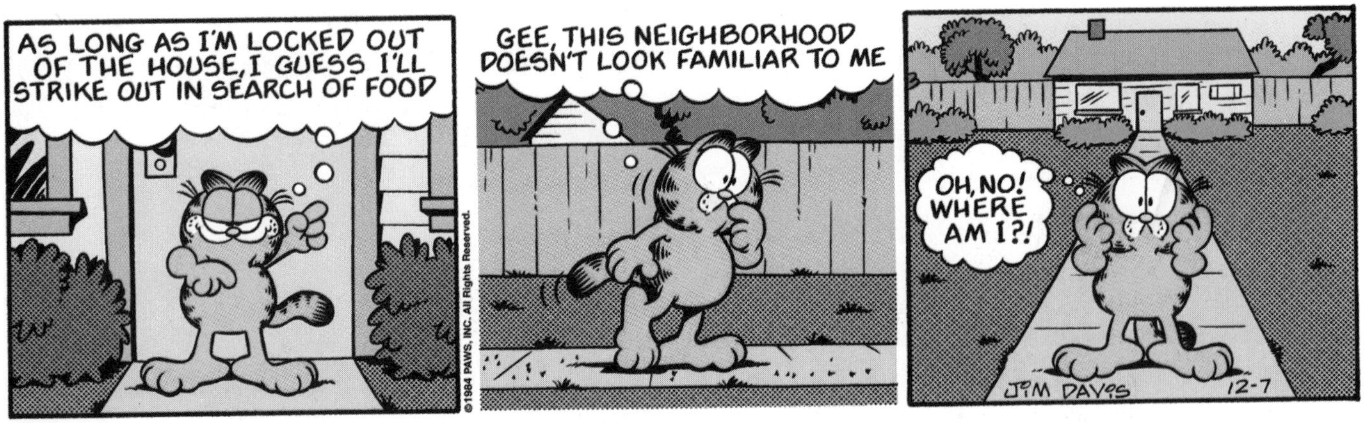
AS LONG AS I'M LOCKED OUT OF THE HOUSE, I GUESS I'LL STRIKE OUT IN SEARCH OF FOOD
©1984 PAWS, INC. All Rights Reserved.
GEE, THIS NEIGHBORHOOD DOESN'T LOOK FAMILIAR TO ME
OH, NO! WHERE AM I?!
JIM DAVIS
12-7

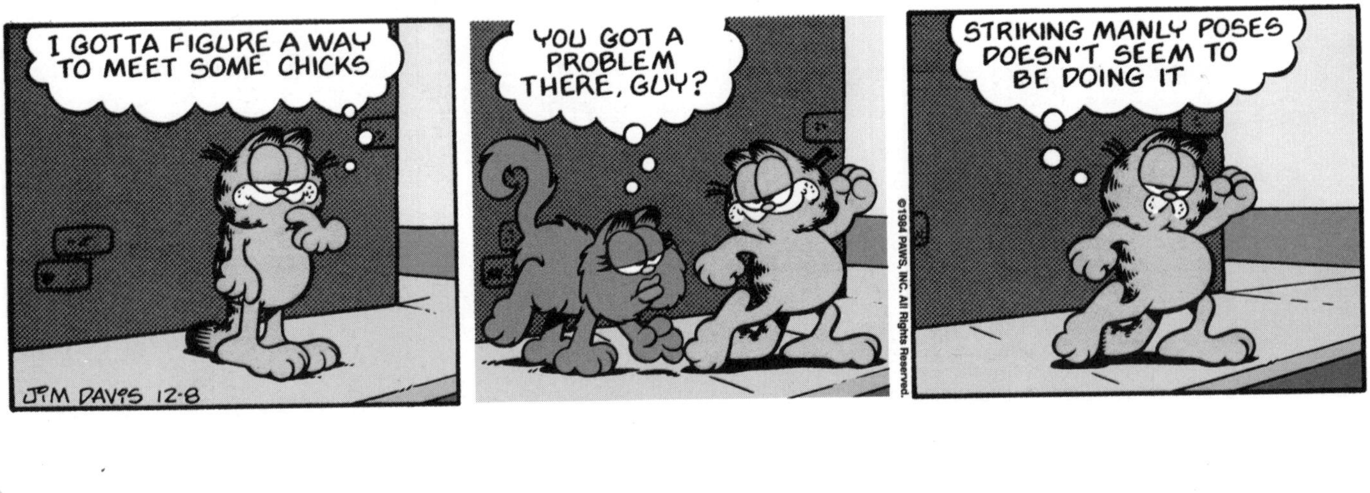
I GOTTA FIGURE A WAY TO MEET SOME CHICKS
JIM DAVIS 12-8
YOU GOT A PROBLEM THERE, GUY?
©1984 PAWS, INC. All Rights Reserved.
STRIKING MANLY POSES DOESN'T SEEM TO BE DOING IT

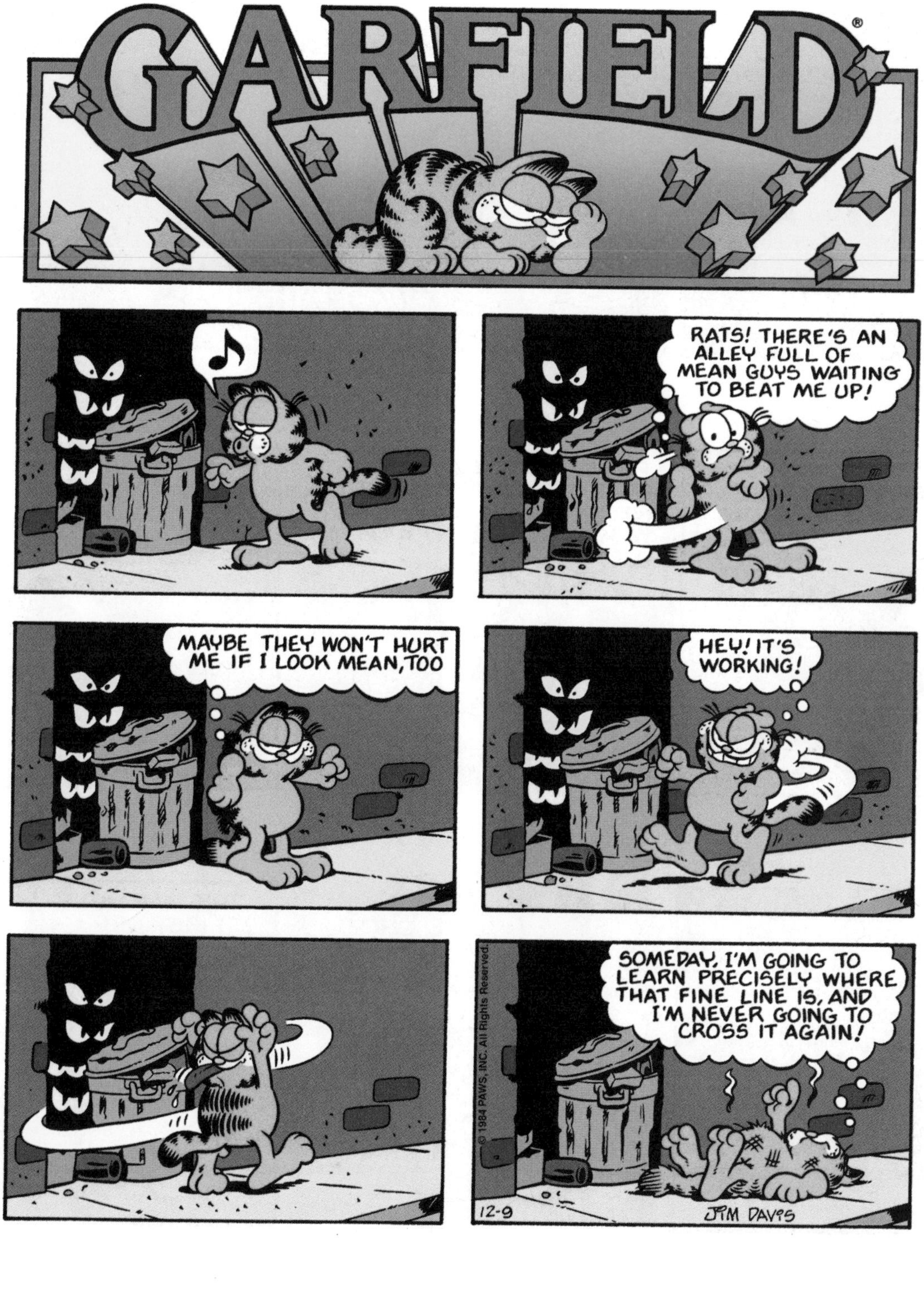
GARFIELD
♪
RATS! THERE'S AN ALLEY FULL OF MEAN GUYS WAITING TO BEAT ME UP!
MAYBE THEY WON'T HURT ME IF I LOOK MEAN, TOO
HEY! IT'S WORKING!
© 1984 PAWS, INC. All Rights Reserved.
SOMEDAY, I'M GOING TO LEARN PRECISELY WHERE THAT FINE LINE IS, AND I'M NEVER GOING TO CROSS IT AGAIN!
12-9
JIM DAVIS

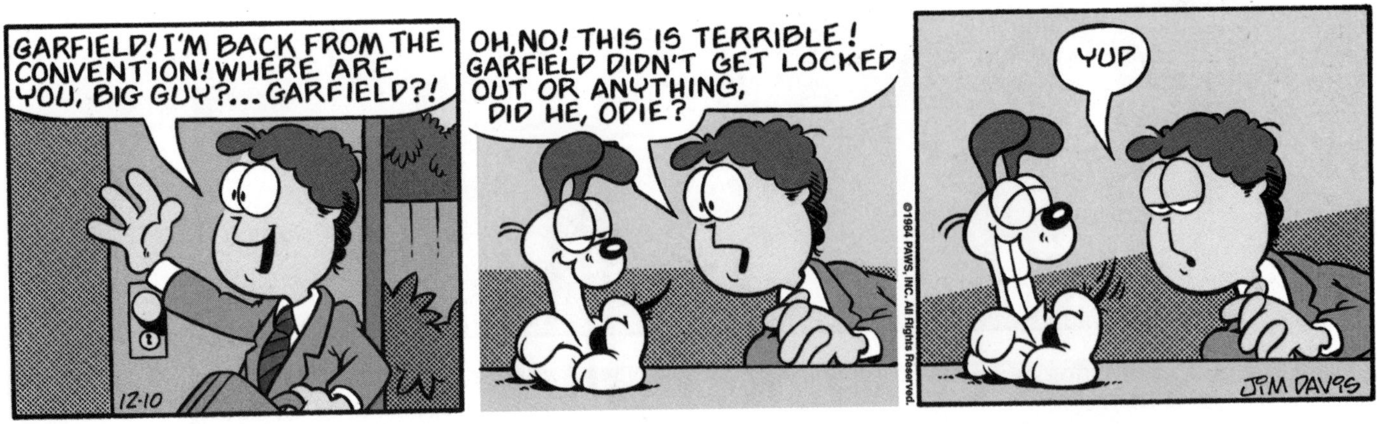
GARFIELD! I'M BACK FROM THE CONVENTION! WHERE ARE YOU, BIG GUY?... GARFIELD?!
12-10
OH, NO! THIS IS TERRIBLE! GARFIELD DIDN'T GET LOCKED OUT OR ANYTHING, DID HE, ODIE?
©1984 PAWS, INC. All Rights Reserved.
YUP
JIM DAVIS

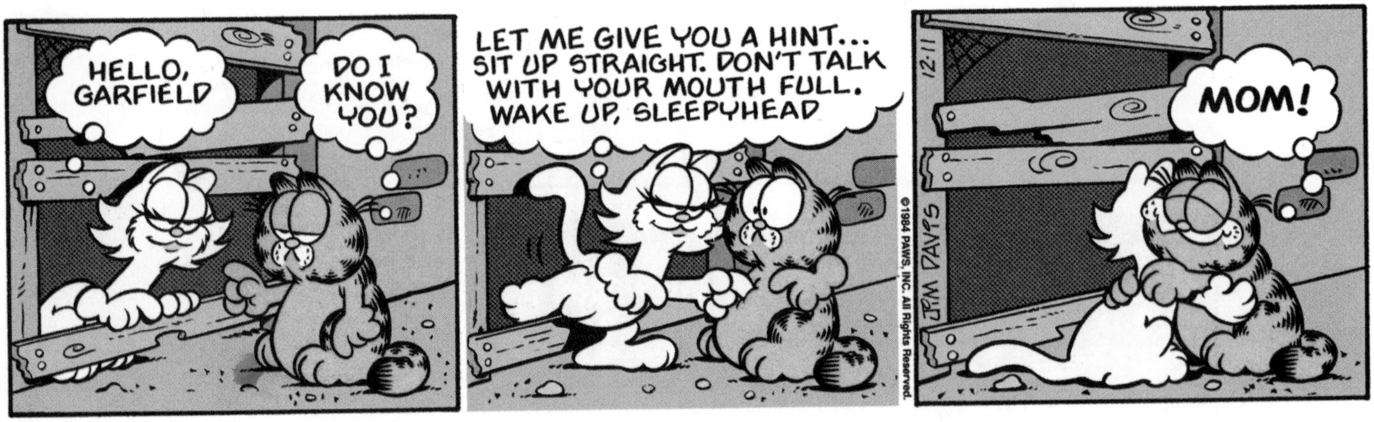
HELLO, GARFIELD
DO I KNOW YOU?
LET ME GIVE YOU A HINT... SIT UP STRAIGHT. DON'T TALK WITH YOUR MOUTH FULL. WAKE UP, SLEEPYHEAD
©1984 PAWS, INC. All Rights Reserved.
12-11
JIM DAVIS
MOM!

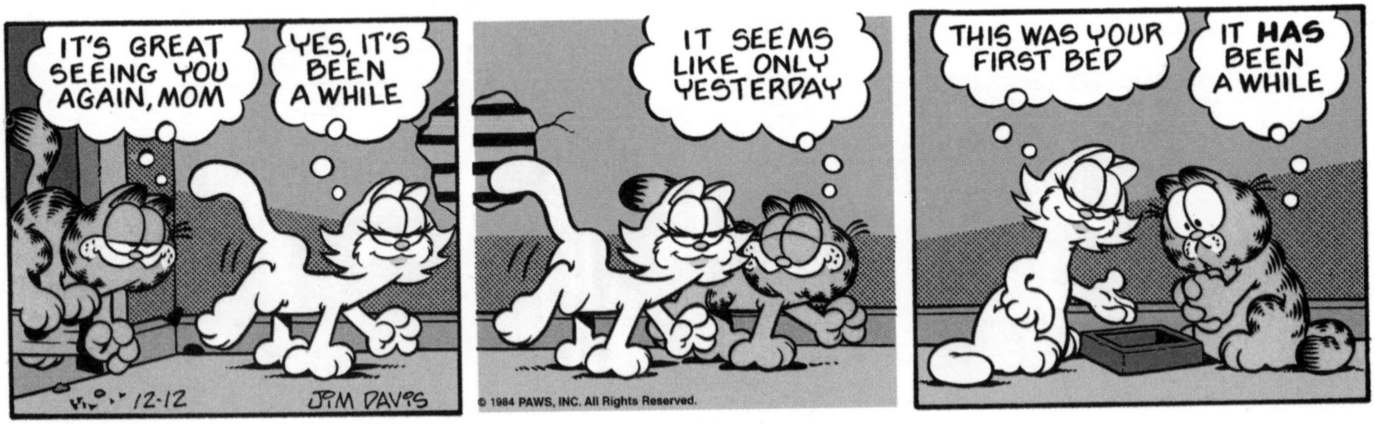
IT'S GREAT SEEING YOU AGAIN, MOM
YES, IT'S BEEN A WHILE
12-12
JIM DAVIS
IT SEEMS LIKE ONLY YESTERDAY
© 1984 PAWS, INC. All Rights Reserved.
THIS WAS YOUR FIRST BED
IT **HAS** BEEN A WHILE

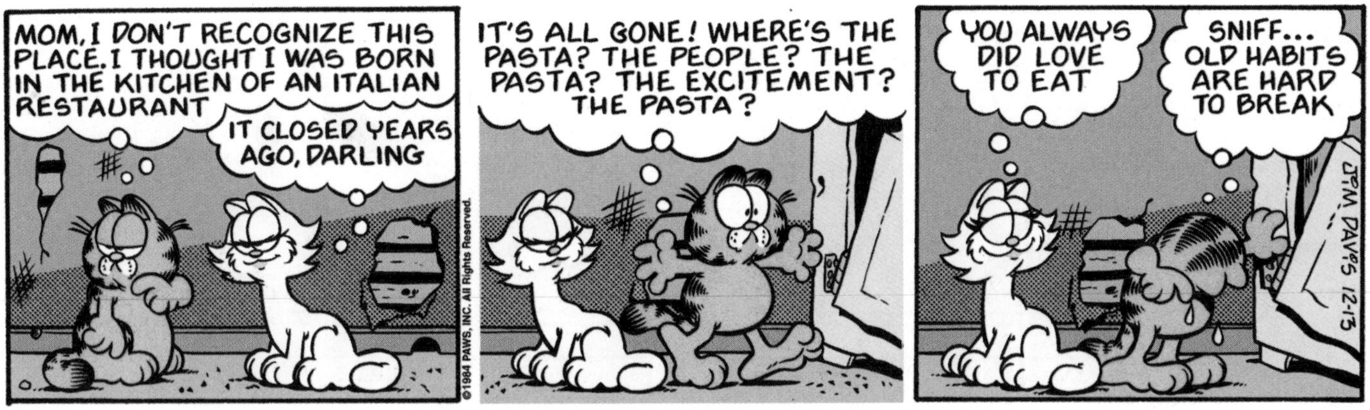
MOM, I DON'T RECOGNIZE THIS PLACE. I THOUGHT I WAS BORN IN THE KITCHEN OF AN ITALIAN RESTAURANT
IT CLOSED YEARS AGO, DARLING
©1984 PAWS, INC. All Rights Reserved.
IT'S ALL GONE! WHERE'S THE PASTA? THE PEOPLE? THE PASTA? THE EXCITEMENT? THE PASTA?
YOU ALWAYS DID LOVE TO EAT
SNIFF... OLD HABITS ARE HARD TO BREAK
JIM DAVIS 12-13

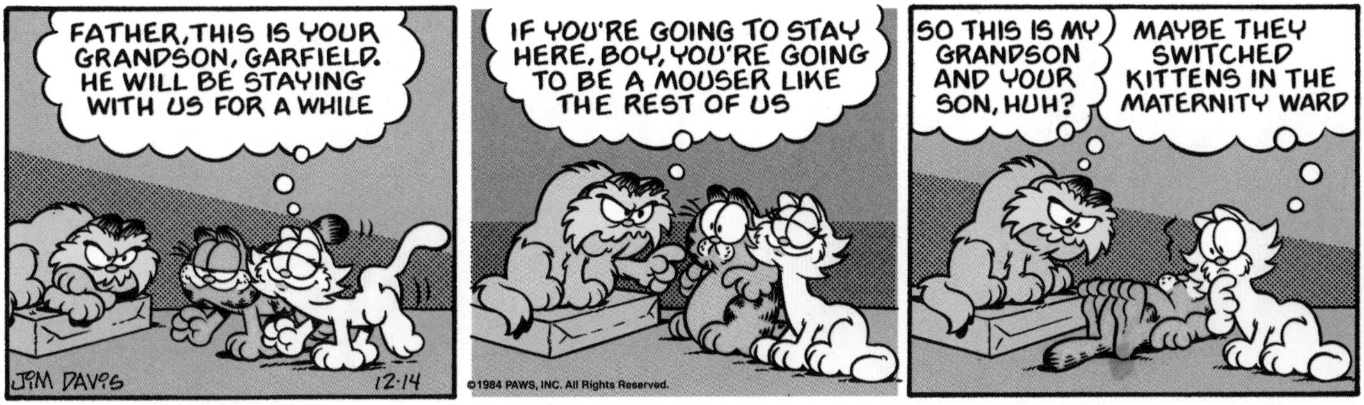
FATHER, THIS IS YOUR GRANDSON, GARFIELD. HE WILL BE STAYING WITH US FOR A WHILE
JIM DAVIS
12-14
IF YOU'RE GOING TO STAY HERE, BOY, YOU'RE GOING TO BE A MOUSER LIKE THE REST OF US
©1984 PAWS, INC. All Rights Reserved.
SO THIS IS MY GRANDSON AND YOUR SON, HUH?
MAYBE THEY SWITCHED KITTENS IN THE MATERNITY WARD

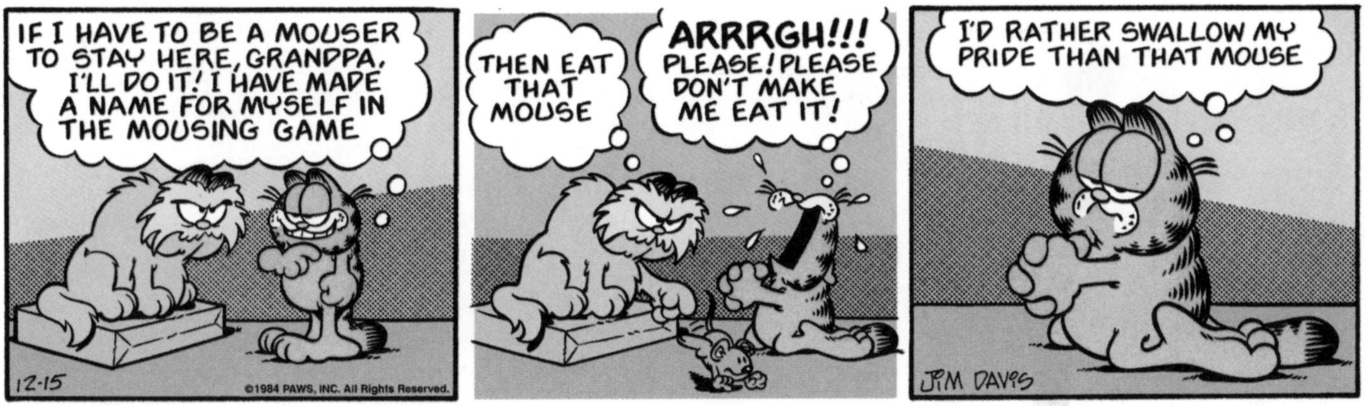
IF I HAVE TO BE A MOUSER TO STAY HERE, GRANDPA, I'LL DO IT! I HAVE MADE A NAME FOR MYSELF IN THE MOUSING GAME
12-15
©1984 PAWS, INC. All Rights Reserved.
THEN EAT THAT MOUSE
ARRRGH!!! PLEASE! PLEASE DON'T MAKE ME EAT IT!
I'D RATHER SWALLOW MY PRIDE THAN THAT MOUSE
JIM DAVIS

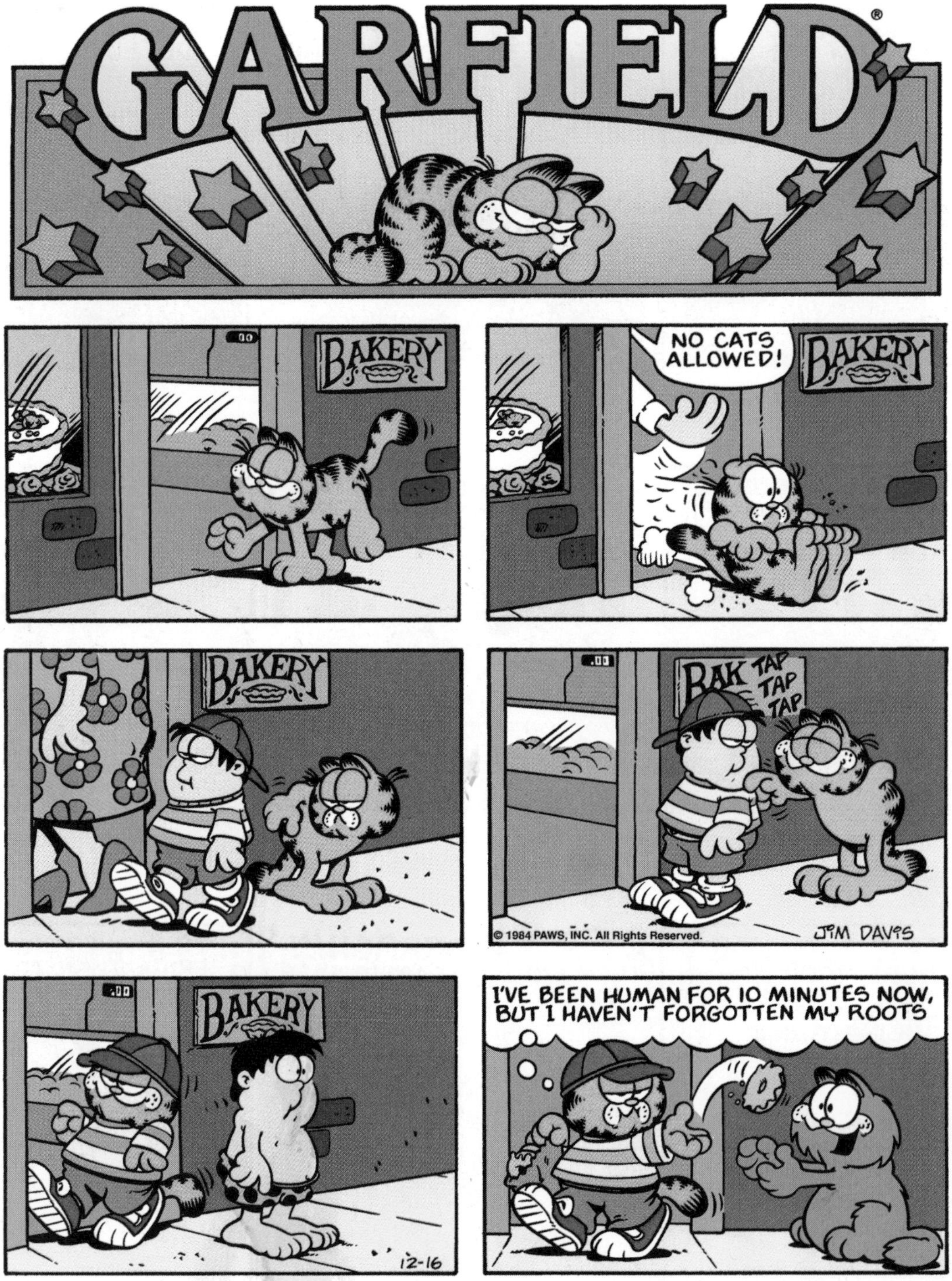
GARFIELD
BAKERY
NO CATS ALLOWED!
BAKERY
BAKERY
BAK
TAP TAP TAP
© 1984 PAWS, INC. All Rights Reserved.
JIM DAVIS
BAKERY
12-16
I'VE BEEN HUMAN FOR 10 MINUTES NOW, BUT I HAVEN'T FORGOTTEN MY ROOTS

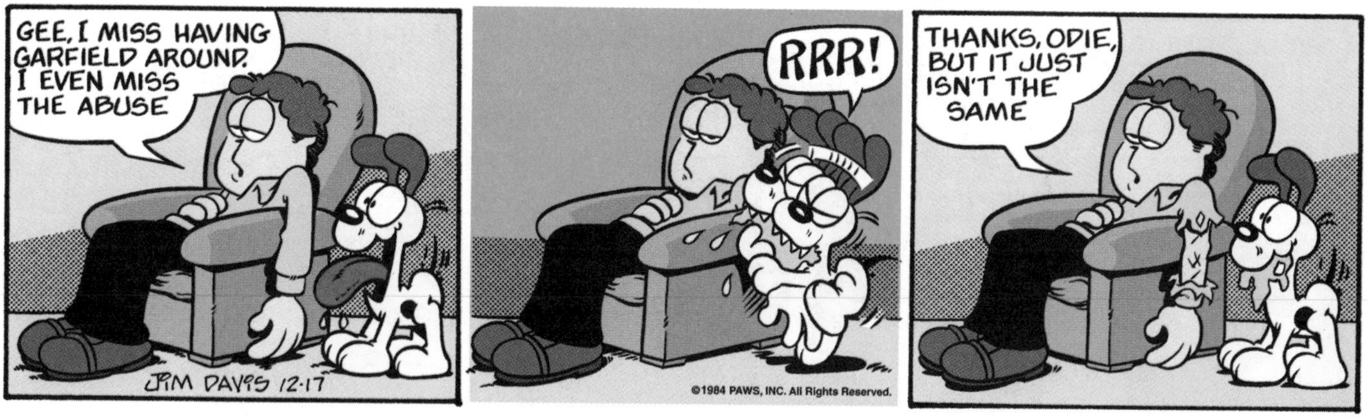
GEE, I MISS HAVING GARFIELD AROUND. I EVEN MISS THE ABUSE
JIM DAVIS 12·17
RRR!
©1984 PAWS, INC. All Rights Reserved.
THANKS, ODIE, BUT IT JUST ISN'T THE SAME

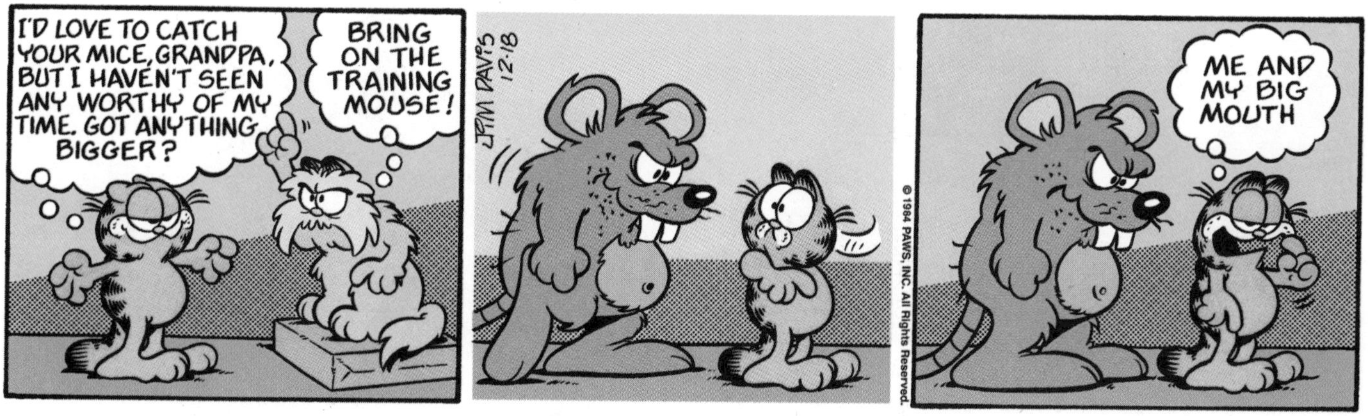
I'D LOVE TO CATCH YOUR MICE, GRANDPA, BUT I HAVEN'T SEEN ANY WORTHY OF MY TIME. GOT ANYTHING BIGGER?
BRING ON THE TRAINING MOUSE!
JIM DAVIS 12·18
©1984 PAWS, INC. All Rights Reserved.
ME AND MY BIG MOUTH

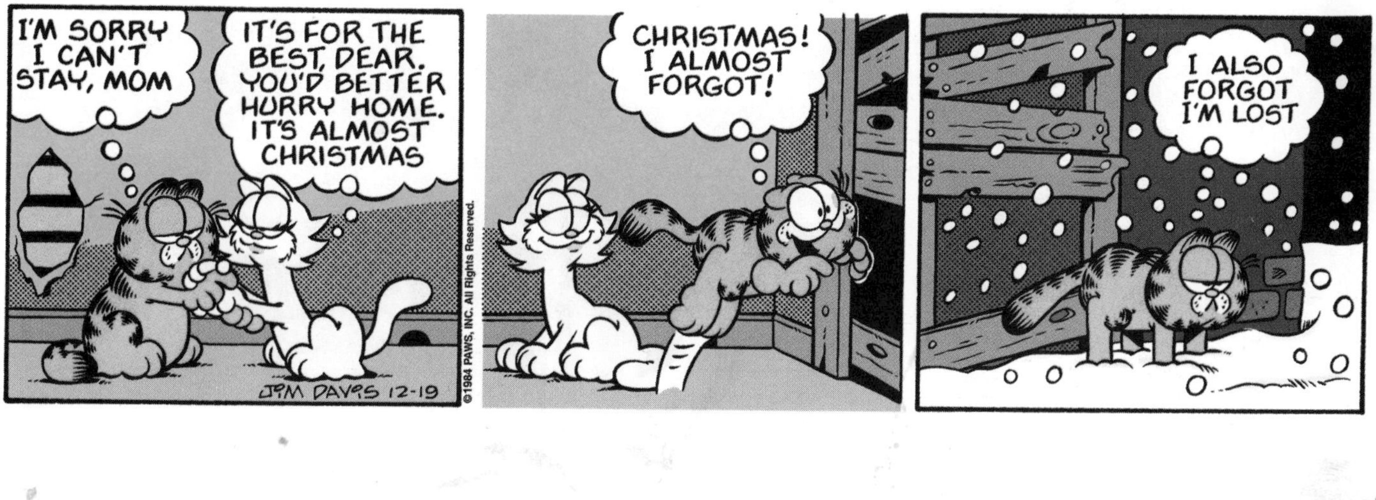
I'M SORRY I CAN'T STAY, MOM
IT'S FOR THE BEST, DEAR. YOU'D BETTER HURRY HOME. IT'S ALMOST CHRISTMAS
JIM DAVIS 12-19
©1984 PAWS, INC. All Rights Reserved.
CHRISTMAS! I ALMOST FORGOT!
I ALSO FORGOT I'M LOST

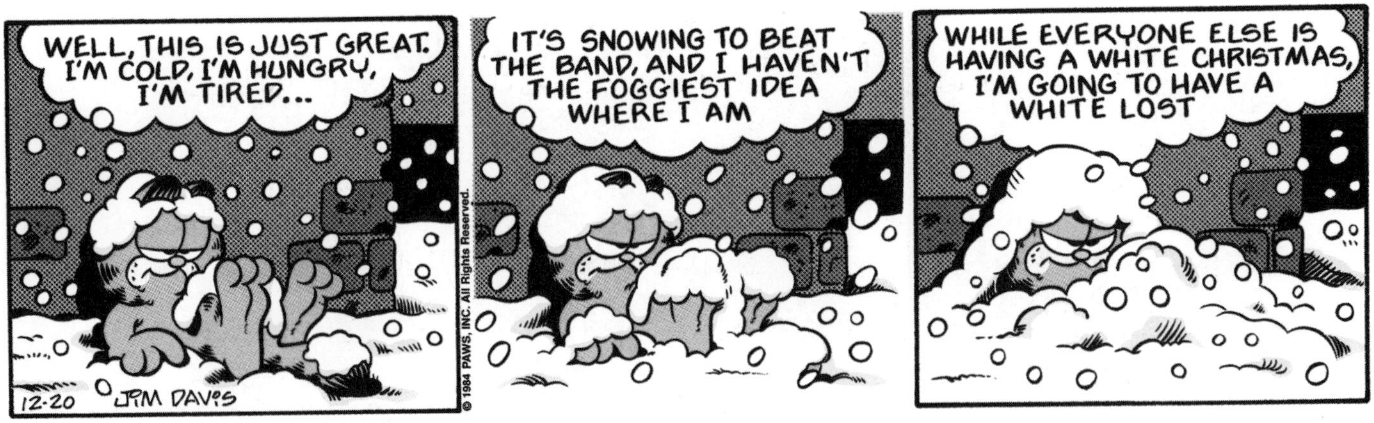
WELL, THIS IS JUST GREAT. I'M COLD, I'M HUNGRY, I'M TIRED...
IT'S SNOWING TO BEAT THE BAND, AND I HAVEN'T THE FOGGIEST IDEA WHERE I AM
WHILE EVERYONE ELSE IS HAVING A WHITE CHRISTMAS, I'M GOING TO HAVE A WHITE LOST
12-20 JIM DAVIS

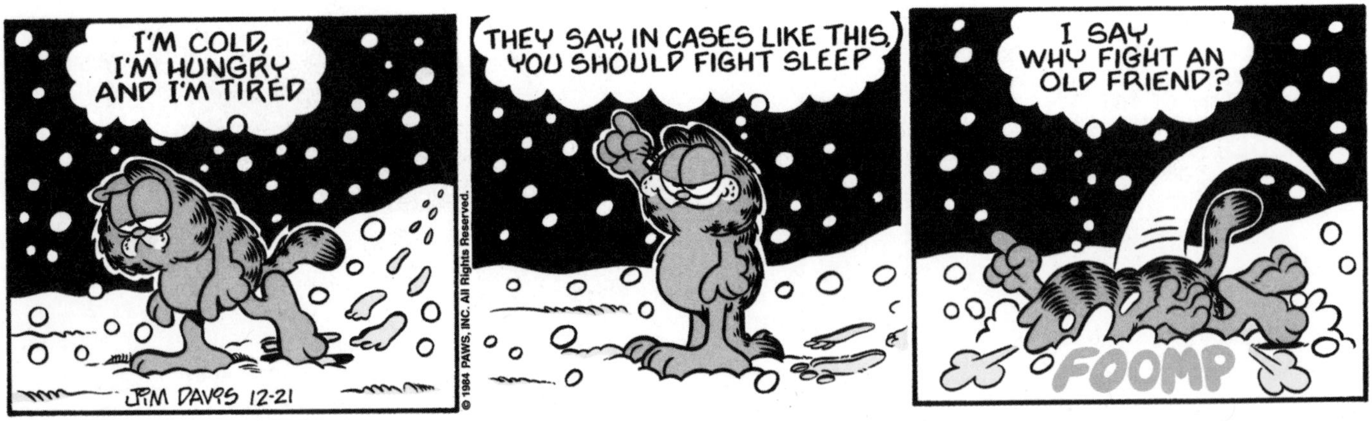
I'M COLD, I'M HUNGRY AND I'M TIRED
THEY SAY, IN CASES LIKE THIS, YOU SHOULD FIGHT SLEEP
I SAY, WHY FIGHT AN OLD FRIEND?
FOOMP
JIM DAVIS 12-21

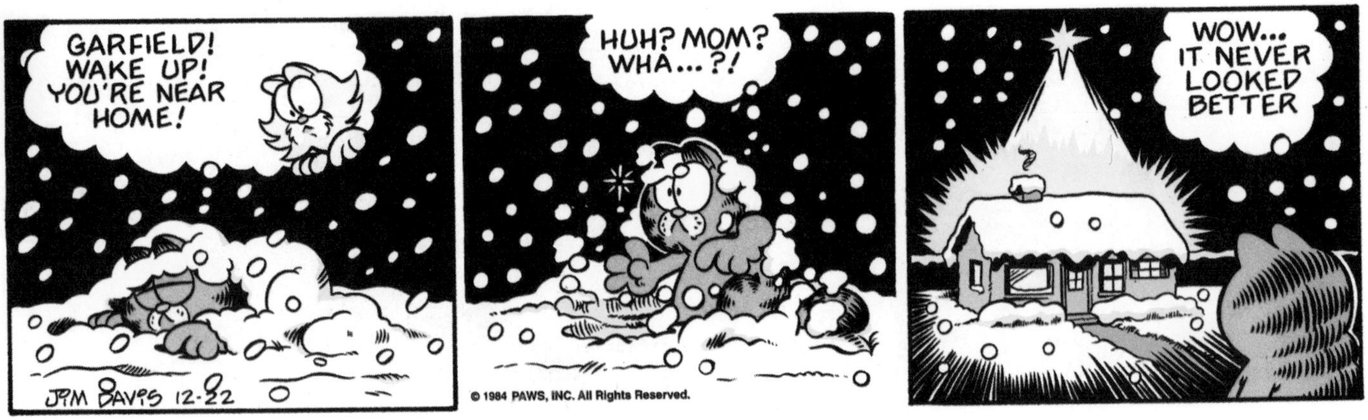
GARFIELD! WAKE UP! YOU'RE NEAR HOME!
HUH? MOM? WHA...?!
WOW... IT NEVER LOOKED BETTER
JIM DAVIS 12-22

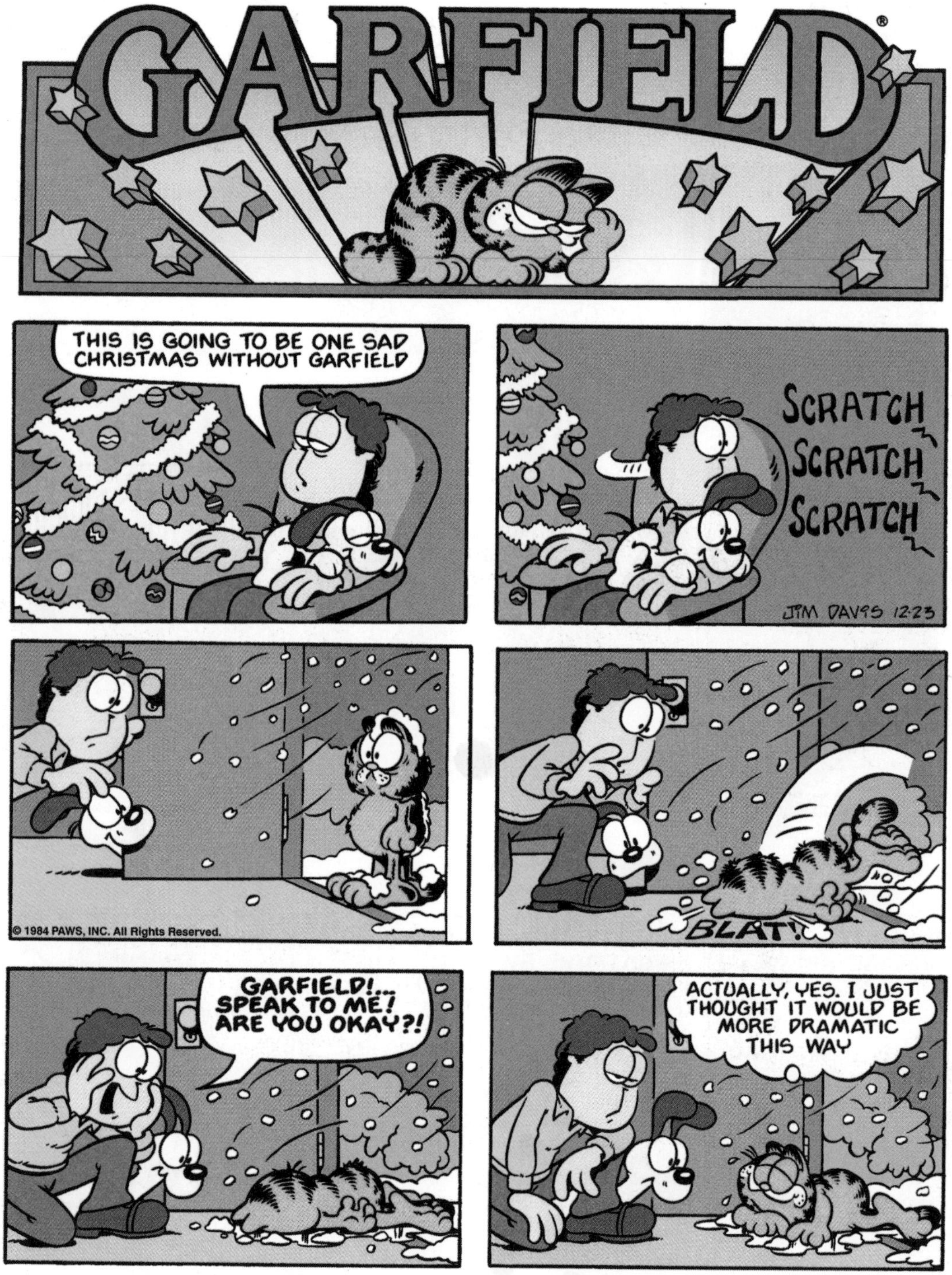
GARFIELD®
THIS IS GOING TO BE ONE SAD CHRISTMAS WITHOUT GARFIELD
SCRATCH
SCRATCH
SCRATCH
JIM DAVIS 12-23
© 1984 PAWS, INC. All Rights Reserved.
BLAT!
GARFIELD!... SPEAK TO ME! ARE YOU OKAY?!
ACTUALLY, YES. I JUST THOUGHT IT WOULD BE MORE DRAMATIC THIS WAY

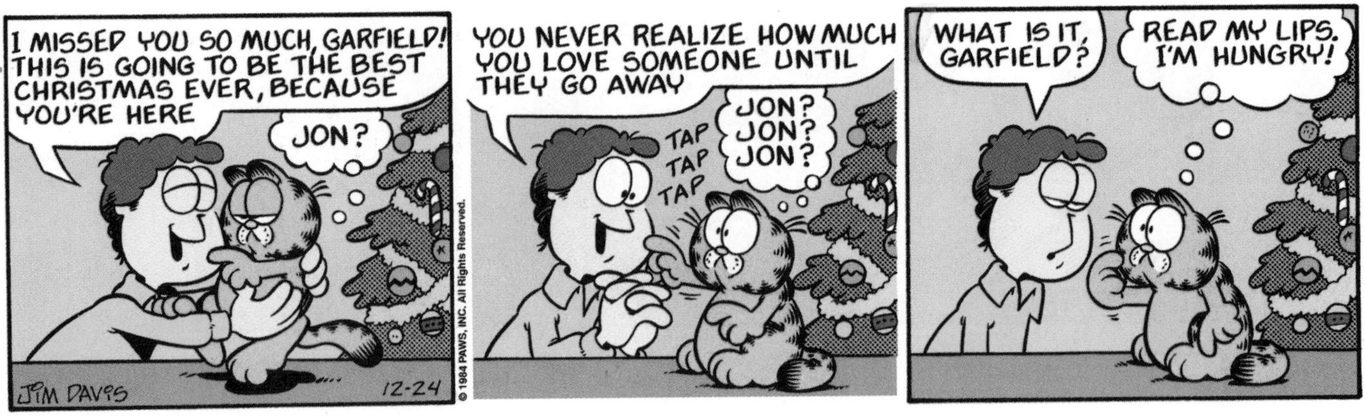
I MISSED YOU SO MUCH, GARFIELD! THIS IS GOING TO BE THE BEST CHRISTMAS EVER, BECAUSE YOU'RE HERE
JON?
JIM DAVIS
12-24
© 1984 PAWS, INC. All Rights Reserved.
YOU NEVER REALIZE HOW MUCH YOU LOVE SOMEONE UNTIL THEY GO AWAY
TAP TAP TAP
JON? JON? JON?
WHAT IS IT, GARFIELD?
READ MY LIPS. I'M HUNGRY!

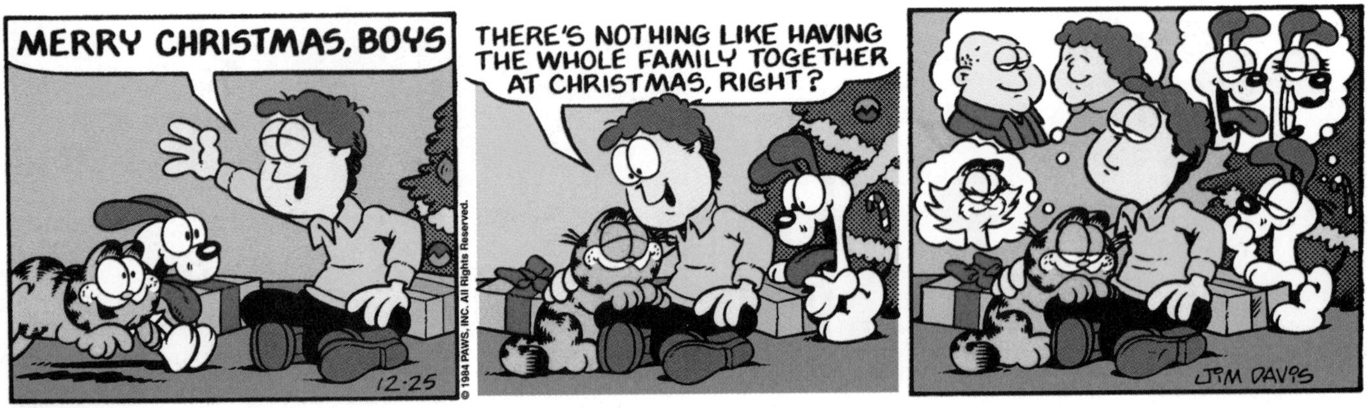
MERRY CHRISTMAS, BOYS
12-25
© 1984 PAWS, INC. All Rights Reserved.
THERE'S NOTHING LIKE HAVING THE WHOLE FAMILY TOGETHER AT CHRISTMAS, RIGHT?
JIM DAVIS

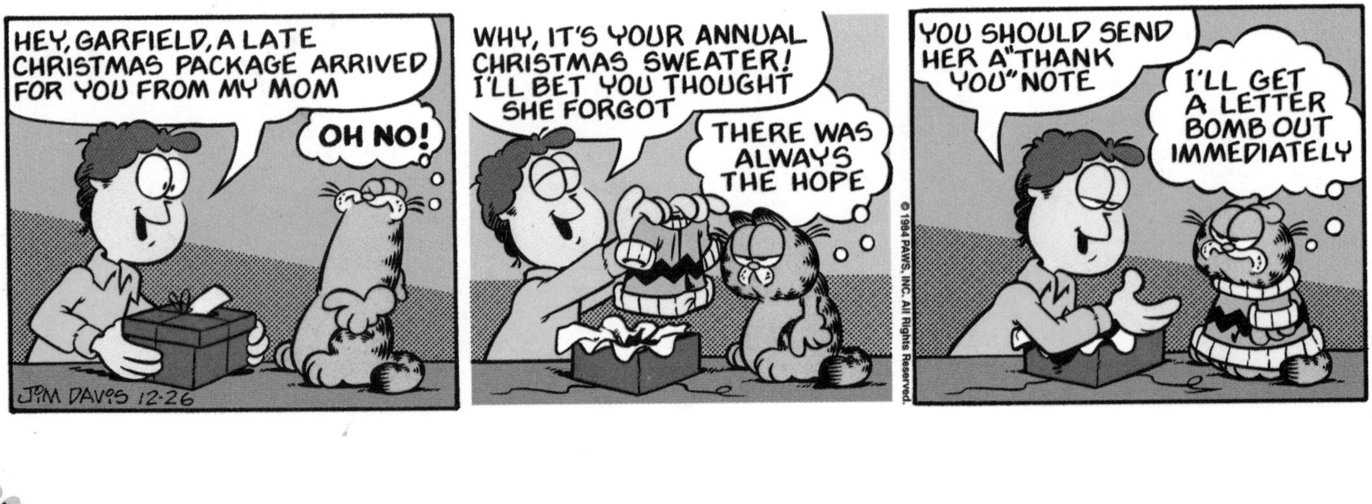
HEY, GARFIELD, A LATE CHRISTMAS PACKAGE ARRIVED FOR YOU FROM MY MOM
OH NO!
JIM DAVIS 12-26
WHY, IT'S YOUR ANNUAL CHRISTMAS SWEATER! I'LL BET YOU THOUGHT SHE FORGOT
THERE WAS ALWAYS THE HOPE
© 1984 PAWS, INC. All Rights Reserved.
YOU SHOULD SEND HER A "THANK YOU" NOTE
I'LL GET A LETTER BOMB OUT IMMEDIATELY

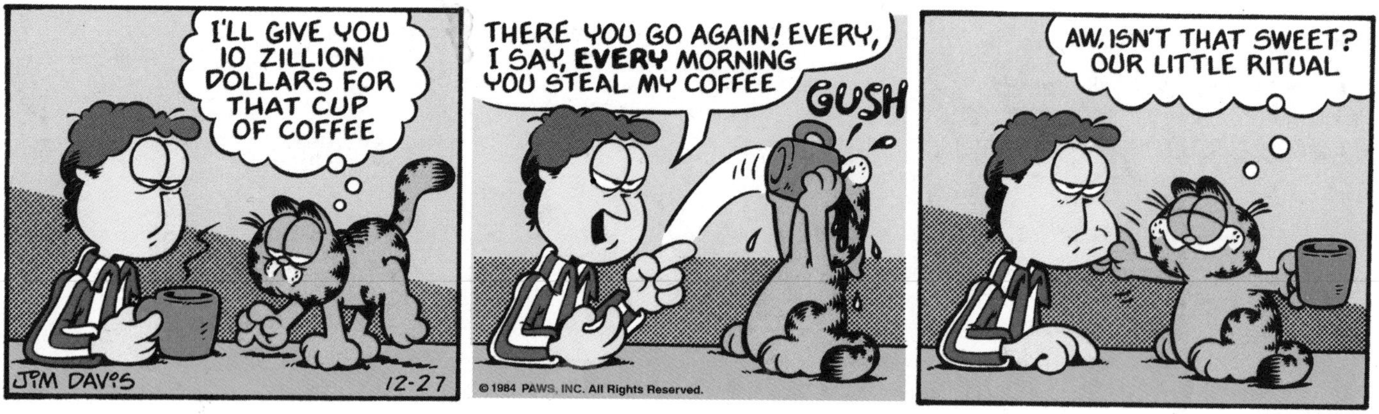
I'LL GIVE YOU 10 ZILLION DOLLARS FOR THAT CUP OF COFFEE
JIM DAVIS
12-27
THERE YOU GO AGAIN! EVERY, I SAY, EVERY MORNING YOU STEAL MY COFFEE
GUSH
© 1984 PAWS, INC. All Rights Reserved.
AW, ISN'T THAT SWEET? OUR LITTLE RITUAL

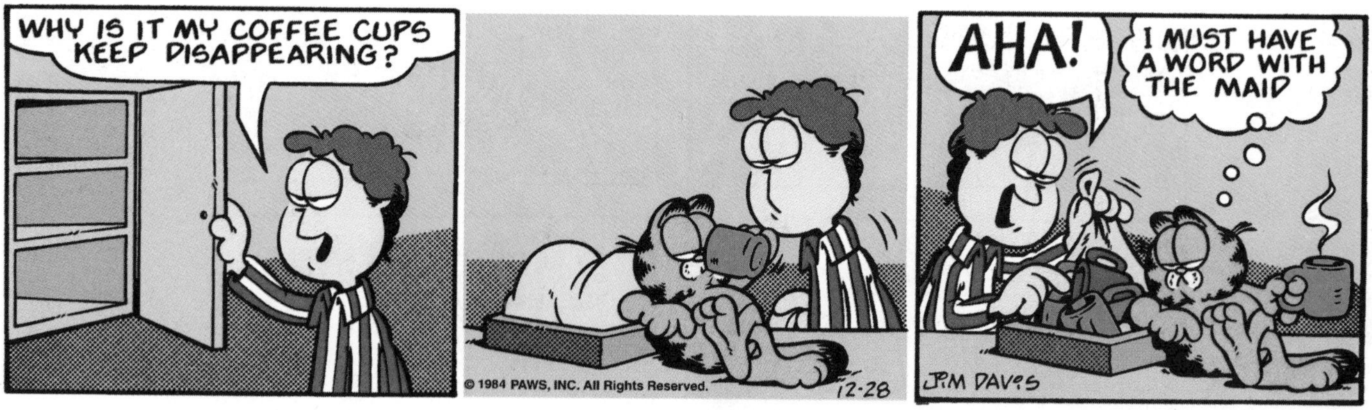
WHY IS IT MY COFFEE CUPS KEEP DISAPPEARING?
© 1984 PAWS, INC. All Rights Reserved.
12-28
AHA!
I MUST HAVE A WORD WITH THE MAID
JIM DAVIS

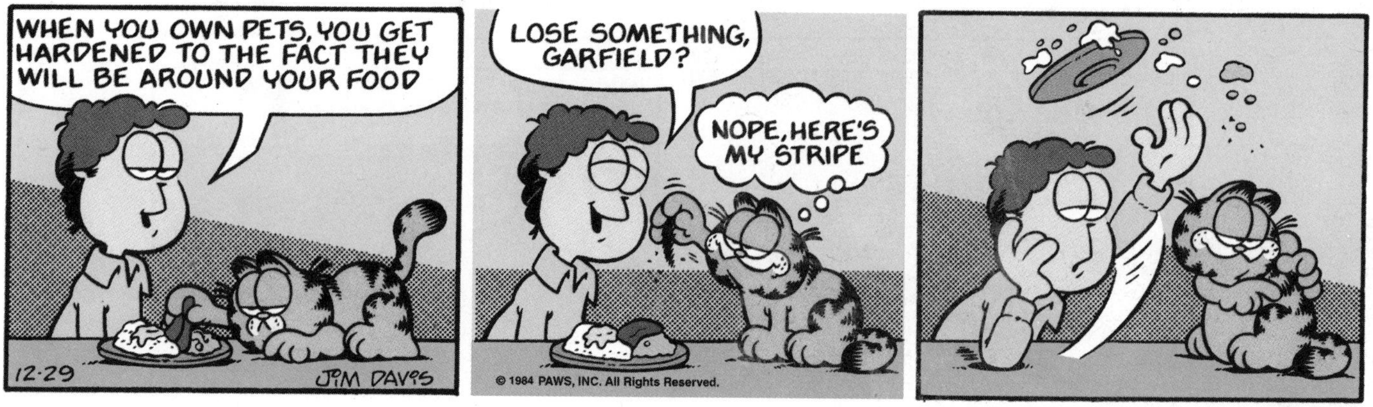
WHEN YOU OWN PETS, YOU GET HARDENED TO THE FACT THEY WILL BE AROUND YOUR FOOD
12-29
JIM DAVIS
LOSE SOMETHING, GARFIELD?
NOPE, HERE'S MY STRIPE
© 1984 PAWS, INC. All Rights Reserved.

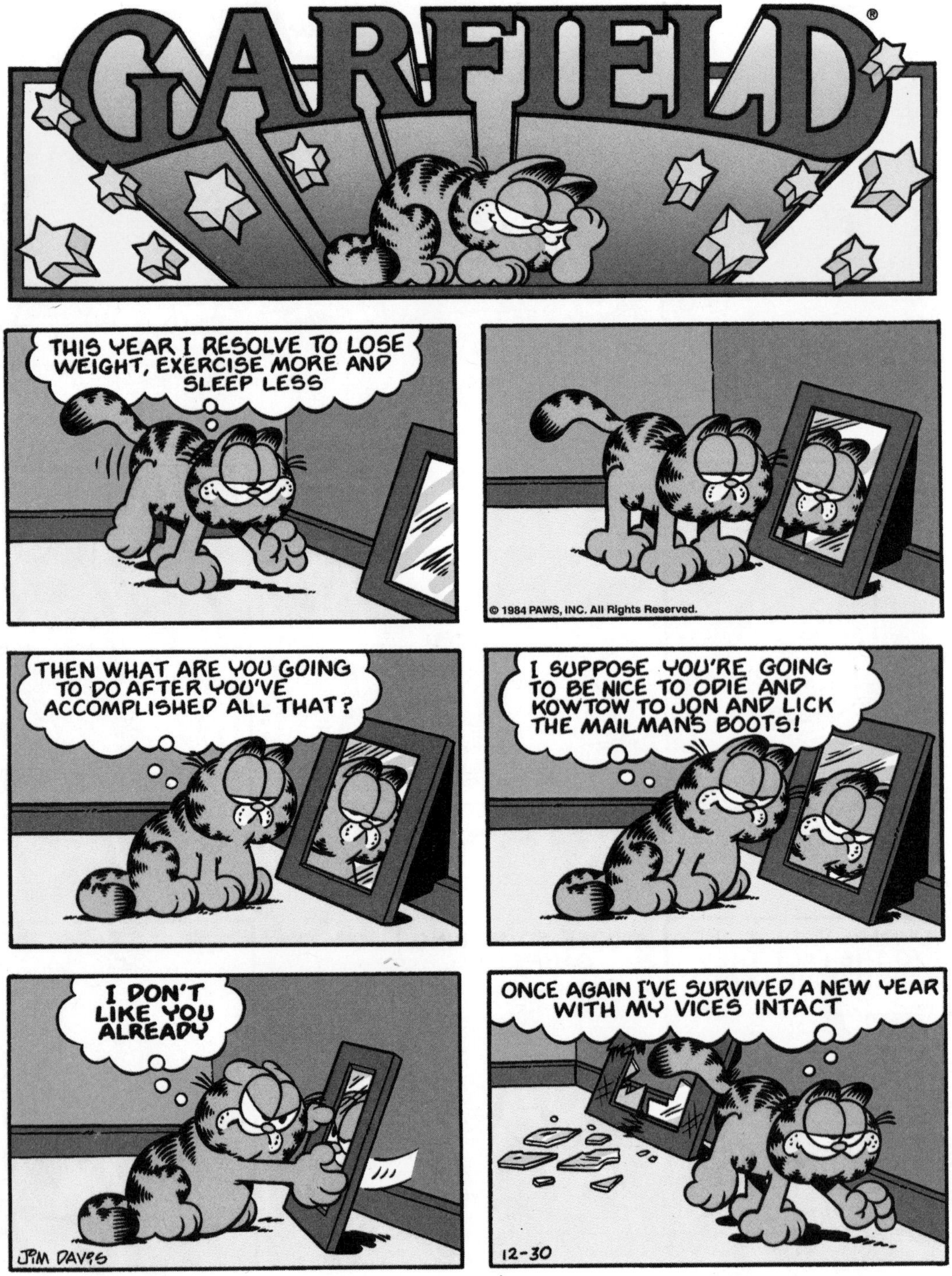
GARFIELD
THIS YEAR I RESOLVE TO LOSE WEIGHT, EXERCISE MORE AND SLEEP LESS
© 1984 PAWS, INC. All Rights Reserved.
THEN WHAT ARE YOU GOING TO DO AFTER YOU'VE ACCOMPLISHED ALL THAT?
I SUPPOSE YOU'RE GOING TO BE NICE TO ODIE AND KOWTOW TO JON AND LICK THE MAILMAN'S BOOTS!
I DON'T LIKE YOU ALREADY
JIM DAVIS
ONCE AGAIN I'VE SURVIVED A NEW YEAR WITH MY VICES INTACT
12-30